PRIVATE WARS

For my father Lawrence

PRIVATE WARS

Personal records of the
Anzacs in the Great War

G R E G   K E R R

There are strange hells within the minds war made
Ivor Gurney (1890–1937)

OXFORD
UNIVERSITY PRESS

OXFORD
UNIVERSITY PRESS

253 Normanby Road, South Melbourne, Victoria, Australia

Oxford University Press is a department of the University of Oxford. It furthers the University's objective of excellence in research, scholarship, and education by publishing worldwide in

Oxford New York

Athens Auckland Bangkok Bogotá
Buenos Aires Calcutta Cape Town Chennai
Dar es Salaam Delhi Florence Hong Kong
Istanbul Karachi Kuala Lumpur Madrid Melbourne
Mexico City Mumbai Nairobi Paris Port Moresby
São Paulo Singapore Taipei Tokyo Toronto Warsaw
and associated companies in
Berlin Ibadan

OXFORD is a trade mark of Oxford University Press

National Library of Australia
Cataloguing-in-publication data:

Kerr, Greg, 1964–
Private wars: personal records of the Anzacs in the Great War.

Bibliography.
ISBN 0 19 550799 1.

1. Australia. Army. Australian Imperial Force (1914–1921). 2. Soldiers—Australia—Diaries. 3. Military nursing—Australia—Correspondence. 4. Military nursing—Australia—Diaries. 5. World War, 1914–1918—Personal narratives, Australian. 6. Soldiers—Australia—Correspondence.

940.48194

Edited by Wendy Sutherland
Text designed by Steve Randles
Typeset by Eugenio Fazio
Printed by Kyodo Printing Co. Pte Ltd, Singapore

Front cover pictures: Sapper Austin Laughlin in a Gallipoli dug-out (private donor);
Lance Corporal Percy Whiteoak (private donor).
Back cover: 'Hellfire Corner' Menin Road, Belgium (State Library of Victoria).
Prayerbook of Corporal William Lowe (Marie Rumsey).

Contents

ILLUSTRATIONS

Author's note: Contributors wishing to remain anonymous have been credited as 'private donor'.

ACKNOWLEDGMENTS

Private Wars is a collaborative project for which I thank many people. Firstly, the soldiers of the AIF who documented their experiences of war—their images and words are the sustenance of this book.

I am indebted to the descendants of these soldiers and the private collectors who have preserved letters, diaries and photographs from Australia's involvement in the Great War, and who have generously lent material, much of which unfortunately could not be placed because of space limitations and style considerations.

Thank you to Bob Sutherland, the conscience of this book, for his generosity and tireless help, and to Major Ian Barnes, Alan Bennett and Wayne Sutherland for their contributions.

To Ian Affleck, of the Australian War Memorial, for his belief in the project and co-operation, and to his colleagues Andrew Jack, Ian Smith, Paul Mansfield and Ashley Ekins, Mark Whitmore and Tony D'Amico.

I am appreciative of the memorial's generosity, as I am for the assistance of the State Library of Victoria where Dianne Reilly, Lois McEvey and Shona Dewar were particularly helpful.

Thanks also to Museum Victoria for its contribution, and to the guidance of Ruth Leveson and Steve Ether.

To Bruce Ruxton and his staff of the Melbourne RSL, particularly Merle Merchant, Joy Tiley, Major Frank Bell, Brigadier Keith Rossi, Brigadier John Deighton, Bill Hall and Keith Walker. My gratitude extends to the staff of F-16 One Hour Photo, Hawthorn, and to Bob Martin.

The donors to this book are too numerous to name, but acknowledgments and thanks are especially due to those whose photographs and written accounts appear: Keith Herrod, David Dalgleish, Grace Connor, Carmen Johnston, Betty Law, Peter and Robyn Morrison, Bertha Moran, the Ross family, the Aitken family, Malcolm McInerney, Frank Mason, Zoe Mason, my parents Laurie and Vivienne Kerr, George Kerr jnr, Jim Kitchin, Marie Rumsey, Peter Tate, Fred Bradley, Margaret Mackin, Dianne Quinert, Brian Jackson, Gillian O'Brien, Annette Haworth, Matthew Darby, Kate and Warren McDonald, Mavis

Philpott, John Lord jnr, Pam Rudgley, Walter Smith, Marlene MaGee, Harry Johnston, Bob Cochrane, Mrs G. Ellem, Elaine Brooke, Nerralee Hinder, Marie Lewin, Keith Gregory, Vi Lanham, Loes Pearson, Judy Kelly, Heather Everingham, Ailsa Rolley, Helen Walker, Mrs J.W. Makeham, Norman Grouse, Ann Mackereth, Betty Pollard, Michelle Entwisle, Lynne Gibbs, Alex McGoldrick, Dominic Scally, Kate and Dan Webb, Marcia Wordsworth and Frank Lloyd.

Thanks also to the many who have assisted the production of *Private Wars* in other ways: Peter Rose, Sir James Balderstone, Mary and Rebecca Sutherland, Phong To, Allan A. Murray, Alison Stewart, Tom Roberts, John Flannery, Alf Batchelder, John Potter, Stephen Kerr, David Green, Steve Westh, Tony Simmons, Louise Dew, Vera Jagow, Rob Perkins, Margaret Barnes, Richard E. McGarvie, Alison McKenzie, Sheila Stevens, John Meyers, Lieutenant Colonel Neil Smith and the Military Historical Society of Australia (Victorian branch).

I am also grateful to a number of authors whose works have guided my research: Captain Charles Bean, Ken Inglis, Chris Coulthard-Clark, Bill Gammage, Alistair Thomson, Richard Holmes and Peter Dennis.

Lastly, I am ever grateful for the support of my family and the enduring faith and encouragement of my wife Susan.

INTRODUCTION

The men whose impressions form the heart of this book are an unlikely grouping of informants. Their backgrounds and fates varied, as did the tenor of their writings and the content of their photographs. War shaped them in ways understood only by those who have known combat, yet their observations evince an understanding of the impact of the Great War on a human level, generations later.

Few of them knew one another yet their paths meet here, some eight decades later, because their experiences and impressions of war are published for the first time. Others appear not as voices, but as a consequence of what has been remembered of them or the fact that they appear in significant photographs.

Some of the images in this book are the last visual remnant of men who never came home; others capture moments in battle when the sway of life and death hung precariously. Some would seem unremarkable were it not for a vital piece of captioned information such as *6 a.m., 25 April 1915* or a name like *Simpson* or *Birdwood*. The writings are similarly diverse. A flow of letters suddenly ends, the spidery ink of a diary gives way to emptiness, and one learns that the writer fought at a place called Lone Pine or Fromelles the next day. Others brim with optimism: *A glorious May morning; said Hullo to the sun as usual*; or meander monotonously before igniting with the words *went over the top today*. A letter written in anaemic pencil marks the final composition of a mortally wounded soldier wishing his baby daughter happy birthday.

Much of it runs contrary to the stuff of myth. When an improbable Gallipoli hero first tried to enlist he was rejected for having a hare-lip, while another youngster knew it was time to get a uniform when a white feather turned up in the mail. On the way to war, a chauffeur from Bacchus Marsh learned of a terrible family secret that was to haunt him to his death in a German shelling barrage, while a baby-faced officer with the weight of a company on his shoulders broke his leg then almost drowned before he had arrived at the front, and a young star of the cadet force system tried to reassure his mother: 'Who wouldn't be a soldier?'[1]

At Gallipoli, an ex-miner from Broken Hill defiantly smoked a cigarette in view of the enemy, while death hovered, moments away; a lieutenant told his father how killing Turks was better than a wallaby drive; and a field ambulance colonel prayed that he might be killed rather than endure the prolonged agony of injury. On a lighter side, a lieutenant enjoyed reading the contents of Fanny Bourke's widely circulated love letter, and a sergeant who had been a stock agent before the war wrote that Gallipoli would make a good sheep run.

Away from battle, an officer from Mount Gambier rejoiced in the fact that roses were almost in bloom, and that he was about to reunite with his 'little Olive' in London; an anonymous soldier and art lover mapped in his diary the bicycle route through 'Constable Country' in England; a former lacrosse star from Melbourne assured his mother: 'About the actress, you needn't worry about her—I am not seeing her or writing to her'.[2] But it soon got back to war. The rose lover spent two days with his Olive while on leave and returned to die in battle near Merris; the fate of the art lover is not known, while the lacrosse star limped through a German trench, a Luger bullet in his thigh, and led 6th Battalion soldiers to one of the most resounding and brutal raids by Australians in the war.

In a trench somewhere in France an artillery driver, who had just been blown off his horse for the third time in one year, confided: 'You do not know the minute you will be blown to pieces';[3] meanwhile, in England, a mob of dis-gruntled soldiers waged their own war when they burned down a 'low-class music hall'.[4]

And in 1917, as an Australia-bound ship carrying convalescents entered the sweltering tropics, a shell-shock victim sat trembling in his great coat, destined to see out his days in a Sydney psychiatric hospital.

Back home, an anonymous soldier, eyes haunted by the dread of the battle-field, walked into a Korumburra studio, removed his shirt and asked to be pho-tographed so that the gaping wound around his midriff would remind someone, some day, of how the war emasculated many Australian soldiers.

A decade after hostilities ceased, the widow of a soldier who had died in a tangle of barbed wire in France was still writing to military mental hospitals in Melbourne on the off chance that her husband might have miraculously turned up. And the children of returned soldiers, however many it will never be known, started to wonder why their fathers became moody, aloof and drank so much, or why they wheezed and coughed up bile every morning. And the children of these children, removed from the entanglements of flesh and blood, began to see it in a new way. Possessed by a yearning to find out more about the war, they began to read old cloth-bound diaries—some torn by shrapnel or stained in blood—and to sift through the sediment it lodged into the streams of their family consciousness.

To the best of my knowledge, most of the photographs and quotes that appear in *Private Wars* have not been published before, with the exception of several quotes from my paternal and maternal grandfathers, and my great-uncle, who served in World War I, and whose accounts are detailed in my earlier book *Lost Anzacs: The Story of Two Brothers* (1997). Some published war diaries and the works of some other authors are referenced although not quoted in my book. A simple criterion has been applied to the selection of primary material: that the images and words convey the experience of going to war in a unique and interesting light, with an emphasis on points of view that reflect the personality of the informants and the impact of environmental and circumstantial factors on them.

Material has been drawn from private collections of dozens of contributors from around Australia, as well as collections held at Museum Victoria, the State Library of Victoria, RSL branches and the Australian War Memorial in Canberra. The 200 photographs have been chosen from thousands of images viewed at these sources.

It is hoped that the hundreds of small fragments of soldiers' impressions acquired and, in some cases, salvaged for this book convey and reflect the composition of the Australian Imperial Force, its attitudes, its physicality and humanness. The diaries and letters, while they are in every case believed to be genuine, are not to be regarded as completely authorative as it is likely that some accounts were influenced by hearsay and rumours, and that some facts were distorted amid the delirium of battle. Some accounts present disparate views of the one incident; they are to be regarded as impressions that imply a wider truth. An example is the description of a 'friendly fire' explosion that killed three 26th Battalion members and wounded several others in a trench at Gallipoli in September 1915. Two of the survivors concur that the blast was caused by an Australian bomb meant for a Turkish trench just six metres away but they conflict on a crucial point—one says it exploded as it was being thrown;[5] the other, more damning account, describes the bomb going off after the thrower (who is not named in either account) got 'dumfounded at something & dropped it'.[6]

I have avoided the kinds of image that tend to reappear in military books, particularly images that correlate to mythology which has been popularly and, in some cases, erroneously accepted as being true to the diggers of World War I. By doing so I hope I have trod some new ground among the heavily ploughed fields of Australian military history, and that, in giving infantrymen and frontline officers a 'voice', this record conveys psychological and emotional resonances considered secondary in many unit histories and battle analyses. Of all that is horrific, wasteful and inhumane about war, I believe that a diary or a candid snapshot conveys a spark of emotion, an immediacy or a totality that cannot be measured for authenticity except by the experience of combat itself.

Certain diary accounts under consideration for this book were later withdrawn because they were found to be inaccurate or they proffered misinformed generalisations. Some images were omitted on the grounds of being technically unpublishable because of blemishes, fading or incorrect exposures. Perhaps the most difficult omission was a shot taken on the morning of the Gallipoli landings showing a group of Australian invaders splashing through the shallows of Anzac Cove. Regrettably the middle of the frame had been obscured by an emulsion bubble. Occasionally, some shots considered to be 'originals' recurred in other sources, and at times, tantalising leads evaporated, such as the anecdotal account of a young private fatally wounded on 25 April while taking photographs.

There has been no censorship applied to the diaries and letters used in this book, which is not to say its preoccupation has been with the macabre and the brutal. Rather than studying the strategies and outcomes of battles, I have focused on individuals and their points of view, their vernacular and the *thusness* of war that their writings and photographs convey. I have endeavoured to illustrate the chronological movements of the AIF throughout the war, from the early enlistment period, the sea voyage to Cairo, the Gallipoli campaign and the battles of the Western Front, as well as experiences of soldiers on leave and the passage back to civilian life for those who survived.

Considerable effort has been made, with the assistance of soldiers' relatives, to trace the biographical details of each individual identified in *Private Wars* as a photographer, a subject of a photograph or written account, a diarist or a letter-writer, but it should be noted that army records are at times fragmented and contradictory and, as such, are to be considered as a reference rather than a definitive source.

If I have been conscious of a theme, it is the notion of war as a journey that penetrated distant horizons, opened minds, aroused new hostilities and promoted a fraternity of unshakeable loyalty; a lottery that exposed 337 000 Australian participants overseas to a reality of savage, rapid attrition which killed 60 000 troops, mostly in their mid-twenties, and prematurely ended the lives of an additional 60 000 returned soldiers between the end of the war and 1932.[7]

I was propelled to write this book by a desire to know how a diary entry or letter reflects an individual's inner being or what it conveys about a time when young Australians, most of whom had not travelled outside their own state, strode unquestioningly, often to certain death on soil half a world away.

I have been enthralled by snapshots that reveal a forgotten or untold aspect of the war, black and white portraits so clear as to render a moment or a face timeless, so full of elation and spirit. I have been moved by photographs of personalities who might otherwise have been a name on a wooden cross, expressions that brim with hope when so much was to be loathed and dreaded. I have been thankful for knowing something of these men, saddened to know that many died before their time. I have lingered over the sorts of lives they might have led were it not for this, and the imprint they most certainly would have left on Australia. The process of communing with them begins with brittle yellowing letters and perhaps a diary, cloth-bound, dank to the touch and emitting the sorrowful whiff of myrrh. Identifying them begins with bare clues: a serial number, a crucial date, a photograph in a sleeve, the name and address of a next of kin.

I am thankful to those who have helped construct profiles from these clues, and to those who have kept these primary documents in safe custody, as I am to the unknown soldiers who, in some cases, risked their lives to retrieve written accounts and photos from the dead and the dying, and ensured their safe return to Australia. One such man, Private Septimus Wilson of the 2nd Australian Light Horse, wrote to the mother of his dead mate Eric Mulvey and promised he would get 'Mul's' camera back to her from Gallipoli if it were God's will that he survived himself.

While *Private Wars* is about Australian infantrymen, many of their experiences and points of view were shared by the New Zealanders who travelled and fought heroically alongside AIF troops under the 'Anzac' (Australian and New Zealand Army Corps) banner. If this book has any other leaning, it may be that its primary sources are at their most poignant and diverse at Gallipoli. Australians spent more time there (eight months) than any other battle location, adapted to it like no other place, and wrote about it and photographed it with unequalled enthusiasm. By the time AIF troops commenced their 2½ year slog at the Western Front in mid-1916, the war had lost its sense of newness, and soldiers became further estranged from the old Australia. They consequently wrote less about what they saw and felt less inclined to take photographs, notwithstanding the fact that security provisions prevented them from using cameras. The famed light horsemen are covered in this book in so far as they served as infantry, travelled with and trained alongside regular troops; their triumphs as mounted cavalry in the Middle East are well explored in other texts.

The seed for this book was sown several years ago when I came into possession of a cigar box of photographs and two shorthand diaries recorded by my soldier grandfather Corporal George Kerr while he was a prisoner of the Turks. The photographs transported me to a terrain inhabited by forgotten POWs; the flame-licked diaries, translated in 1995, permitted me to meet the grandfather I never knew. 'If I ever write anything about military life,' he wrote in December 1915 from a Constantinople prison, 'I see no reason why I should not describe the life exactly as I have found it. This might seem to savour of sensationalism and would possibly be attacked on the ground that it tends to undermine the faith the general public has in its army and navy.'[8]

The business of survival and raising a family kept my grandfather from attempting to publish anything about the war. He had lost his only brother

Hedley—also an avid diarist and photographer—on the day of the 25 April landings, and while George was shot and captured at Gallipoli, narrowly escaping execution, who really wanted to read about it when the war's grieving had seeped into every second Australian household? Although I never knew George, something compelled me to fulfil the unfilled *If* of his Constantinople diary entry, eighty years later.

When they enlisted, men like my grandfather unburdened themselves of their civilian pasts and arrived at a new freedom made all the more profound because of the imminence of injury or death. Youthful as they were, some seem possessed of a knowledge that their warrior status was the honour one earned and the price one paid for being born in a heroic age, as the British soldier-poet Ivor Gurney once put it. Observations of this kind are noticeable among the sombre hues of photographic studios where new recruits are being observed as soldiers for the first time, or in trench snapshots when a soldier's sixth sense has reasoned that his odds of survival are slimming by the hour.

Some fill their plain uniforms awkwardly; the men they are supposed to be are betrayed by a hint of boyish diffidence in the eye, a lilt of adolescence that emanates from the spirit. Others face the camera with resolute purposefulness, as if in recognition of the fact that their time of reckoning has arrived. Later, they think nothing of bearing their torsos to the sun, carving their initials in the pyramids or resting an elbow in the dirt beside a mate's grave. In their casualness and ease they evoke chapters from the days when Australia was a sprawl of colonies: a slouch hat with the chin-strap slung between the lower lip and the chin, the way some bushrangers used to; the kind of half-smile bending to a grimace evident in photographs of swagmen around the turn of the century; a hat with the front rim turned wide-awake in a fashion popular on the goldfields of the 1850s. Subtleties like waxed moustaches, ramrod postures, pith helmets and canes reveal another strain of the Australian Imperial Force: its indelible links to the public school system and Australia's old master, Britain, the birth place of one in every four men who served in the AIF.

Some of the group photographs divine elusive qualities like optimism, brotherly love and the kind of *grace under pressure* Hemingway spoke of in reference to courage. They celebrate the prime of life before it is recognised and torn asunder in battle; they strike veins of raw emotion, group purpose and camaraderie rarely, if ever, found outside the topography of war. They catalogue the diversity of a newly federated nation's manhood, for 417 000 men—about half its eligible male population—had enlisted out of a total population of less than five million people. There is the bare-chested mounted trooper with the he-man physique, the jockey-sized private with the face of an altar boy, the newly enlisted father whose mallet-sized hands tenderly embrace his two young sons in their last photograph together, the wiry boxer with the dragon tattoo across his chest, the lanky officer who has dressed up as his native guide 'Abdul' for the day, and his mate who has affected a monocle for the occasion…Two out of every three of them would go on to be killed or wounded in battle, or in mathematical terms 64.8 per cent of the AIF, representing by far the highest casualty rate of any allied force in the war.

They present an irony to this author who, three generations later, writes about them as men mostly younger yet seemingly older, more knowing, than he.

Romantic superlatives outlive them. The British correspondent Ellis Ashmead-Bartlett called the Anzacs 'a race of athletes'[9] after watching them take the hills of Gallipoli; John Masefield, another Brit, thought the men of the AIF 'walked and looked like Kings in old poems'.[10] Such allusions to physical bearing and nobility were echoed by Australia's official war historian Captain Charles Bean's theory that several generations of battling the elements under the Australian sun had forged a superior all-round specimen to the average Briton born into the drudgery of life in industrial cities. The difference was accentuated later by the fact that the Australian volunteer talked louder and walked taller, broke leave more often and generally made more of a spectacle of himself than the average Brit who was paid less and who conformed to tight-fisted discipline.

Yet by then Australian recruits, while sowing myths of their own, began to see through the polish of a myth that held the British soldier to be superior in all ways. The Brits they saw in Egypt were mostly non-professional Territorials or First New Army soldiers smaller in size and not as well trained as the Regular Army originals who had been engaged at the Western Front since 1914. Many Australians were dismayed to see them looking like timid schoolboys in pith helmets, not the stoic fighting men from the pages of Kipling's war stories. 'We are harder than they are & easily beat them on the march,'[11] observed Private Peter McConnachy. Trooper John McGrath adopted the mantle of protector 'and saved a Tommy soldier from drowning', in the surf at Alexandria.[12]

Afer being wounded at Gallipoli, light horseman Private Percy Virgoe jotted in his diary, '…a lot of Tommies aboard this boat [hospital ship]—Territorials & some of Kitcheners Army—They are on the whole a puny lot & miserable looking and very dirty & greedy in their habits. Am rather disappointed in them'.[13]

Just how big and robust were the Australians? Some of the photographs in *Private Wars* allude to physical stature and the suggestion of strength, but are specious gauges of actual traits like height and brawn. The Australians were no doubt physically impressive, particularly during the early recruitment waves, but collectively they were a long way short of the 6 feet or 180 cm ascribed to almost every man in some exaggerated newspaper reports.

The war artist George Lambert, whose famous work shows Australian light horsemen in various death throes at the Nek, observed that the average

Australian, if indeed such a man existed, was short and stout.[14] Lambert's view concurs with an analysis of No. 9 Platoon, C Company of the 3rd Battalion[15] formed in Sydney in 1914, a typical segment of the early AIF. The average height of 52 men surveyed in the platoon was 5 feet 8 inches or 171 cm (almost 10 cm short of 6ft); the average weight was 10 stone 12 lbs or about 69 kilograms, which is lighter than any senior player in the modern Australian Football League.

A physical survey of the AIF's most highly decorated soldiers, its Victoria Cross winners, showed that most of them were actually below medium height, which is not to say that the shortest men made the best soldiers. One of the most famous of them, Albert Jacka, stood 5 feet 6½ inches (166 cm) tall.[16]

A writer risks further impartiality by alluding to a certain '*je ne sais quoi*' that the Australians possessed or perhaps why their pea-soup coloured uniform began to stand out as noticeably as the blue-grey tunic of the French. Captain Bean has been maligned for compulsively linking the AIF to the bushmen of the outback, Australia's finest sportsmen and the warriors of the *Iliad*. Other authors and soldiers themselves have endeavoured to explain this quality by describing diggers as men of wit, courage and flair; simple blokes who had a go, smoked a lot and liked a 'blue'; dashers who spoke in a drawling mongrel Cockney and used 'lingo' like *strewth*, *blimey* and *bonzer*; 'sentimental blokes' who missed home and inscribed their wallets with mottos like *talk clean, live clean, fight clean, play the game*;[17] dark horses who did not look much but were as solid as bricks under fire; risk-takers who got high on the smell of cordite and the roar of gun thunder; scrappers who produced their best in the teeth of grave danger.

If indeed the Australians were imbued with a special élan, it might account for the fact that young naval midshipmen produced khaki uniforms after they had steered rowboats ashore at Gallipoli, and joined the invading infantry. It might explain what motivated Melbourne *Age* reporter Phillip Schuler, some of whose photographs appear in this book, to lay down his notebook and serve with them until he died of wounds in France in 1917.

It rubbed off on commanders too. As he lay bleeding to death on a hospital ship off Gallipoli, General Bridges skited that he had at least commanded an Australian division,[18] while General Birdwood declared that no offer of promotion could ever entice him away from the Anzacs after watching them storm Lone Pine.[19] It might also explain reports of French refugees following Australian divisions from front to front, safe in the knowledge the Australians would do the job against the Germans when others had failed.

To a new generation, the popularly synthesised *way* of the Anzac is both emulated and reflected through a prism of modern life-styles and altered sensibilities. Their coarse trench dialect echoes through work sites, markets and sporting club changing rooms. Their courage is epitomised obliquely in peaceful times by a Country Fire Authority crew racing to the scene of a wildfire or a visually impaired person tapping quietly through crowded city streets or a young police-man who vows to be back on the job two months after being shot through the chest. Their egalitarian attitudes thrive in close-knit communities where no one is less than equal, where newcomers with new customs are embraced and give the best of themselves in return.

It is not that World War I diggers were any better, any more dignified. They dropped the 'F' word, stole from one another, drank themselves stupid, fre-quented brothels and burned them down. Some foreign journalists wrote them off as an undisciplined rabble; British generals, while impressed with their size, doubted their worth as soldiers, particularly during the restless days before Gallipoli; the Germans thought of them as murderers and thieving scum. But they were elevated by an extraordinary hour, and proved their mettle in the cru-cible of fire that it seems each young nation must brave. The young lacrosse star, Sapper Austin Laughlin, sensed it at Gallipoli: 'Our chaps crept down the sap connecting the trench, with bayonets fixed and a something in their eyes that I have seen in the eyes of mortal men but once before'.[20]

Today's army draws heavily on the legendary steel of the Anzac for training and motivational purposes. An Australian Army instructional publication titled *Junior Leadership on the Battlefield* says today's soldier is fit but 'most lack the physical and mental toughness of previous generations'.[21] The journal says one of the AIF's most celebrated soldiers, Bert Jacka, was more than a fighter, 'he was a genius'.[22] There is a presumption that we have softened as a nation, and that the likes of Jacka belonged to a golden breed.

Only three of Australia's Gallipoli veterans were alive at the time this book went to the publisher. Each had celebrated his 100th birthday, yet not one was among the 16 000 to land on the shores of the Aegean on 25 April 1915. We have made them torchbearers of times when more was given for less. We have asked them to sit, wheel-chair bound, shrouded by grey drizzle, one April day every year; to rehash clichés and to be mouthpieces for causes like the republic. They would wonder why all the fuss about a word like 'mateship' going into the pre-amble to the Constitution; they would sigh at news of more instability and fight-ing in the Balkans, the flashpoint for World War I. Mostly, these old soldiers want to be left in quiet dignity.

Meanwhile, accounts of their deeds are being respun in classrooms, and dis-torted in pubs like loose orders passing along a line of tired soldiers, or forgot-ten altogether. And their ideals and reasons for fighting—loyalty to king and country, honour, an assertion of manhood, redemption and the desire to be in it—are being revised, dismantled and reassembled by minds bordered by the logic of 20–20 hindsight.

For a preciously brief time they are with us still. As their world retreats further from ours, and as we wrestle with questions like 'who are we', the rendering of their war recollections has never been more relevant. World War I, like no other event, blooded Australia into the reality of modern industrial civilisation, and set a watermark by which we gauge ourselves as an emergent nation.

Whilst many primary accounts from the war are protected by conservation processes in public institutions, alarming proportions of documents in private hands are in danger of deterioration, or being lost with the passing of generations. In many instances, the true historical worth of material is simply not known and its neglect poses the likelihood of rare gems—perhaps a first-hand account of Lone Pine, a Robert Capa-style snapshot or a spontaneous trench portrait of Billy Sing the sniper, or Bert Jacka—being cast into oblivion. It is no less neglectful to discard the ordinary, the seemingly banal. What may read as mundane discourse might be the only existing link to a unit's movements during a vital operation; a name interpolated among reams of narrative, the only clue to the real fate of a soldier whose army file ends with the words: 'missing in action'; an impersonal-looking typed document in the sleeve of an officer's diary the final communiqué that sealed the fate of thousands in a single battle, and alluded to the culture of sacrifice that permeated the thinking of military planners.

The author of one such document, Colonel E. G. Sinclair-MacLagan, had run out of time to brief the 3rd Brigade's four battalions individually about their role as the initial AIF strike force at Gallipoli. Instead he issued the commanding officers of each battalion with a vague, sweeping statement that began: 'In an operation of this kind there is no going back...'[23]

Amid the thousands of pages composed over the span of forty or more battles the AIF contested from that time on, classic handwriting-styles that stamp a man's station in life, prefacing greetings—*Dear Father & Sisters, Diar Mrs Turner, To my Loving Wife, Now Dear Old Dad*—and the formality of a generation for whom the written word held a certain intimate majesty; traces of deep affection that could not find a voice when less mattered, an emergent confidence emanating from the writings of youngsters whose opinions counted for little before they wore a uniform; rough, inconsistent scrawl that tells of a position under fire, the effect of shell shock—'... *P.S. Please excuse scrawl, my hand is not too steady*'[24]—or the presence of a second party dictating a dying man's last letter. Margins listing the names of women met in French estaminets; meanderings to pass the hours: '*Nothing doing*', or '*The name of this place is Fleurbai [sic]*', and invariably a 'first-time': a soldier's first taste of champagne, his first glimpse of snow, the grey form of a German appearing over a trench in no man's land...

A touch of the ironic and the surreal: entire battalions cheering wildly as they march past a kangaroo in an enclosure at the Cairo Zoo; opposing forces opening fire on a flock of birds flying over Gallipoli; a soldier in women's clothes walking through the ruins of a French town; men playing a piano left on a road in the middle of a battle zone. A concise allusion to weakening inner fortitude and fading morale: 'Our C.O. has gone to hospital with nervous breakdown', wrote Private Arthur Sanger in 1916.[25]

Another day, another flourish of pencil, another blank assessment of a day in battle: '4/6/15 Saturday', began Private Virgoe. 'Very heavy bombardment of our trenches by Turks, shrapnel. Casualties—W.M. McGregor (killed), M.P. McCabe (wounded), Sgt Murray Storrer (died of wounds), C.R. Phillips (shrapnel wound in head—critical), L.H. Dare (shot himself in hand with bullet).'[26]

Only the pen to reassure that love stood firm and that everything would be all right. 'Well old girl you must be having a struggle to make both ends meet. I wish it was over and we were together again but cheer up we will later on have a good time',[27] wrote Private George Levens before embarking for Gallipoli. Levens, of the 7th Battalion, disappeared on the day of the landings.

'Friday May 15th Many happy returns of the day, dear wife. I wish I were with you to speak these words',[28] pined 52-year-old Colonel Alfred Sutton from Gallipoli.

The act of writing was a way to try to make sense of it, to make it bearable. As he watched yet another German flare light up the sky one night, Lieutenant John Barton joked that it 'was generous of Fritz to supply all the lighting'.[29] To another extreme, Sergeant Allan Tongs declared that what he saw in France was not fit for the pages of his diary. 'I will not try to sully your mind you are better far better never to know...' Yet it was a matter of time before the unutterable filled every frame. 'If there be our guardian angel[s] above they must surely weep',[30] Tongs wrote at Pozières.

Some for whom the angels wept left prefaces to their own epitaphs. The day before he died at Lone Pine on 25 April 1915, Corporal Hedley Kitchin wrote: 'A Coy. issued with the wire cutters of the Batt...It strikes me that wire cutting is the first step to the next world'.[31] Sergeant Albert Goodsir's last written words were: 'Going up to support someone on a hop over'.[32] Hours before Lieutenant Geoff McCrae was shot through the neck at Fromelles, he wrote: 'Farewell, dear people, the hour approacheth, Love from Geoff'.[33]

By the time Jack Lynch's August 1915 letter arrived from Warracknabeal his brother Pat, a corporal with the 26th Battalion, had been killed when a fuse bomb was accidentally dropped into a Gallipoli trench. A condolence letter is sent to a mother in mourning over the death of her Fred at Pozières. 'Will you kindly accept my deep sympathy in your great loss...'[34] The letter takes on a deeper resonance when it is learned that the author of the letter, Bert Jacka, had been shot seven times in the same battle.

Some documents map the inner workings of a personality yet speak for the mindset of thousands. 'By the time this reaches you, I am likely to have received my baptism of fire', wrote Private Peter McConnachy, the miner from Broken

Hill, mortally wounded by sniper fire while he smoked a cigarette in view of the enemy on 25 April. The circumstances of McConnachy's 'baptism' reveal a reckless wilfulness to do things on his own terms. Earlier in Cairo, he had rejected promotion to corporal on the grounds that corporals did 'all hands dirty work'.[35] He was obstinate in the extreme, maybe incredibly game, even stupid, but his attitude equated with the reputation of Australian servicemen for exposing themselves unnecessarily to the dangers of incoming fire.

A number of correspondents who survived long enough were able to convey how war hardened them and prised them away from the lives they once knew. Private Murray Aitken, a sentimental young accountant, told his mother of his revulsion at the idea of using a bayonet and, during the first few terrible days at Gallipoli, hugged the earth closer than he 'ever hugged a girl'. A month later, he confessed: 'Mother, I'll admit to a certain savage pleasure in firing to kill'. And in July 1916, when Aitken, a lieutenant by then, was asked what should be done with a German buried to the waist in mud, he said: 'You can shoot him or dig him out; please yourself.'[36]

From amidst this hardening came the will to live and a desire to rekindle a future in a country many vowed never to leave again. 'Tell Tom to tell them down the sugar house to keep my job for me cause I will get a wooden leg on and will be as good as new,'[37] wrote Private Roy Oldroyd, a 19-year-old sugar refinery worker who was hit five times in the lower right leg by machine-gun fire at Gallipoli.

Upon discovery or closer reckoning, some private records reveal an omission in Australian war literature or are simply riveting yarns. The story of Private David McGarvie is both. McGarvie was rejected because of a hare-lip when he first tried to enlist, but later was accepted when it was realised he was something of a crack shot. At Gallipoli 12 months later, 'I don't know how many I fired. Head and shoulders at 10 or 12 yards, was just easy shooting'.[38] He was referring to the day 372 light horsemen were shot down during the charge for the Nek. Few battle histories, including Captain Bean's opus, credit the light horsemen at the Nek with inflicting a single enemy casualty with the rifle that day. Somehow it has been overlooked that a 23-year-old dairy farmer who was handy with a .303 killed up to a dozen enemy soldiers.

The examination of such accounts has made it clear to me that the soldier generation of World War I was a group whose ilk will not be seen again. Strict censorship prohibitions and the high incidence of Allied imprisonment prevented World War II diggers from recording their experiences with as much freedom. A new kind of world weariness and cynicism stopped them writing about going away to fight with the same *joie de vivre* of the 1st AIF volunteers, to whom keeping a diary was seen as a noble, Victorian activity,[39] and to whom keeping a positive frame of mind was imperative.

Photographs of Australian forces in the two wars bear obvious similarities, as many World War II servicemen were the progeny of ex-AIF members. There are the same lean, sun-tanned frames, the same raw, open faces of unfinished manhood, the furrowing around the mouths of battle-fatigued men, vacant stares from beneath helmets, a sense of belonging, or at least, getting by, whatever the surrounds, dry smiles that translate to mean: *She'll be right*. But unlike private photographs from World War I, such images lack intimacy and spontaneity as most of them were taken by newspaper photographers or official correspondents who, because of their links to propaganda channels, were not to be entirely trusted.

The men of the 1st AIF were the symbolic and, in some cases, ancestral offspring of the Australians who fought in the Boer War, from 1900 to 1901. But open a World War I album beside a comparatively rare Boer War collection and the physical and attitudinal differences become clear. A face from an Australian Boer contingent was typically gaunt and bewhiskered; a subject did not so much *look* at the camera as glare at it or gaze somewhere between the eye of the lens and the edge of the frame. He gave the impression of quaint old-worldliness and slight bewilderment; he left one to think that his uniform was not quite right and that he had not consciously defined himself in the eyes of foreign beholders.

In contrast, photographs of Australia's World War I soldiers convey an unmistakable sense of self-assurance and composure on an individual level, although the camera was a common accessory by then and it may partly explain why these men seem more at ease than their Boer War counterparts. Moreover, the Great War was arguably the photographic event of the century, and Australian soldiers compiled what is probably the most significant pool of amateur photographs from any war. Bound by fewer censorship restrictions than other forces, the Australians were tickled by a new gimmick in technology, Folding Kodaks and Vest Pocket Kodaks, and were able to shoot film and get it developed cheaply while away from the front, then send home snapshots or photo-postcards. Australian soldiers were keen to document the journey there, too, a fact which explains this book's strong representation of photographs taken in Egypt. More than 300 000 AIF servicemen trained there, making it the largest movement of Australians on foreign soil in any one period since white settlement. The availability of cameras enabled them to accumulate the first photographic profile of Australia's population, albeit a male-dominated one transposed against backdrops of pyramids, desert sands and back alleys.

Meanwhile, the world was watching. Outsiders knew little of Australia beyond that it had been a dumping ground for British convicts, it was somewhere south of the equator and that it got warm. Now Australians were being observed collectively for the first time, in the dawn of their testing in battle. Conversely, these men with slouch hats and a keen appreciation of all that was exotic and new had entered into the next most significant phase of Australia's sociological metamorphosis since the 1850s gold rushes when, at one time, one in every nine men in Australia was Chinese. The country they left behind—and returned to in lesser numbers—would never be the same by virtue of the fact they had departed its shores.

At Gallipoli AIF troops became key witnesses to history where, through an astonishingly short-sighted reasoning, the Australian Government had not appointed a single photographer to document the campaign. Captain Bean sensed a black hole looming in the coverage of Australia's military effort and took it upon himself to take photographs, but it was impossible for one man to convey the magnitude of the fighting or the demographic fibre of Australia's 45 000-strong Gallipoli contingent. With the exception of an occasional foray by a newspaper photographer or a movie reel cameraman, Australian soldiers were in the unique position to record their own war and define the visual elements of their own legend. What made the position of Australian soldier-photographers all the more unusual was that some were encouraged to take photographs by their unit commanders.

By the end of the Gallipoli campaign, they had documented the action so thoroughly that it may explain why the AIF, in Australian eyes at least, seemed to have a virtual monopoly on every strategic development on the peninsula. Other armies like the Turks and the Gurkhas did not possess the resources to compile an archive, while the British had more pressing concerns on the France/Belgium border to warrant recording the Dardanelles with any concerted historical purpose. It is often overlooked that the British suffered more terribly and fought as courageously as any Allied army at Gallipoli: 21 000 of its troops died there, the next highest toll being the French with 10 000, followed by the Australians with 7600. The Turkish Army, whose death toll was officially 87 000, probably more, comprised mainly illiterate peasant classes who did not write of their experiences, and private cameras were banned in their trenches. Regrettably, because of the absence of private written and pictorial records from the Turkish front line, let alone any comprehensive burial records, the depth of Turkey's sacrifice at Gallipoli has never been fully appreciated.

To the Australian soldier, writing about the war meant that he could record a significant event, and that he could one day look back and make sense of how it affected him. Studies of AIF war letters and diaries reveal an expressiveness and narrative skill that challenges the opinion that the army was comprised mostly of coots, larrikins and facetiously named 'deep-thinkers', or as Manning Clark once put it, 'men who never could find words to explain anything they did in life'.[40] As a letter writer and diarist, the Australian had an eye for detail and the capacity to know what was going on. He was not a linguist, he made a rough kind of a poet, and his grammar and spelling lapsed, yet his writings demonstrate a basic degree of literary proficiency and a knack of conveying a point of view. The 'roo shooter, the clerk and the solicitor alike had been encouraged to think for themselves yet to conform to the high standards of a state education system, though some members of the AIF barely knew how to sign their own enlistment papers. Some soldiers contributed yarns, illustrations and humorous verse to troopship and trench publications which became barometers for collective thinking and digger vernacular. Others sent stories and photographs to be published by newspapers, but these 'trench correspondents' were generally regarded as grand-standers and beat-up artists, and certainly not much better than the British journalists assigned to cover the action.

'Did a Turk and Australian fight on edge of a cliff and fall into sea?'[41] postured Sapper Laughlin. 'There is no such place at Anzac where such an occurrence could have occurred. Most of those yarns are all borax…Those special correspondents combine their reports from the wanderings of patients under chloroform at some base hospital.' And from Lance-Corporal Henry Pepper, later in France: 'There will be a lot of heroes at home after this war who have never seen the front. The best letters in the papers come from fellows who have never seen the front'.[42]

Even so, soldiers remained a major conduit for the dissemination of war news until mid-1916 at the Western Front where there was a strict prohibition on the use of private and press cameras. Taking a photograph not only put one at risk of being hit by sniper fire, one could be court martialled. A few Australian soldiers continued to take photographs in defiance of these odds; some of these shots appear in *Private Wars*.

The first official photographer attached to the AIF, Lieutenant Herbert Baldwin, an Englishman, did not arrive until November 1916, but the stress of covering the action saw him invalided after the battle of Messines in June 1917. The next to arrive were Captain Frank Hurley and his assistant Lieutenant George Wilkins, both Australians fresh from documenting separate polar expeditions in the Antarctic and Arctic respectively. The two were placed under the authority of the Australian War Records Section, given their own staff, and specific policy directives. They were escorted around Australian lines by Captain Bean, who had lobbied for their appointments, insisting on the importance of a true and accurate record of the war. Both photographers courageously pursued their work, often while under threat of shellfire, but the system had its failings.

Although their cameras were more sophisticated than the amateur version, they were bulkier and difficult to set up on tripods in the Flanders mud. And while Wilkins was dedicated to photography for historical record, the aesthetically-inclined Hurley grew frustrated at not being able to capture the full panorama of battle, and experimented with composite images as well as colour. He regarded the overlaying of composite scenes as a necessary artifice to convey war's true theatre, albeit from fragmented frames taken at different locations. Although Hurley was working to a brief of generating images for propaganda and publicity purposes, he eventually fell out with Bean who argued that doctored photographs should not be released as 'official'. It was also Bean whose influence led to Hurley's transfer to cover light horse operations in Palestine in late 1917.

୬

No photograph, no matter how emotive or contrived, can fully convey the experience of war. Words can engender a sense of the smell of burning paint when Lieutenant Bert Heighway's lighter was engulfed by machine-gun fire on the morning of the Gallipoli landings; but how can even the most eloquent narration fathom how Private Arthur Findlay's stomach knotted in anticipation of his first trench raid at Fleurbaix—'my nerves are all on the jump endlessly waiting, it will be Hell tonight'[43]—or Driver Claude Ewart's sense of rage when he discovered the body of a kidnapped woman in a trench full of dead Germans? Words and images together cannot generate anything quite so elegiac as the scene after the battle of Fromelles when a recovery party found the body of young Major Geoff McCrae with his hand outstretched, pointing a pistol towards enemy lines.

Only those who have known combat can know what it is like to live with the dead, to see a mate blown to pieces, to mercilessly club an opponent in hand-to-hand fighting, or to train the bead of a rifle on to the form of another human being and to see the target fold to the ground. We can only guess what might have been going through Major Ernest Gregory's mind when he wrote in June 1915: '9th Regiment man had both legs bombed off. Smoked his pipe while Dr. was cutting off the pieces of flesh—not a word'.[44]

While there is no substitute for reality, the trench photographs selected for this book convey an actuality, an undistorted moment in time. Because they were not equipped with telephoto lenses or automatic accessories, the cameras used to take these shots encouraged closeness and precision, and emphasised a recognition among the men of the AIF that they were participating in the pivotal event of their lives. The black and white images they generated encourage the beholder to look for qualities like emotion and definition. Many of them possess a clarity that holds, amazingly so, after the passage of decades. They are without pejoratives; they are seen not to lie. If a subjective bias is evident, it is in the moment of the taking, and the subject a photographer chooses to illustrate—or the photograph this author has been moved to select.

Sometimes the subjects project an air of positiveness to convey the impression they are doing better than circumstances permit. A laboured smile might hide the fact that a subject's best mate has just died; the lifting of one's chin and the straightening of the posture may conceal for an instant that a man is on the verge of exhaustion. It is for the beholder to see subtleties that pare to the essence of the thing: eyes that have lost their lustre, lines of disillusionment and mental strain around the mouth, the hand of a nurse resting gently on the wrist of a wounded soldier, a captioned date that reveals a certain soldier is days away from death.

The men brought to life by such photographs (and the passages that accompany them) deserve admiration and compassion. They are viewed by those in safe possession of the facts; passengers who attach themselves to the journey for a while, then return unscathed to the comfortable stations of peacetime.

Photographs of actual combat are scarce because of the obvious fact that the cameraman presents himself to danger, the closer he gets to the action. The nearest Captain Bean got to recording such an image was a set-up shot of a posse of Australian soldiers, bayonets drawn, charging toward an imaginary Turkish position. The game is given away by the smiles of some of the participants. Later, he had occasion to photograph the real thing at Krithia as Australians strode into a storm of gunfire so thick that men held shovels in front of their faces to deflect bullets. Bean, who was crouched in a nearby trench, instinctively reached for his camera but realised he had left it behind. And so dissolved one of the photo opportunities of the war.

Robert Capa's 1936 photograph of a Spanish Loyalist soldier falling backwards, rifle in hand, is regarded as being the most powerful war photograph produced. Although grainy and out of focus, it grimly expresses the outcome of combat—death, at the precise instant of its arrival. Over the decades, the pursuit of the *ultimate* war picture has cost the lives of dozens of photographers, including Capa, and some soldier cameramen. While *Private Wars* contains no such images, it has photographs of dead soldiers, Turks, Australians, Germans, to illustrate the finality of battle, as well as some amateur shots of Australians in the act of fighting. One shows a bomb thrower in a Gallipoli trench, wound sidelong in the motion of launching a 'jam-tin' bomb; several more depict snipers engaged in duels with Turkish opponents. Some images taken of soldiers at 'zero hour', moments away from attack, are equally dramatic.

The process of compiling *Private Wars* was at its most invigorating when a second glance at a discarded shot registered recognition in a face somehow permanently cast in the mind. A hunch, a diary sentence and an irrefutable date have then combined to prove that face belonged to a John Simpson Kirkpatrick or a Brigadier General 'Pompey' Elliott.

In one instance, a staged photograph, depicting Australian two-up players being 'devastated' by an enemy bomb, was knowingly selected on the basis that it is theatrically impressive and that it reflects the inventiveness and humour of Australian troops.

Contrivances aside, the photographs of and by Australians in World War I are the most vivid article of that war we possess. An impulse of mind and heart or a reflex action, they are a permanent frame of what another set of eyes saw, of what one witness deemed important, horrific or life affirming. They invite alluring questions. *What happened next? Did he survive? The colour of his eyes?* They fire the imaginations of young history students and form intrinsic links to the thematics of literature and movies,[45] which in turn shape popular consciousness and deepen public appreciation of war's consequence.

Of the 163 AIF servicemen who became 'informants' for this book, fifty-eight died or received mortal wounds at Gallipoli or the Western Front, while one sergeant drowned en route to war; another five who had been wounded died prematurely after returning to Australia. An additional forty-three, probably more, received significant wounds. In round terms, two out of three of the men in this book were killed or wounded, reflecting the wider trend of the AIF.

৵

Author's note: Some readers may be encouraged to seek the service records of their soldier ancestors. This can be done by writing to National Archives of Australia, World War I Personnel Records Service, PO Box 7425, Canberra Mail Centre 2610 (Fax: 02 6212 3499).

I

OUTBREAK

When George Kitchin Kerr picked up the 25 September 1914 edition of the *Snowy River Mail* and saw his name on its front page new recruits column, he knew his appointment with destiny had come. The art student had gone to make a proper quid felling trees at Orbost, in eastern Victoria, and it seemed for a while that nothing could penetrate the remote, densely timbered world he inhabited.

Until, that is, a group of assassins calling themselves the 'Black Hand' on the other side of the world uncoiled a chain of circumstance that soon commanded attention even in far-flung Australia. At first, the shooting murder of the Archduke Franz Ferdinand, heir to the throne of Austria-Hungary, in Sarajevo on 28 June 1914 generated more more sympathy than alarm in local newspapers. Another mob of agitators had settled an old score in the Balkans, but what did it have to do with Australia, other than the fact that the Archduke had once charmed Sydney with a visit in 1893?

The first sign that Australia might somehow be affected was a fall in prices on the Melbourne and Sydney stock exchanges on 22 July[1] in response to a deterioration of relations between Austria and Serbia. In the ten days that followed, Europe's intricately woven quilt of insoluble treaties began to lose its seams, and other countries entered the fray, motivated by honour, fear, territorial lust and ancestral ties. Austria declared war on Serbia, Russia mobilised to support its Slav cousins, the Serbians, while Germany, whose rulers were drunk on territorial ambition, declared war on Russia, which in turn, saw France go in on the side of the Russians. Europe was at war and it had only taken six weeks.

Australia had no complaint with any neighbour, and its military capability amounted to a fledgeling navy and a weekend army of teenagers. It did not have much to gain materially or territorially by going to war, yet heredity and sentiment bound Australia inexorably to its parent, the British Empire.

On 4 August Britain entered the fray as the reluctant opposing superpower to Germany, and the protector of Belgium, whose borders had already been crossed by German troops. Australians could no longer passively observe. They knew their ultimate security against any covetous aliens depended on the intervention of Britain's Royal Navy, so it followed that their sovereign protector could do with some support, however small, in an hour of need. National opinion swayed between wanting to go and having to go; dissenting voices receded. Either way a commitment of Australian troops seemed inevitable. But it was not all about helping Britain: an equally emotive secondary notion held that if the oppressive 'Hun' could be stopped in his tracks then it was a cause worth fighting.

The Liberal Prime Minister Joseph Cook had actually cabled London with the offer of a force of 20 000 infantry, as well as the Australian navy, on 3 August, a day in advance of Britain's war declaration. Reg Cooke, a student who would enlist two weeks later, was in Melbourne the next day. 'Walking up Collins Street we stopped a while outside the "Age" office where an orator relieved the tension by a semi-comic speech. His question "Who'll never eat German sausage again" met with a vigorous reply.'[2]

News of the offer spirited a frenzy of pro-war sentiment and by the time the offer had been accepted by Britain two days later, a patriotic movement had sprung up almost instantaneously through every town and city. Brass bands played British war tunes from city trams, diners in cafes stood to toast the King and sing the National Anthem, fundraising rallies were staged for the war effort, while newspapers published letters recommending that Australian troops be issued with stockwhips and boomerang-shaped bayonets, among other contraptions.

For a country so young in military tradition, the logistics of raising and mobilising an expeditionary force in six weeks presented difficulties. Enlistment booths in cities swelled with volunteers, many of whom had registered their names at barracks before Australia's involvement in the war became official.

Never before had such a physically impressive or enthusiastic representation of manhood stepped forward at one time in Australia's history, and enlistment standards were set deliberately high.[3] No man was to be under the age of 19 or over the age of 38, nor was he to stand less than 5 feet 8 inches tall (170 cm) or have a chest measurement less than 34 inches (86.4 cm).[3] It was preferable that he had served time in the military cadets, that he was of firm Anglo-Celtic cast, and that he had no obvious physical defects like bad teeth or hare-lips.

Each state formulated brigades of 4000 or battalions of 1000 according to the density of its population. Volunteers were allotted according to the timing of their enlistment, their place of origin, even their calling. Reg Cooke, a graduate of Trinity College, was one of about 500 volunteers from Victoria's elite public schools in the 5th Battalion; the 6th was full of tradesmen and blue-collar workers from the suburbs of Melbourne; the 11th was almost exclusively Western Australian because of its formation in Perth; the 3rd contained a balance of men from the suburbs of Sydney and regional New South Wales; while the 14th was dominated by miners and labourers like George Kerr from rural Victoria.

Motives for enlisting were equally diverse. It was popularly believed that the Germans would be dealt with in six months, so many were impelled to sail away on the next available boat, the scent of adventure and danger in their nostrils. Others knew that as soldiers they would be accorded status for the first time in their lives. Edward Edwards, a clerk from Wangaratta, found that his name had been put on his office honour board before he had even enlisted.

Some desired to escape unsatisfactory domestic arrangements or dead-end jobs; others, including clergymen, who enlisted as rank and file soldiers, became aware that a spoke in the wheel of history was about to turn and that Australia's 'baptism of fire' was imminent. It prompted them to articulate concepts like loyalty to king and/or or country and notions of honour and sacrifice. 'I sincerely trust that you will look at my move in the right light, as you do most things, and recognise that out of a family of three sons, one can be spared for the defence of Australia',[4] wrote Private Eric Mulvey, of 2nd Australian Light Horse, to his mother.

As the months passed and casualty lists brought home the reality of it all, some joined up to avenge the death of an older brother or a mate; others enlisted out of guilt. Private Thomas Sibson, a 5th Battalion reinforcement, told his parents: 'I got the white feather given to me so I thought it was time I went I am having the time of my life since I have been out here… P.S. Who would not be a soldier its a great life'.[5] A few months later, Sibson had the audacity to write: 'I think it is time that Walter Wells enlisted or has he got what the Australians term it (cold feet)'.[6]

The British Government wanted Australia's troops structured so that they could be absorbed into its own armies, but the Inspector General of the Australian military, William Bridges, insisted the force should retain its Australian identity. Their induction as soldiers consisted of physical training, fire-arms handling and marching drills that never seemed to end. As keen as they were to have a go, Australian volunteers were reluctant to conform to the rigid traditions of the British Army. They contravened lights-out rules at base camps and were often to be found loitering in bars and cafés till the early hours. They did not take well to punishment either, as exhibited by the occasion at Broadmeadows camp, north of Melbourne, in October 1914, when troops rallied to secure the release of a 5th Battalion soldier who had been shackled on the ground like a convict as part of Field Punishment No 2. 'The men started to give them a pretty bad time so the Officers sent for the Brigadier (McCay) and he stood on a box & addressed the men, and said that he would hold an inquiry about the matter and that he would ask the men to go away quietly. All the men walked away after giving 3 cheers for the Brigadier',[7] recalled Private Allan Horner of the 6th Battalion.

When they marched for all to see, they looked strong and keen, but commentators noted how they lacked finesse and were sloppy on detail. Rows of bayonets tended to run askew, boots not infrequently stepped 'out of synch' and there was a tendency for talking along the lines. Some doubted whether these raw colonials with the dull uniforms were ready to match the fighting traditions of the British Regular Army. Ready or not, the first 12 000 of them went to war in October 1914 with the name 'Australian Imperial Force' on their badges. A second contingent of 12 000 sailed two months later; more than 300 000 Australians would follow them over the next three years.

Troops set sail with ambivalent emotions, knowing they might never see Australia and their loved ones again, yet sensing they had begun Homerian journeys that would eclipse the lives they knew.

'Cheers and much waving was exchanged on both sides, and the watchword to the girls to "keep single" was taken up with much avidity. In the afternoon the submarine Miners Band steamed round the vessel and among other tunes played "It's a long way to Tipperary", "The Girl I Left Behind Me" finishing up with the National Anthem',[8] wrote Lance-Corporal Harry Smith, as the 3rd Battalion left Sydney on the *Euripides*.

The brigades from south-eastern Australia set sail to the West Australian port of Fremantle where they linked up with the rest of the contingent. From there thirty-eight transport ships and three cruisers headed north-west through the Indian Ocean, destined for Egypt. The cramped monotony of the five-week journey would test the patience of restless soldiers and the invention of their officers. 'We just laze about & read & fight all day long. There are over 2000 on board so you can guess we are packed just like sardines [in hammocks]',[9] grumbled Private Murray Aitken on the *Ascanius*.

Physical drills were conducted on the decks, along with musketry parades, boxing, church services and lectures. Distractions came in the form of a pod of whales lolling by, a school of flying fish or a rough swell on the Great Australian Bight. A book-making ring started up on one ship in anticipation of the Melbourne Cup, while ex-newspapermen formed a soldiers' publication on another. Jokers staged mock court martials; some of more serious mind like Harry Smith read novels and listened to gramophones; others fished, worked on sun-tans or mused at how their ancestors were transported *to* Australia in much the same manner.

'We are all like convicts just now, everyone has his hair cut clean off. All of us has a different number',[10] wrote Private Harold Marsden, a 9th Battalion signaller.

Heavy swells prompted outbreaks of sea-sickness, particularly through the Great Australian Bight, while cramped conditions and changing climates spread influenza, measles and pneumonia, among other ailments, some of which proved fatal.

It seemed a matter of time before restlessness would breed discontent.

The first fatal casualty of the 7th Battalion was the loss of Colour Sergeant John O'Meara, aged 22, from the *Hororata*, at sea near Albany.[11] It is not known whether he jumped, fell or was pushed, and his mishap was not the first nor the last of its kind. When the *Kanowna* berthed at Fremantle for coaling, an order prevented all shore leave. But indignant troops refused to allow the coaling to take place until the Major agreed to let them go ashore. The Brigade got their leave and returned drunk, almost to a man. Private Frank Lesnie, of the 17th Battalion (and former school captain of Norwood Orphanage in London) was sober enough to remember: 'I witnessed 24 fights in 3 hours, which was followed by a general scrum. We retired that night some with black eyes, others with a few bruises and aching limbs'.[12]

Private Jack McInerney noted, with typical understatement, that troops aboard the *Malwa* were 'a little rowdy in Fremantle'.[13] Sergeant Jack Chugg wrote of trouble of a different kind:

> Derby day & 1000 miles away from Melbourne, the weather is very muggy ... I might tell you it is something awful down in the mess room. Most of us go about half naked. Driver Jarman was discharged through refusing to be inoculated, also being home sick. He has a wife & 6 children & I'm sure thats what is making him down hearted, he often has a weep...[14]

Private Aitken found himself in disgrace.

> Nov 7th Well, Mother dear, at last I've fallen foul of the Captain. Yesterday afternoon we were having a life belt drill & I, with the others, was laughing and joking. He singled me out + sent me to the detention cell...I felt very much like a criminal, behind iron bars, with no literature & sitting on the floor. At any rate, its been an experience for me.[15]

As to the European crisis, news came through that war had been declared between Britain and Turkey in November; the following month Greece had emerged as a potential enemy because of developments in the Balkans. 'I feel glad that I am on my way to take a part and the boys are all anxious to have a run at the Greeks',[16] Private McInerney wrote.

On 9 November, any doubts that a war was really happening were dispelled by news of the first convoy's escort ship, HMAS *Sydney*, disabling a German raider, the *Emden*, near the Cocos Islands. The victory over the Kaiser's fleet generated celebrations all round. Sergeant Chugg wrote: '... our Colonel shouted for every man aboard to drink to the luck of the "Australian Navy" which we all did willingly'.[17] Sergeant Tom Allsop's diary entry on the same day read: 'Well our officers were like a lot of school boys for awhile, and we cheered & cheered again then we had a lot of extras put on our table for dinner'.[18]

The *Emden* celebrations spilled over into 'crossing the line' ceremonies a few days later. The custom, which marked the passing of a ship across the Equator, involved a dunking in a canvas bath for anyone deemed fit to 'see the mysteries of the deep'. Light horseman Private Dolph Musgrove recounted: 'King Neptune and all his followers came aboard about two o'clock. Major Baker took the part of King and the band master was his wife, he looked very good too as a woman. The officers were the first to go through...'[19]

A month after setting sail, the voyagers began to anticipate land: a thick breeze laden with the smell of freshly rained-on earth, a locust blowing on board, the sight of smoke on the offing. Soon Colombo had come into view, giving most of the men their first glimpse of a foreign land. Such was Private McInerney's anticipation that he wrote: 'I hope that their relapse [at Fremantle] will not prevent us going on shore at Colombo. I hope to taste the mangoes and paw-paws, ride in the rickshaws; see as many sights as time will allow and then the roof can fall in...'[20] But to the great disappointment of many, leave was denied to all but officers and a few lucky soldiers. Private George Kerr, of the 14th Battalion, was among a few who risked punishment and jumped ship, not to be denied a once-in-a-lifetime opportunity. Private Henry Geyer, also of the 14th, settled for staying on board.

> We arrived at Clomber and their was hunderds of natives came around the ship in boats, some of the natives was selling fruit and cigettes, and we throw money down to them and they dived into the water for it. Clomber is the prettiest place ever I saw on my travels...[21]

The last leg of the journey steered a course through the Red Sea—'water same as other seas of course',[22] joked Major Ernest Gregory—up the Suez Canal to the port of Alexandria from where troops disembarked for training camps around Cairo.

CORPORAL JOHN FLEMING

Because of an anachronistic regulation that prevented men whose bodies bore letters D. (Deserter) or B.C. (British Convict) from being accepted into the AIF, tattoos of any kind caught the attention of medical examiners at enlistment booths. But this soldier, Corporal John A. Fleming, with the dragon tattoo on his chest, had no trouble getting a uniform. Fleming sailed from Hobart to enlist in the 38th Battalion in Melbourne in January 1916 at the age of 26. A carpenter by trade, he kept himself in supreme physical condition by boxing, but the adverse conditions of trench warfare wore him down. He was gassed in France in 1918; earlier he suffered a dose of malaria as well as a continual bowel complaint. His wife also experienced the ignominy of receiving an official letter stating that a 1917 Mentioned in Despatches notification had actually concerned another John A. Fleming. Fleming attained the rank of lieutenant and returned to Australia in 1919.

Melbourne tattooist John Entwistle said every war fought by Australians has attracted a queue at tattoo shop doors. 'The enemy can take your possessions, your freedom or your life, but that tattoo stays with YOU.'[1]

HENRY HERROD

With a six-shooter in his hand and the world at his feet, a teenage Henry Herrod seems ready for anything life can throw at him.

HENRY HERROD *with three friends before enlistment*

Shortly before enlisting in the 14th Battalion, a dapper Henry Herrod, back left, poses in a studio with a group of mates whose identities are not known. Herrod was employed as a timber worker at Cuming, Smith & Co. in Victoria's Yarra Junction. Judging by the robust frames and weathered hands of the other men, they too were labourers.

AUSTIN LAUGHLIN *(below), and the Melbourne University lacrosse team (above)*

Austin Laughlin's scholarly air might have seemed out of place in a trench. The 21-year-old Melbourne University student lived with his parents in the wealthy suburb of Malvern, dabbled in poetry and captained the university and Victorian lacrosse teams. He held his own on the battlefield as well. In fact, a successful trench raid led by Laughlin at Fleurbaix in 1916 was criticised by the official war correspondent Captain Charles Bean for being excessively brutal. Laughlin is standing hand in blazer pocket, second from the left in the back row of the Melbourne University lacrosse team photograph.

PRIVATE SIDNEY TATE *and his two sons*

Some diarists were as much concerned with the lives they left behind as the action around them. Private Sidney Tate's entries for the month of October 1917 included a brief description of a trench raid in which he 'took a watch from a prisoner', then 'Ernie's birthday 4 years old [24 October]…' and 'Dave's 8th Birthday [31 October]'.[2]

In this studio portrait taken before Tate went away to war, Ernie is sitting on his father's right, Dave is to his left. Tate, a 38-year-old former builder's labourer from Sydney, died as a result of a gunshot wound to the head, near Amiens in 1918.

PRIVATE HUGHIE LOWE

By September 1915 Australia had been in the war for over a year, and Hughie Lowe decided he could wait no longer to be with his half-brother Corporal William Lowe in the trenches. So he went to the enlistment booth with a bounce in his step and a letter from his mother saying it was okay by her if he enlisted. What the Sydney recruiting depot didn't know was that Lowe was 14 years old, and that he had blackmailed Mrs Frances Lowe into signing the consent letter by threatening to enlist under an assumed name. 'You'll never know if I get killed or not',[3] he warned her. He gave his age as 18 years, 2 months, and fluked his way in as a driver with the 4th Field Artillery Brigade. Somehow his deceit held up until January 1918 when his mother put the authorities wise and he was sent back to Australia. He had not yet turned 18. Mrs Lowe had good reason to want him home; a few months earlier her other boy William, whose story is told in the caption on page 265, had been discharged because of 'delusional insanity'.

After he was sent home, Hughie Lowe worked as a telephone technician in Sydney, married and had four children. A daughter, Marie Rumsey, said: 'My Dad had a scar on his neck and we'd ask him how he got it, and he said "he was a German with a bayonet and he came running across this field with a bayonet and got me on the side of the neck". Whether it was true we'll never know'. Lowe's casualty papers contain no mention of him suffering any injuries.[4]

PRIVATE DAVID McGARVIE

When David McGarvie strode into a recruiting office at the Victorian grazing town of Camperdown in September 1914, he declared that he could shoot, ride a horse, and that he was ready to fight for Australia. 'But they were only taking fit men. Well, the doctor wouldn't have anything to do with me at all. He said, "Go and put your clothes on, you're only wasting my time". Because I had a hare-lip you see'.[5] The following Saturday he rode 40 kilometres to Colac and successfully enlisted as a private with the 8th Light Horse. He proved himself an unlikely hero at a place called the Nek a year later.

Private George Haskell *and an unidentified soldier*

Perhaps these two Australians are trying to emulate the fighting 'bulldog' spirit of the British Army, although their mascot appears to be of dubious breeding. The photograph was located during a search of Australian War Memorial collections. The name Geo. Haskell appears on the back of it. George Haskell, a Victorian farmer, served as a private with the 1st Division Signal Company. The identity of the other man is not known, nor is it known which of the two is Haskell.

PRIVATE EDWARD EDWARDS *and his brother* PRIVATE CHARLES EDWARDS

'I have to go to the swearing in depot and take the oath as soon as you sign them [enlistment papers]. Now don't make a fool of me. I got two hours off this morning to go down and enlist, and they are that proud of me in at work today I scarcely did a stroke',[6] wrote Edward Edwards, in a 15 July 1915 letter to his mother.

The 18-year-old clerk from Wangaratta, Victoria, had earlier told his father that one of his reasons for joining the 8th Battalion was to avenge the death of a former Wangaratta High school mate Charles Powley, 7th Battalion, at Gallipoli on 25 April.

His brother, Private Charles Edwards, a 19-year-old ironmonger, enlisted the same day in the 8th Battalion. In this 1915 photograph taken during a meal break at the Seymour training camp, Victoria, Edward is seated to the right on the chest, Charles is seated on the left, emptying the contents of a can of bully beef on to a plate on his lap. Private Edward Edwards was killed in action at Pozières on 26 July 1916. Charles Edwards survived the war.

27TH BATTALION SOLDIERS

Lieutenant Lindsay Ross' 'A Windy Day' photograph of 27th Battalion soldiers could have a number of interpretations. It was taken during a break at Broadmeadows camp, north of Melbourne, in November 1914, shortly before these men sailed to the front with the 2nd AIF contingent.

PRIVATE IVAN POLASKI

'Pte Ivan Polaski', the young soldier who appears in this soldiers' vaudeville routine at Broadmeadows, could not be traced in AIF records. It is possible that he was one of an estimated 15 000 Australian soldiers who enlisted using an alias to conceal their true identity. In Polaski's case, it might have been a ploy to detract from being under age. He was photographed by Lieutenant Ross.

Lᵗ. W. Freeman.   Meinself.   Lᵗ. G. Beith

Gordon Beith.   A feed of watermelon.   The Missing Link.

LIEUTENANT WILLIAM FREEMAN, LIEUTENANT LINDSAY ROSS,
LIEUTENANT GORDON BEITH

These young Victorian lieutenants at the Broadmeadows training camp were star products of Australia's cadet force system. Not one was past the age of 22, yet each was given the daunting responsibility of leading citizen soldiers to war. William Freeman, of the 13th Field Artillery Brigade, appears top left, Lindsay Ross, 27th Battalion, top middle as 'Meinself', Gordon Beith, 24th Battalion, top right, and eating the watermelon below. Freeman, a Warrnambool farmer, was awarded the Military Cross for bravery at Broodseinde in October 1917, but died of wounds three months later at the age of 23. Ross, a teacher from Ballarat, was invalided back to Australia in 1917 as a result of a severe arm wound, re-embarked early in 1918 and survived the war. Beith, a clerk from Ballarat, was shell-shocked as a result of a Turkish bombardment on Lone Pine in 1915 and suffered a breakdown. He was admitted to Mont Park Military Mental Hospital upon his discharge from the army in April 1916.

The sequence of photographs appeared in an album belonging to Lieutenant Ross, which is housed in the State Library of Victoria.

Members of the 4TH FIELD AMBULANCE BRIGADE

Members of the 4th Field Ambulance Brigade take a respite from field dressing practice at Broadmeadows training camp. This photograph is from the James McPhee collection held in the State Library of Victoria. Sergeant McPhee, a bank clerk from Essendon, joined the 4th F.A.B. in October 1914. He was presented with the Military Medal for bravery under fire in France in 1918. His war diary reveals an eye for the surreal: on one occasion a wounded Irishman assisted by McPhee gave his religion as 'Ration Carrier'; on another he described how a priest by the name of Devine was put under arrest for 'stretcher bearing'.[7]

18TH BATTALION TROOPS *wearing in new boots*

'Excellent way to make boots fit', wrote Sergeant Henry Roberts in a caption to this photograph. The soldiers are believed to be members of the 18th Battalion, detouring via a New South Wales river on a route march in 1914. Generations of Australian soldiers have worn in new boots in this way.

Main guard parade, 1ST LIGHT HORSE

'Dear Bertha, Am sending you post cards of the guard as promised. They are not very good ones. They were taken about five oclock in the afternoon and we were looking straight into the sun. I am showing plain enough in it but cannot see Bill. I think that is him with the shodawow [*sic*] of the rifle down his face…Your affectionate Brother Ted.'[8]

Driver Edward (Ted) Chave is standing in the front row of this guard parade at Cootamundra Military Camp, New South Wales, behind the young boy. Chave's younger brother Bill is slightly behind and to his left, face partially shadowed.

EDWARD *and* BILL CHAVE

'This is a snapshot of Bill and I in our dungarees. I am nearly ashamed to send it to you as I think it is a very poor photo. Well Bertha, I suppose you will be surprised to hear that Bill and I are leaving here for Liverpool tomorrow night',[9] wrote Ted Chave from Cootamundra Military Camp, New South Wales.

Everywhere Ted Chave (right) went, younger brother Bill seemed to wear him like a shadow. The farm labourers of Yarrangobilly, near Tumut, enlisted as reinforcements to the 1st Light Horse Regiment, then later transferred as drivers to the 5th Division Artillery. That way they could take advantage of their horse-handling skills and Ted, 27, could keep an eye out for 22-year-old Bill. Tragically, though, Ted Chave was accidentally killed on 17 March 1917 when a tree limb fell on him while he was cutting firewood behind the lines in France. Bill Chave survived the war and was returned back to Australia in 1919 but he was grief-stricken over Ted's death, according to relatives. He took his own life in 1925 at the age of 32.

A third Chave brother, Harry, enlisted in 1916, aged 31, as a driver with the 2nd Reinforcements to the 56th Battalion. He survived the war and returned to the family farm. He died in 1966 at the age of 81.

27TH BATTALION SOLDIERS *march through the streets of Adelaide*

Lieutenant Lindsay Ross, saluting, leads 27th Battalion reinforcements on a march past South Australia's State Governor shortly before embarking for France in December 1917. Ross was invalided to Australia after being badly wounded in France in 1916, then rejoined the battalion while it was being replenished with the 20th Reinforcements in Adelaide. Tall, strong-looking soldiers have been posi-tioned at the head and tail of the columns in this photograph. Some of the smaller reinforcements would not have been accepted in the AIF when more stringent physical standards applied in the early part of the war. Processions like this one through the streets of Adelaide took on a solemn air as battle casualty lists increased alarmingly.

5TH BRIGADE TROOPS *waiting to board the* CERAMIC, *Sydney*

Troops believed to be from the 5th Brigade muster in Sydney in preparation for their voyage to the front on board the *Ceramic*.

This photograph appeared in an album belonging to Sergeant Roberts from the 18th Battalion.

The troopship BERRIMA *is farewelled from Sydney*

2nd AIF Contingent soldiers cram the decks of a troopship, believed to be the *Berrima*, as it is farewelled from Sydney in December 1914. The streamers and cheering crowds were typical of the national fervour during the early enlistment period. The photograph is from an album compiled by Major Edmund Milne of the 1st Railway Supply Detachment.

27TH BATTALION *reinforcements wait to board the* ULYSSES

With the *Ulysses* lurking in the distance, these 27th Battalion reinforcements commence their odysseys from a near-empty Station Pier, Port Melbourne, on 22 December 1917. The pier was a point of departure for tens of thousands of AIF troops, particularly in 1914 and 1915. This photograph was taken by Lieutenant Ross.

2

EGYPT

Several reasons prevented the Australians from proceeding to England to prepare for the Western Front. The German Army had been momentarily checked by the British and the French, and training facilities for new troops were not yet available. A second, more pertinent factor was the fear that the Turks would strike the Suez Canal, and make a play for the vulnerable British possession of Egypt.

Having disembarked at Alexandria, the 1st Contingent commenced a six-hour train journey to Mena, a lie of sand within view of the pyramids. That the troops would camp and train beside one of the Seven Wonders of the World seemed a fair compensation after most of them were denied leave at Colombo. Once tents had been pitched, troops were allowed leave. Some slunk away to Cairo, but most of them flocked to the pyramids. Private Harold Jude, a fireman of Ballarat, was among them. 'Australian soldier first white man to climb this pyramid',[1] he wrote. Lieutenant Lindsay Ross had his fortune told in the King's Chamber of the Great Pyramid. 'Here it is',[2] he told his mother. 'About 7 months ago I was worrying about something. (Perhaps it was I wanted to go to the war)…'

In their haste to climb the pyramids, some soldiers fell to their deaths. Others developed a mysterious 'pyramids cough' after crawling through the chambers of the pharaohs. To climb a pyramid and to carve one's name linked a man to Napoleon's army, some of whose names could still be seen on the rocks. This rite of soldiers was later formalised by portraits on the lower steps of the pyramids or beneath the cold stare of the Sphinx. This patch of sand became a photographic tolling point for almost every member of the AIF, whose units were never more complete, never stronger than in Cairo.

Most photographs from the pyramids are buoyant and spontaneous, reflecting the glee of the ingenue who glimpses immortality as the setting Sahara sun bathes him in the glow of a crucible. It was typical for brothers like Hedley Kitchin, of the 6th Battalion, and George Kitchin Kerr, of the 14th Battalion, to reunite there; for soldiers who grew up in the one town, like Pat Lynch and the other 'Warrack [Warracknabeal] boys' to get together for a shot for the folks back home. Yet there is a sad valediction tinged to them—it became a statistical certainty that two out of every three men in those photographs would be killed or wounded in the war.

While the pyramids transmitted an enduring allure for most Australians, the city of Cairo offered more sensual and venal enticements. True to any great odyssey, the sensibilities of these journeymen were broadened and affronted as never before. Letters and diaries brim with wonder and excitement, others are puritanical, or reflect disdain and intolerance of 'inferior' cultures that emanated from the xenophobic attitudes of a 'White Australia'. If an Indian or a Gurkha was fighting alongside an Australian, he was considered a decent fellow, but if the dark-skinned character approaching down an alley was a pedlar with something to sell, he was to be mistrusted and despised. Driver Duncan McCrae told 'Miss Turner' that the Cairo natives 'only wash every time it rains and that is every twenty years'.[3]

Lieutenant Ross, a school teacher from Ballarat, explained that if you wanted respect from a black man 'you must show that you are the boss otherwise they get cheeky'. Later, the lieutenant joked: 'I forgot until the other day that it was Sam's birthday. I'll send him a "fez" to wear to Sunday School'.[4]

When Private McConnachy found out his younger brother Cliff had just joined up he wrote:

> My advice to Cliff is not to take any spirits from the niggers...one lot taken to an analyst contained a quantity of human wine—these dirty beggars will do anything for money... Also tell him (Cliff) not to interfere with the black women wearing a veil, they have some high religious standing among their people and it is a serious thing to meddle with them.[5]

Some accounts hint at the kind of mischief and cynicism that inspired C. J. Dennis' creation of the larrikin digger in *Songs of a Sentimental Bloke*, a hit among soldiers after it was published in 1915. The Australians commandeered trams, raced donkeys through brothel districts and refused to salute British officers. They splurged their pay-packets wantonly, earning themselves the nickname the 'six-bob-a-day tourists'. If they weren't being ripped off by Arab hawkers, they were roughing them up, upturning their stalls or, in lighter moments, teaching them how to swear in English.

'You can have every sort of amusement at this place for pretty well all the Hotels have a hall at the side with girls dancing and singing and you can have donkey races up the main street with no one to interfere',[6] rejoiced Private Young, a labourer from the Melbourne suburb of Brunswick.

Private McInerney of Mount Gambier might have been a fan of Kipling's *Kim*. 'What a pity you must miss these sights. It is a wonderland. Picture me threading my way through narrow lanes with crowded native traffic of a very cosmopolitan nature. See me on my white donkey with Said, the boy, yelling behind me'.[7]

Private Geyer, a barman from Bendigo, told his parents:

> Cariro [sic] is 8 miles from where we are camped, it is the most Imorial place in the world, it wont do for me to explain it to you. The most beautiful women are here to be seen. And they all carrier on a fast life with all their beautiful ways— ways they will never be able to entice me to do wrong so bear that in mine.[8]

Sentiments like this were common in letters home, particularly to parents, wives and girlfriends, yet many soldiers succumbed to a 'temptation of a certain kind, which had best be left unsaid',[9] as Private Lesnie put it. Some spoke of it euphemistically: a tour of the 'fish market', or a bit of 'jiga-jig' with a 'bint' (black prostitute). However it was expressed or confessed, the highly paid Australian soldiers frequented Cairo brothels in large numbers and the casualty sheets of 10 per cent of them became marked with the words 'Venereal Disease', 'Gonorrhoea' or 'Syphilis'. Thousands of others escaped infection only by law of chance.[10]

So alarming was the problem that King George V voiced his concerns to Australia's Governor General, and AIF authorities enforced curfews in brothel districts with patrols to round up deserters, many of whom were drunk. Attempts were made to extend YMCA recreational facilities at base camps, and to issue soldiers with prophylactics, but still some persisted, and, in early 1915, AIF authorities transported a few hundred offenders home and discharged them from the army. Captain Charles Bean was summoned by General Bridges to write to Australian newspapers explaining the situation. Wayward veterans from the Boer War were blamed for stirring up trouble among younger, more impressionable elements. In the long run the episode probably did more to generate bad feeling among the ranks towards military bureaucrats than to alleviate the incidence of trouble around Cairo.

After seeing the Bean article posted up, Private George Levens wrote: 'McBain is going to get what his [illegible] not from the wasters but from the South Africans [ex-Boer War servicemen]. I know a lot of them and they are the finest fellows I have ever met'.[11] Private Mulvey, a light horseman, said: 'Many who have read his report in the Sydney M.H. [*Sydney Morning Herald*] suggest that the only army uniform he ever wore before was a red guernsey it would be ridiculous to expect an expeditionary force to be all members of the Y.M.C.A. wouldn't it'.[12]

The Australian presence abated in Cairo for a while after the purge. Training hours were extended and commanders went about promoting men seemingly to shore up discipline and morale, rather than for any outstanding performance. Private Mulvey was sceptical when promoted to lance corporal in Heliopolis in

March 1915. 'It means that I carry a stripe on my arm and with my rather fine moustache, it makes me look rather military. It came as a shock to me, I seem to have done nothing to earn it except keep off the crime sheet'.[13] Around the same time, Private McConnachy knocked back a promotion to corporal. 'Corporals do the Officers and all hands dirty work and that would not suit me, they are paid only a little more than a private'.[14]

When leave was permitted, soldiers looked to other attractions: a visit to Heliopolis, the 'Toorak of Cairo', with a Luna Park 'almost the same as the one in St Kilda with a water slide thrown in', a felucca ride down the Nile River; a visit to the City of the Dead on the outskirts of the city, or the Muslim Citadel where visitors ran foul of fastidious attendants once it was learned the acoustics generated a decent echo. Diaries describe music halls like the *Kursaal*, where one could see a French diva perform to the accompaniment of an orchestra, or a juggler that Private Aitken had recognised from a show in the Australian gold mining town of Kalgoorlie.

Out in the light horse camps, troopers, who would die as foot soldiers at the Nek, tried their hand at buck-jumping. The Cairo Zoo was popular, and sometimes entire brigades were marched through it to break the routine of desert training or to keep them away from the city. Private Harold Aisbett recalled one such march: 'We passed an enclosure in which there was an old man kangaroo & and when the boys at the head of the column first saw him they started to cheer & the cheers went right down the whole length of the column some 2200 men'.[15]

A diversion came in early February when Turks attempted to seize part of the Suez Canal. The 7th and 8th Battalions were called in to support Indian and British garrisons, but by the time the Australians got there, the Turks had retreated in defeat. The Suez flare-up was technically Australia's first infantry engagement since the Boer War, but the over-trained AIF still had not had the chance to prove itself. Rumours of the AIF's departure for one front or another came and went, leaving soldiers in a state of limbo. Authorities, meanwhile, had to contend with fresh outbreaks of disease, more restlessness at base camps, more insubordination and desertions.

Private John Makeham wrote from Cairo in February 1915: 'Monday, general review by Sir Ian Hamilton [commander of the Allied Dardanelles forces], he expresses general satisfaction with the troops and says that the Australians are the largest type of men engaged in the present war'.[16]

On Good Friday, 2 April, Lance Corporal Mulvey contended: 'Within the past two weeks we have been reviewed on separate occasions by the High Commissioner of Egypt, Sir A. MacMahon and Sir Ian Hamilton, so surely that must portend something'.[17] Mulvey's prediction that 'something' was about to happen was correct but it had nothing to do with fighting Turks or Germans.

That night violence erupted in the Haret el Wasser red light district when a New Zealand soldier was stabbed during an altercation with an Arab brothel minder. Immediate retribution was sought on the Arab, as well as the brothel, and it soon spilled into adjoining venues. At least one soldier was reportedly shot dead, scores more were injured.

Lieutenant Geoff McCrae described it as a 'regrettable incident';[18] Sergeant Chugg saw it as a 'little disturbance'.[19] He was dining in a 'Wazzer' café when he heard gunshots and rushed out to see 'red caps' (British military police) firing at Australian and New Zealand soldiers who had recently been placed under the same corps banner.

> By this time there was a bon fire in the centre of the street & breaking windows all over the place. One chap got shot near me and another got it in the leg & I aided him a little but the firing was too hot & I didn't want a piece of lead in me. It was funny to see the tables & chairs coming out of the windows, mattresses & all sort of things…Some of the men broke up the fire engine & cut up the hoses in foot pieces with their 'Reid' knives.

The riot was the first of two rampages at the Wazzer, the second, less spectacular 'battle' occurred in July 1915, with mostly Australian and New Zealand reinforcements featuring in the action, driven by much the same reasons. Some omens, seemingly biblical in portent, preceded the first riot. A locust storm swept through several AIF bases a few days before, and, at night, restless sentries fired shots at stray dogs in the desert. The day before the riot, April Fools Day, ushered in the news that the 1st Australian Division was to proceed to the Front—but which front, against whom, when?—then a series of pranks at base camps and a sand storm. But what caused Anzac troops to snap? Boredom, growing resentment over the ruses of Cairo traders and prostitutes. In their hunger to fight, were some driven by a quixotic motive to release women, some from war-torn Belgium, kept in bondage by pimps and hashish dealers? Was it a pagan rehearsal for their true 'baptism of fire'? One thing remained clear: they had been stuck in a 'dirty filthy place' called Cairo, without a war to fight. The day after the Good Friday riot, troops were ordered to strike camp and embark for the front.

5TH BATTALION SOLDIERS *on the* ORVIETO

5th Battalion soldiers sort through kits and rifles before making their way to sleeping quarters on the *Orvieto*. This photograph was taken by Melbourne *Age* correspondent-turned-soldier Phillip Schuler on 21 October 1914, the day the former Orient liner left for the front. Other passengers included General Bridges and the staff of the 1st Australian Division. Men on this ship sailed in luxury in comparison to soldiers who sailed on converted meat and wool carriers.

The MARATHON *encounters a heavy swell in the Great Australian Bight*

Rough swells in the Great Australian Bight made it difficult for many soldiers, especially those at sea for the first time, to find their 'sea legs'. The Bight was remembered as being notoriously rough, with big waves occasionally breaking over the bows of ships. This photograph of the *Marathon* was taken from another troopship as a fleet of AIF reinforcements headed for the Western Front in May 1917.

Sea-sickness on board the BALLARAT

Incidences of sea sickness were high particularly during the early part of the voyage to Egypt. This was due to a combination of rough seas, disagreeable food and fumes from ship engine rooms. In this photograph taken on board the *Ballarat* a number of soldiers appear to have been overcome by the problem. The *Ballarat* was torpedoed and sunk on Anzac Day 1917 in the English Channel.

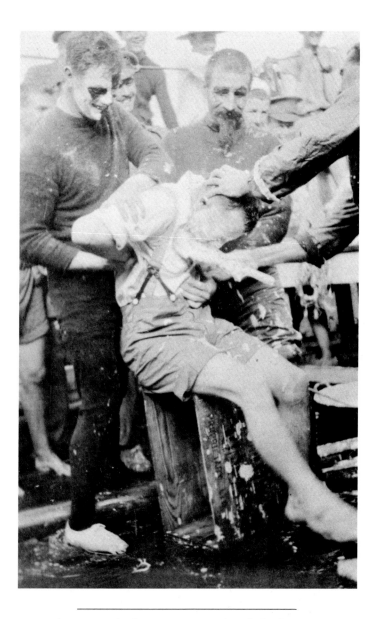

A crossing the line ceremony on board the AENEAS

Father Neptune's gang prepares this soldier for a dunking during a crossing the line ceremony on board the *Aeneas* in October 1916. Traditionally staged to celebrate a ship's passing across the Equator, the light-hearted custom was not always popularly received by Neptune's victims. In one case, a fight broke out on the *Hororata* when a corporal took exception to being chosen and threatened the participants with a knife. The ceremonies were eventually banned by AIF authorities because of the risk of injury and sickness but were revived on transport ships returning to Australia in 1919.

This photograph was donated to the Australian War Memorial by Lieutenant Alexander McMillan of the 3rd Division Artillery.

Armed guard for captured EMDEN *crewmen on the* ORVIETO

These soldiers stand rigidly to attention during an inspection on the *Orvieto* after it had taken custody of fifty-one prisoners from the *Emden*, a German raider sunk by the *Sydney* on 11 November 1914 near the Cocos Islands. The POWs included Captain von Muller who refused to give assurances that he would not try to escape. General Bridges ordered an armed guard and denied von Muller the courtesies he might have otherwise received. The photograph was taken by Phillip Schuler.

Sack-racing on the ULYSSES

'Wednesday Dec. 26th Boxing Day [1917]. Like the people on land we are having a holiday today and we have held sports on board ship. All day long on the boat decks teams and individuals have been indulging in various competitions for the champi-onship of the ship at boxing, tug of war, skipping, jumping, potato race, sack race and many other forms of sport.'[10]

Lieutenant Ross, 27th Battalion, diary, on board the *Ulysses*. Ross also took the photograph.

Native diving for money from Australian troopship at Colombo

'Nigger diving for money from the davit at Colombo', said the caption on the back of this photograph by an unknown AIF soldier. Shore leave was mostly denied to all but senior officers when AIF transport ships moored at Colombo, their first port of call in a foreign land. Frustrated troops amused themselves by throwing money to natives who had paddled alongside the fleet offering fruit or feats of athleticism for a few loose coins. The term 'nigger' was common parlance among Australian servicemen. The expression was said to have derived from the 'Nigger' brand of boot polish.

7TH BATTALION *troops marching, Mena, Egypt*

Young Melbourne officers Captain Geoff McCrae, 25, and Lieutenant Bert Heighway, 21, leading C Company, 7th Battalion, back to base camp at Mena, Egypt, after a desert drill in early 1915. McCrae, left, collapsed after one such march. 'I have been in bed for three days with a chill and had a temperature of 102', he wrote on 16 March. '…I caught it in the same manner as many of these people get pneumonia. We had a very hot march and my clothes were thoroughly saturated with perspiration. We went straight into the trenches and had to stand in there from 6 p.m. until 4 a.m. in the cold night breeze and a drizzle of rain. Dear old Swift looked after me like an anxious mother'.[11]

This photograph was donated to the Australian War Memorial by Brigadier General H. E. 'Pompey' Elliott.

BRIGADIER GENERAL H. E. ELLIOTT, MAJOR IVIE BLEZARD
and CAPTAIN CHRISTOPHER FINLAYSON

Brigadier 'Pompey' Elliott, standing left, was wounded leading the 7th Battalion into battle on the day of the Gallipoli landings, as was Major Ivie Blezard, reclining on cart. Captain Christopher Finlayson, standing right, was wounded later in the campaign. The photograph was taken at Mena Camp near the pyramids.

Elliott stood out for his tempestuous personality and his affection for his troops. He did not like the nickname 'Pompey' but took it sportingly, as he did when 2nd Brigade troops stole his unusually large size 10 digger's hat and posted it back to his wife in Melbourne.

Musketry drill

'First Catch—the point where the bullet has descended sufficiently to strike the head of a man, whether mounted, kneeling or lying…'[12]

Notes from the diary of Private Percy Virgoe, 4th Light Horse, 1915, Egypt. AIF troops regularly conducted war man-oeuvres under simulated conditions in the desert but the soldier pointing his rifle at the camera (second from right) appears to be treating it more like a game. In fact, he is in breach of an army regulation forbid-ding the pointing of a weapon at anyone other than the enemy. The pyramids are visible in the background of this shot taken by an unknown soldier.

Australian trench systems along the Suez Canal

'For the Defence of the Canal': this undated photograph was probably taken early in 1916 when Australian forces were involved in the fortification of trenches east of the Suez Canal. In February 1915, however, some companies of the 7th and 8th battalions were diverted to the canal to quell an abortive attack by Turkish forces on the strategically important waterway. The photograph was taken by Lieutenant Ross.

22ND BATTALION *soldiers, including* LIEUTENANT WILLIAM MAY,
swimming at Mena House, Egypt

Lieutenant William May, of the 22nd Battalion, sent this photograph home to his wife in Port Melbourne. May appears in the front with his hands out of the water. A caption beneath it read: 'Swimming pool Mena House Lt Buckley (adjt) behind me'. The pool was in the grounds of the Mena House Hotel where some AIF commanders stayed. It was not far from where 1st Division AIF troops trained.

LIEUTENANT MAY

PRIVATE FRANCIS KENNEDY

Lieutenant May was attached to the headquarters of the 22nd Battalion while in Egypt. His batman, Private 'Snowy' Francis Kennedy, a driver from St Kilda, enlisted in the service corps but later decided he wanted to join the infantry.

He was killed in action in Belgium in 1917 at the age of 34. A batman's role ranged from that of clerk to cleaner. Many batmen were chosen because they were seen not to measure up to the daily grind of regimental life.

CORPORAL ROBERT MILLER *and* 5TH LIGHT HORSE *mates*

Corporal Robert Miller, right, relaxes with a group of his 5th Light Horse mates outside a tent in Egypt. Emu plumes, the Light Horse trademark, stand out on the hats of the two men in the middle of the group. The light horsemen bemused some inquirers by telling them that the plumes were 'kangaroo feathers'.

PRIVATE ERNEST LESTER

SERGEANT CHARLES MASTERS

'Pte Lester caught napping "Do not publish this"', wrote Corporal Hedley Kitchin of the 6th Battalion on the back of this photograph he took at Mena Camp. Ernest Lester, a 20-year-old gold blocker from North Fitzroy, was discharged from the army in March 1916.

They travelled to war together, ate and slept together, fought and died together... Sergeant Charles Masters, of the 2nd Field Artillery Brigade, is photographed with his horse 'after two hours sleep in the desert'. Australian mounted troops were renowned for the way they cared for their horses; the horses, in kind, were unflinchingly brave. In fact, the 'sleeping' pose of the horse in this photograph was adopted in light horse training procedures to double as a human shield in the case of sudden ambush. Masters, a blacksmith, was killed in action in 1916.

PRIVATE AUSTIN LAUGHLIN

'This is me. Notice my criminal hair-cut. I am preparing to eat a piece of Turkish delight (in my right hand) You will notice how fat and well I am looking. Leo took this snap.'[13]

Austin Laughlin sent this 1915 photo postcard from Mena Camp to his parents in Melbourne. The postcard illustrates a dramatic physical transformation in Laughlin from his university days, on page 27.

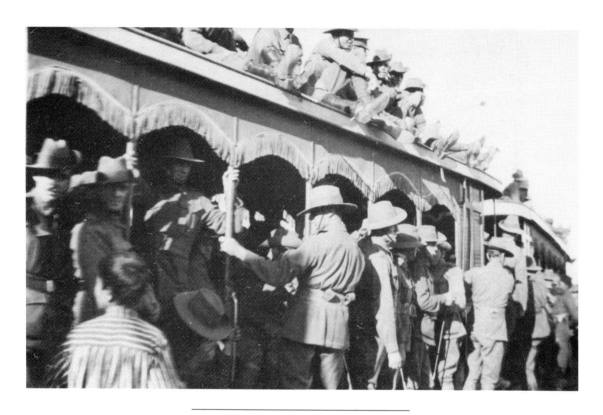

AIF SERVICEMEN *crowd a Cairo tram*

This photograph shows a group of AIF servicemen on day leave in Cairo. The city's tramcar network was under continual strain from overcrowding, fare evasion and harassment of conductors by Anzac troops. Some trams were commandeered and taken for high-speed jaunts, a feat for which rowdy members of the Imperial Camel Corps gained renown.

Outside a burial chamber at the pyramids

'In old Cairo' reads the caption of this photograph by Lance Corporal William Gornall of the 23rd Battalion. The shot was taken at the pyramids, at the opening of a burial chamber. Gornall was a photographer by profession.

AUSTRALIAN SOLDIERS *in front of the Sphinx*

'Dear Nell, This is not a good photo. The light was a bit strong I suppose. You can recognise Hall and I, the other five chaps of our section...' says the scrawl on the back of this photograph. With their souvenir walking canes, the unidentified Australians seem to be mimicking the aristocracy as they pose with their guide in front of the Sphinx and the Great Pyramid.

3RD BATTALION SOLDIERS *in front of the Sphinx*

'In afternoon went for excursion to pyramids and Sphinx and had our photos taken at foot of Sphinx…a mate and myself went up to the top [of a pyramid] on one side and down again on the other. There is a lovely view to be obtained from here and I further enhanced the importance of the pyramids by engraving my illustrious name on that Stately Pile of Ancient Artisanship.'[14]

Lance-Corporal Harry Smith, 3rd Battalion, 6/7 December 1914, diary, Egypt. Smith, a cadet draftsman and Sunday School teacher from Narrabeen, Sydney, is reclining in the front row of his platoon, third from left, cigarette in hand.

Although only 19, he was a man with a point of view. To most, the way the sun rose on the voyage to Egypt was 'bonzer'; Smith was enraptured by its 'wonderful opalescent tints and reflections'. Most

yarned and gambled in their spare time; Smith listened to a gramophone, wrote an extensive diary and read novels by Russian authors Dmitrii Merezhkovskii and Vladislav Ozerov. To most, the natives of their first port of call, Colombo, were jabbering 'niggers'; to Smith they were 'very pleasant peace-loving and good-natured little fellows'. And being a Sunday School teacher at St Cuthbert's Church of England got him the job of 'altar boy' for services on board the *Euripides*.

As a youngster his sporting and academic achievements earned him a scholarship to Sydney Grammar School where he also served in the senior cadets. Talented all-rounders like him were eyed for quick promotion, but Smith seemed to revel at being in the company of rank and file soldiers. He would die among them at Gallipoli.

I st Feb.1915 "B" Company
at the foot of the Cheops Pyradid
Egypt

AUSTRALIAN SOLDIERS *on the steps of the Cheops Pyramid*

This unidentified company of Australian soldiers presents an atmosphere of casual individualism. A young bugler sits on the ground (to the left) wearing a cheerful expression, while a short soldier near the top left stares into the ether triumphantly, like Napoleon himself. Lower down to the right, a group of soldiers unfurl flags revealing various allegiances, while three soldiers to the bottom right of the frame hold white handerchiefs in what might be a gesture of mock surrender. Judging by the smiles on many of the men, they were amused by a comment moments before this portrait was taken on the steps of the Cheops Pyramid, on 1 February 1915.

SOLDIERS *climb the Great Pyramid*

Climbing the Great Pyramid passed into ritual among armies over the centuries. The 144-metre ascent was not without its dangers, however. Some Australian soldiers were killed or seriously injured attempting to climb it.

PRIVATE DAVID JUDE *and* PRIVATE PERCY MINIFIE

'P. Minafie and Myself on top of Cheops pyramid a good view of the size of one of the stones on top.' This photograph appears in an album sent home to Private David Jude's family after he was killed in action at Gallipoli. Private Jude, right, a fireman who enlisted in the 8th Battalion, had earlier written: 'Australian soldier first white man to climb this pyramid'.[15] His friend Private Percy Minifie rose to the rank of lieutenant and was killed in action at Broodseinde in 1917.

An Australian soldier in Cairo

While in Egypt, a soldier could hire a donkey for a few piastres a day. The humble donkey was used for sightseeing jaunts through Cairo and, in some instances, races through the narrow streets. The soldier in this photograph is not identified.

Cairo water-bag carrier

'EGYPTIAN CARACTERS'. A street pedlar, with a goat skin water bag slung over his shoulder, beams with the realisation that he is the subject of Lance-Corporal Gornall's camera. The blurred outline of an Australian soldier is to the right of the frame.

SERGEANT MASTERS

Sergeant Masters comes under close attention from Cairo street hawkers while waiting to catch a tram. The native immediately to Masters' right is probably selling a soft drink concoction. Australian soldiers became suspicious that beverage dispensers watered down or adulterated their brews, particularly alcohol, with methylated spirits or worse.

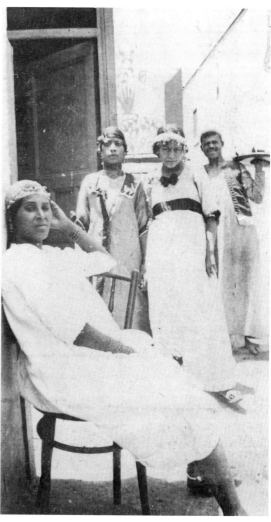

A brothel, Alexandria

Scene outside an Alexandria brothel

'Courteseans and hire ladies' wrote Quartermaster Sergeant John Lord, of the 13th Australian Field Ambulance, on the back of these photographs taken in the port city of Alexandria, where Australian troops disembarked for Cairo. Scenes like these were typical of Egypt's thriving brothel trade. While soldiers voiced apparent disgust over the sex trade, it was a temptation many could not resist. In the image on the right the young woman next to the waiter appears to be pregnant.

AUSTRALIAN SOLDIERS *outside a Cairo brothel*

Two Australian soldiers haggle with a brothel pimp in the Wazzer, Cairo's red-light district, which AIF authorities eventually declared out of bounds because of the alarming incidence of venereal disease among troops. A dispute between a New Zealander and a brothel minder is alleged to have sparked the Good Friday Wazzer riot of 1915.

An Australian soldier and a young hawker

An Australian wearing a pith helmet selects confectionery from a young native trader near the pyramids. The soldier's helmet is decorated with the AIF rising sun emblem, distinguishing it from the British pith helmet.

LIEUTENANTS THOMAS *and* BERTWISTLE

'Lieuts Thomas and Bertwistle' seem to be catching up on news from home. The photograph by Lieutenant Ross was taken at base camp. Wilfred Bertwistle was wounded in action in France and returned to Australia in February 1917. Lieutenant Thomas' army records could not be traced.

Native guide

'Abdul'…'Lt Brice as Abdul' These two photographs were taken in Cairo by Lieutenant Ross. His friend Charles Brice fought with the 20th Battalion and returned to Australia in November 1918. Abdul features in some of Ross' writings.

LIEUTENANT CHARLES BRICE

In a letter to his mother on 25 July 1915, Ross said: 'I was just showing my Arabic writing to Abdul the "guide" + he has written some more for me. The concoction on the right means "very good" the next one means Australia is "very good".'[16]

Unknown mounted division soldier

LIEUTENANT LANG

This bare-chested soldier struts his manliness like a star graduate from the Snowy Baker Physical Culture School in Sydney. The soldier is unidentified but probably belonged to a field ambulance unit. His leather gaiters indicate he was a horse driver. His cocksure stance and well-worn slouch hat contrasts with that of Lieutenant Lang, right, who, with his pith helmet and flexed cane at the ready, has cheekily adopted the airs of a self-important British officer. Both photographs were taken while AIF divisions were training at camps around Egypt. The shot on the left was taken by Quartermaster Sergeant Lord. The shot on the right was taken by Lieutenant Ross. It is not known what became of Lieutenant Lang.

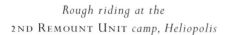

Rough riding at the
2ND REMOUNT UNIT *camp, Heliopolis*

'Blanketing' at the
2ND REMOUNT UNIT *camp, Heliopolis*

A breaker at Major 'Banjo' Paterson's 2nd Remount Unit camp commands a big audience during this tussle with an untamed horse. Paterson, who made his name as a Boer War correspondent and poet sympathetic to the ways of the Australian bushman, was given the command of the unit at the age of 50, partly so he could pursue his love of horses.

This photograph was taken by Cedric Foot, a 2nd Remount lieutenant, at Heliopolis on the outskirts of Cairo. Most of the horses used by Australian mounted units were 'recruited' from the Australian countryside or donated by graziers. About 160 000 horses were transported from Australia during the war. The most common was the 'Waler', a horse with hardy bloodlines that originated from the interminglings of stock mares and brumbies.

'Blanketing' was a popular pastime in cadet training camps before the outbreak of war, and carried on to base camps throughout the war. It involved a large number of participants heaving upwards at the edges of the blanket, propelling a victim skywards, trampoline-style. Authorities frowned upon the practice because of invariable mishaps including broken bones and concussions resulting from victims either missing or falling through tears in blankets. This photograph was also taken by Lieutenant Foot, a Queensland grazier who survived the war.

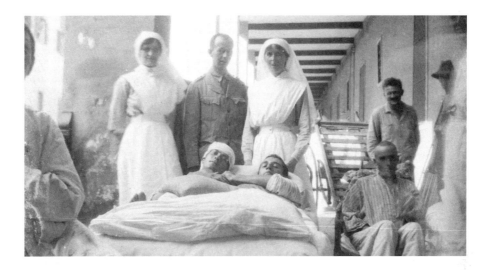

AUSTRALIAN *convalescents and nurses*

AUSTRALIAN *soldiers outside a Cairo hospital*

Hospital facilities around Cairo were over-crowded with soldiers who succumbed to dehydration, pneumonia, flu and various local fevers. The epidemics were brought about by a combination of exotic climate, poor hygiene and over-exertion during training. Facilities were tested even further when the incidence of venereal disease peaked by early 1915.

This photograph was selected from an album belonging to Sister Kathleen Doyle, who is the nurse standing with her hands on the bedhead.

The photograph above illustrates the light blue and white pyjamas worn by convalesc-ing Australian soldiers in Cairo, and as seen by the hundred in the vicinity of hospitals. A caption on the back of the photo read: 'Can you recognise me standing at the back, Love Gus'. It was brought back from the war by Gunstaff Lansberg, a 14th Battalion private from Melbourne. He was discharged in 1917.

2ND BRIGADE *officers outside Brigade Headquarters*

'DEAR MRS COLES, MENA 11-3-15. Here is a group of 2nd Brigade officers at a Pow-wow at the Brigade Headquarters. For indentification purposes I have branded myself x…perhaps we look thin and worried (I don't think)',[17] wrote an unknown officer who sent this card home to Australia.

Of the 130 officers in the 2nd Brigade, fifty-seven were listed as killed, wounded or missing within five days of the 25 April landings, a large proportion of them having been hit by Turkish snipers. Other brigades suffered similar losses.[18] The man in the centre of the group with the white walrus moustache is Major Robert Gartside, a Boer War hero, killed in action while leading a charge near Tommies' Trench, Krithia, on 8 May. In this photograph Major Gartside appears to be rolling a cigarette; at least ten other men can be seen smoking. The apex of the Great Pyramid appears above the ridge line, left of frame.

A sand storm near Cairo

Australian soldiers close ranks as a storm engulfs them near Cairo. The desert sand was a source of perpetual frustration for soldiers training in Egypt—it got into everything from eyes to clothes, guns and food.

SIR GEORGE REID *watches* 1ST DIVISION *troops at Mena Camp, Egypt*

Sir George Reid, top hat raised, reviews troops before addressing the 1st Australian Division at Mena Camp on 30 December 1914. Sir George was otherwise known as 'Sir Greid' on account of his bulk, and 'Yes-No Reid' because of his equivocation during the Federation Convention of the 1890s. Australia's third Prime Minister and High Commissioner to London, Sir George endeared himself to troops by providing items such as clasp knives, but some used their 'Reid knives' to cut fire hoses during the Wazzer riot three months later. This photograph was taken by Phillip Schuler.

A fight between two 1ST DIVISION *soldiers*

'Fight Mena' is the caption on the back of this anonymous photograph. Given their reputation for gambling, some soldiers probably wagered quick bets on the outcome of this altercation between two 1st Division soldiers.

The aftermath of the Wazzer district riot

Cairo's Wazzer district in ruins after Australian and New Zealand troops rioted there on 2 April 1915. A cluster of Australian soldiers surveys the damage in the background while another Australian is riding a donkey, left foreground. This photograph was taken by Quartermaster Sergeant Lord.

AUSTRALIAN *soldiers with a skull found at the City of the Dead, Cairo*

Digging for antiquities and bones became a popular recreation for soldiers around the ancient sites of Egypt. This skull was probably unearthed during a visit to the City of the Dead on the outskirts of Cairo. Some soldiers came to know the site as the 'City of the Dead-tired'.

3

GALLIPOLI

On 11 April 1915 the first Anzac ships sailed in to Lemnos harbour, eighty kilometres from Gallipoli. An initial force of 35 000 Anzac troops began an intensive period of disembarkation and landing manoeuvres, while the intricacies of an invasion of the Gallipoli peninsula were mapped out.

The Allied navy had failed in two earlier attempts (4 March and 18 March) to outbomb Turkish forts along the mouth of the Dardanelles, and the lion's share of the operation had been deflected on to the infantry. They would invade as part of a multinational attack on the peninsula, charge over its hills and secure Maidos on the Dardanelles, knock out the batteries along the Narrows then sail 280 kilometres to Constantinople, the jewel of the Ottoman Empire. With the Western Front in deadlock, Winston Churchill, the most forthright and impatient member of the British War Council, schemed that the conquest of Constantinople (Istanbul) would not only relieve pressure on Russia—at war with the Turks in the Caucasus—but also frustrate German ambitions to expand a railway link via Turkey through to the oil-rich Middle East.

The average Anzac knew little about the wider schemes of the war. Betting men predicted they would be playing two-up in Constantinople within a week. A few of them with a historical bent would have known they were near a place called Troy where heroic armies from the pages of Homer battled to the end, centuries before.

Because of the early harassment of the Dardanelles by the navy, the invasion had become the worst-kept secret of the war, and the peninsula that had been coveted by so many armies over the centuries was well garrisoned by Turks. General Hamilton and his staff, meanwhile, had only six weeks to prepare for the first sea-to-land invasion since the British attack on Napoleon's forces in Egypt in 1801.

Certain details were either rushed or glossed over in the countdown. Staff intelligence officers ignored advice to allocate scouts to reconnoitre the terrain in advance of the infantry, while hospital ship facilities had room for 300 'serious cases' even though a 30 per cent casualty rate was anticipated. If an unwritten mentality justified these oversights, in the Australian instance, it may have emanated from a culture of sacrifice that had been instilled into soldiers since the inauguration of compulsory military training in Australia.

Colonel E. G. Sinclair-MacLagan had no time to brief the 3rd Brigade's four battalions individually about their role as the initial AIF strike force at Gallipoli. Instead he issued each battalion commander with a communiqué dated 21 April:

> In an operation of this kind there is no going back…
>
> One thing I want you to remember all through this campaigning work is this, and it is important: you may get orders to do something which appears in your position to be the wrong thing to do, and perhaps a mad enterprise.
>
> Do not cavil at it but carry it out wholeheartedly and with absolute faith in your leaders because we are, after all only a small, very small, piece on the board.
>
> Some pieces have often to be sacrificed to win the game, and after all it is to win the game we are here.
>
> You have a good reputation you have built up for yourself and now you have a chance of making history for Australia and a name for the Australian brigade— the third—that will live in history…

Soldiers, meanwhile, made the most of their last days as a 'training force'. They strode among olive groves and herds of sheep, wandered into schools and entertained children in classrooms; they swam in Lemnos Harbour and thought longingly of home. Some with questionable ailments remained in hospital— 'cold feet I think',[1] wrote Lieutenant Ross of two 27th Battalion officers. A mate told Private David Mills that he would come back to Lemnos one day for a honeymoon; Mills would be content enough if he could come back to 'this little peaceful corner of the world' on his own and 'have a quiet peaceful rest'.[2] Lance-Corporal Smith attended a church service that was a hit among Australians because they received a glass of whisky upon leaving—'reason why some went in and out a couple of times'.[3]

Doubts persisted over the reliability of the untested AIF troops, but Churchill had not forgotten the tenacious way a previous generation of Australians fought during the Boer War, which he had covered as a newspaper correspondent.

As their battleships steamed towards Gallipoli in darkness, each man privately contended with the reality that judgement hour was at hand. Some turned to prayer, other stuck close to their best mates and chatted and joked to relieve the tension, while hot chocolate and coffee was passed around the decks. They were too anxious for sleep, and as much as many wanted to smoke, they abided by a strict lights-out rule that included the glowing tips of cigarettes. Some earnestly wrote their last letters or jotted in diaries. Corporal Hedley Kitchin pencilled his last diary entry. 'A Company issued with the wire cutters of the Batt. about 48 all told. It strikes me that wire cutting is the first step into the next world. Not if I know it though…'[4]

The aim was to jump the Turks in the pre-dawn with what little element of surprise that remained, but as the first few dozen rowboats neared the shore their cover was blown when a small steamboat that had been towing the landing craft fumed sparks from its funnel. A volley of Turkish gunfire cracked from the barely visible hills almost immediately. The baptism had commenced.

The 3rd Brigade began to scamper ashore just after 4.30 a.m. but some were hit before they could make it to dry ground, while others further back drowned under the weight of their packs. It got worse as the sun rose, and the view of Turkish riflemen, machine-gunners and artillerymen improved. This coincided with the landing of 2nd Brigade troops around 5.30 a.m.

In one devastating burst about 100 members of the 7th Battalion were shot when their lighters approached a machine-gun emplacement at Fisherman's Hut, to the left of the main Anzac thrust. Bert Heighway, a 7th Battalion lieutenant, escaped the initial slaughter, and got his boat within 20 metres of the shoreline when

> One of my men was hit first, through the neck, then I was the next to get it through the chest. It nearly knocked me out of the boat. I quivered like a rabbit, but pulled myself together at once. I was steering the boat at the time so I had to let go with my hands and use the tiller with my feet. I managed to keep the boat nosed for the shore. The poor chaps that were rowing stuck bravely to it, and so did the others. You could see a look of revenge on all their faces. As soon as we bumped the shore they scrambled out, except myself, 3 killed and 7 wounded…I believe a lot of my men were killed when they were stepping on to the shore…The Turks kept up a continuous fire on the boats although they knew they were full of dead and wounded.
>
> While I was lying there one just took the skin off my shoulder, and another ripped my haversack. Dozens of them went within an inch of me. When the bullets cut through the sides of the boat you could smell the burning paint. A shell came screaming towards us once. It touched the side of the boat and went into the water without exploding, but sent up a huge spray that nearly drowned us.[5]

David Mills, the private who had dreamed of returning to Lemnos for a 'peaceful rest', lunged ashore and tucked himself into an embankment. 'Shells screaming everywhere…I have kissed dear little "Nans" photo goodbye, "May God have mercy on my soul" and care for them I have left behind'.[6] Mills closed off by drawing a crucifix beneath the text. A few hours later Mills, 23, of the 8th Battalion, was wounded in the first line of attack then hit again, fatally, while being stretchered to a dressing station.

When pauses in the gunfire permitted, some gamer types, including Lieutenant John McIntyre of the 1st Battalion, produced cameras and took snapshots of the action.

The Anzacs had landed about a kilometre north of their designated landing position, Gabe Tepe, an open beach, which although more heavily defended, might have enabled a speedier movement of troops and munitions ashore. Instead, they were confronted by a series of knolls and fractured ridges, which presented a huge geographical disadvantage to the invaders. Among the first to be picked off below were the young British midshipmen steering the lighters to shore. They held on tenaciously amid a gathering storm of lead, and upon landing their boats, some were seen to pull on khaki uniforms and race ahead with the infantry.[7]

By mid-morning, hundreds had made it well inland, despite the damage inflicted by Turkish snipers who were under instructions to save bullets for 'British' officers and non-commissioned officers. But the invaders continued with one vague instruction in their minds: 'Push on at all costs', and with the help of a not altogether effective Allied naval barrage, some made it as far as the third and highest ridge-line from where the Dardanelles, the initial prize, could be seen gleaming blue, to the south-east.

A surreal stillness descended around midday. Most of the Turkish garrison had been silenced, and for a while, it seemed, Gallipoli was there for the taking. But troops had been muddled in the confusion, communications were in disarray and many officers had been shot. Vital minutes ticked by as soldiers stood around, some digging trenches, some laughing, some smoking. Meanwhile, Turkish reinforcements were converging on the area at the urging of a young Lieutenant Colonel Mustafa Kemal, the future president of Turkey, who correctly deduced that the Anzac push was more than a feint. He knew that if the invaders commanded Hill 971, the highest peak in the near distance, Gallipoli would be theirs.

Still, some Australians basked in the sun with an air of disarming recklessness. Private Tom Leahy took it upon himself to muster a group of soldiers from Broken Hill, and urged them to start digging before the Turks, who were visibly massing on a distant ridge, counter-attacked. His mate Peter McConnachy remarked that the Turkish bastards were not going to stop him finishing his smoke. Minutes later McConnachy was fatally wounded, cigarette in hand, in a torrent of gunfire.

When the counter-attacks swept through, the Anzacs were overwhelmed by greater numbers. Hundreds of Australians and New Zealanders were either killed or wounded, or driven back to the second ridge-line where a series of fierce skirmishes ensued. Captain Joseph P. Lalor, who carried the sword of his grandfather, the Eureka Stockade rebel Peter Lalor, was one of them; Corporal Kitchin another. Lalor's sword was found some time later, but the 12th Battalion captain was never seen again; Kitchin reportedly died when his section was surrounded near Lone Pine, but he too was never located.

Sergeant Basil Newson, of the 2nd, was somewhere near:

> From now on men fell thick and fast around us, their snipers doing great work. 'Crack' and a man would roll down the hill right along side you, with a bullet through his head, then you hear—'The B————s got me' and on the other side of you a man has been hit somewhere else. Our chaps were getting riddled in almost every conceivable part of the body.[8]

By nightfall, as light drizzle fell, opposing troops entrenched themselves, leaving scores of dead and dying men sprawled in no man's land between. A new order swept along the lines: 'Dig in at all costs'. The demarkation zones that were to hold for the eight-month campaign had been set. About 16 000 Australians had landed, and 589 of them were already dead.

The next few days produced the usual turn of mad drama unique to war. Some soldiers died trying to rescue their wounded mates, others saw unutterable things and laughed it through or were reduced to quivering wrecks. They prayed that if their turn came it would be quick, or they shot a finger or two off to get a quick passage out of it. Others 'fielded' Turkish fuse bombs and lobbed them back, hopefully before they exploded. Young privates who had not shown much in the training camps began barking orders and pulling together sections of men after their NCOs fell dead.

The lines were swept by rumours that Australians had been found disembowelled and castrated, so some got a scent for blood and set out with revenge in their hearts. This kind of fighting was mostly never written about. It was ruthlessly exacted with the bayonet or a gun at close range, or with bare hands. Mechanical impulses, adrenalin and bare instinct took over. He who prevailed was usually quicker, stronger or greater in number. Private Fred Robson of the 15th Battalion wrote that he and a group of mates got a Turk who had surrendered and tied him to a tree before shooting him 30 times.[9] One sergeant wrote of shooting a Turk five times in the face at point-blank range to avenge the death of a mate who had been shot through the stomach; another wrote about the 'gorgeousness' of one's bayonet driving through the flesh of an enemy.[10]

Private Aitken of the 11th Battalion confessed, perhaps in a haze of bravado: 'Mother I'll admit a certain savage pleasure in firing to kill'. But the 24-year-old's conscience was less comfortable with the notion of bayoneting. 'Last night I dreamt about a bayonet charge. It worked on my mind all day…'[11]

Others held on grimly under the weight of creeping fatigue and delirium. All knew the sway of fate could tilt their way at any given minute. 'I ordered a volley from the men on my left (Phil Garlick joining in) I only put my head up for the second time (just a second) when a sniper got me through the jaw. I thought I was done… I didn't know I had so much blood in my body, but I dont think there is much now…'[12] wrote Sergeant Newson of his 26 April wounding.

The next day Corporal William Siddeley, of the Australian Medical Corps, was shot by a sniper while studying a map. 'I was struck in the abdomen by a bullet hitting the buckle of my belt, it ricocheted & hit me in the left groin; it was just as if a hot poker had been put against the skin.'[13]

Colonel Alfred Sutton, of the 3rd Australian Field Ambulance, assisted the first casualties.

> I saw men fall + half rise + fall again, yet they went on. One boat of wounded went by us, we cheered them + they cheered us back, + then one fellow with his arm in a sling + his head bandaged sang out 'Are we down-hearted?' + the whole boat yelled 'No'.[14]

The heavy casualties and the confusion meant that units were still in disarray days after the initial invasion. On the night of 27 April, Colonel Ernest Herrod, of the 7th Battalion, held a sector with fifty men from sixteen different battalions, half of the men being New Zealanders. None of them had rested since the landings.

As the days progressed, a siege prevailed. Most casualties were inflicted by snipers' bullets, artillery shells and the occasional bomb lobbed from nearby trenches. Keeping your head down generally meant survival. The lull gave soldiers the opportunity to absorb the momentous events of the first few days, and to begin the process of remembrance. When Eric ('Mul') Mulvey of the 2nd Light Horse died in a raid on Turkish trenches two days after arriving at Gallipoli, a fellow squadron member, 'Sep' Wilson wrote: 'I cannot realise it and am always expecting to see his face in the trenches'.[15] Corporal Charles Lewis' mate Harry Bailey fell as the pair charged Turkish positions on the day of the landings. 'He [Bailey] was lying just behind me and talking away while I was firing. I think he knew he wouldn't live because he kept on saying "Oh well we've had some good times together".'[16]

Some diarists and photographers demonstrated an eye for an angle, an intuition for history in the making. When Colonel Sutton first started taking photographs of his 3rd Field Ambulancemen training before Gallipoli, a young private with a sloping smile captured his attention. The same private featured in Sutton's diary a few weeks later, not for any textbook heroism, but for going about things in an unorthodox, efficient way. 'Pte Simpson has shown initiation in using a donkey from the 26th to carry slightly wounded cases & kept up his work from early morning till night every day since.' And later: 'Simpson shot thro chest by shrapnel bullet/ + wounding forearm of Fraser'.[17]

And at precisely 11.30 a.m. on 15 May, Sutton was on to one of the biggest stories of Gallipoli before it had time to become a rumour: 'General Bridges has just been shot through the thigh, there was considerable haemorrhage but it is not known whether the femoral artery is cut'.[18]

The sight of General Bridges strolling through the trenches was a morale booster for the men at Gallipoli. He had made them what they were—a purely Australian fighting force—and diggers curiously admired how he got around from post to post, upright like an old Spartan, refusing to duck or wait while bullets whizzed by. Bridges continued in his cavalier style, until he was shot by a sniper while moving between sandbag buttresses in Monash Valley.

As he lay dying, Bridges skited that he had at least commanded an Australian division. His pride in the Australians was cemented by their courage a week before when the 2nd Brigade and a brigade of New Zealanders tried to storm Krithia, an old village, south of Anzac Cove. They were ordered to attack in daylight to avoid confusion, marching across open fields toward the well-defended village, beyond which lay the strategic prize of Achi Baba peak. British and French troops had failed to take the village in the preceding days. British troops in reserve positions cheered and waved their helmets, as the Anzacs pressed on through walls of flame and bullets. As Private Gerard Cochrane, of the 5th Battalion, trudged into the roar he was distracted by the sound of a young AIF soldier near him, singing *Australia Will Be There*. The soldier kept singing till he fell dead. About 1000 Australians eventually fell before reaching the village. Albert Young, who had been promoted to sergeant that morning, was shot several times in the right leg and left to lie bleeding all night. 'Another day and night of horror, most of our company being wounded',[19] he wrote. Young died on 22 May after his wounds turned gangrenous.

Corporal Siddeley tended to the wounded.

> Arms & legs blown away & hundreds of others were about ¼ mile from the firing line & bullets were landing all round us & would often hit our medical kits... I heard someone saying 'for God's sake shoot me'; he was beyond aid (being shot in the stomach). I gave him morphine …

If the scene were not surreal enough, a gangly red-headed figure later appeared, wearing wire-rimmed spectacles. Siddeley recognised the stranger as Captain Bean, the official correspondent. 'I felt like putting him to his doom for what had been written by him in the Melbourne papers, but there were wounded to be looked for and no time for revenge. Capt Bean offered me a drink of fresh water which was accepted and appreciated. I would have drunk stagnant water, he also offered me some assistance & you can bet your life I soon gave Mr. Bean a job [to take kerosene tins of water around to the wounded]'.[20]

Eleven days after Krithia, the ledger was squared when the Turks launched a massive assault centred at Quinn's and Courtney's Posts in an attempt to drive the Anzacs into the Aegean. An estimated 42 000 of them charged just after midnight, shouting to the glory of Allah. About 10 000 of them were mown down in a blaze of gunfire so relentless that the barrels of the Anzac rifles became too hot to touch. Some broke into vulnerable points in Australian trenches but were dealt with by the likes of Private Bert Jacka who killed nine Turks in hand-to-hand fighting on his own, earning him Australia's first Victoria Cross of the war.

The 19 May attack heralded a change in attitude among opposing commanders, who up until then had been trying to break the stand-off by launching futile assaults for contested territory or a presumed weakness in the lines. A burial armistice was agreed upon, five days later on 24 May, to bury thousands of rotting corpses, and to minimise the incidence of disease spread by flies.

The interlude gave units a chance to count their dead. Of the fifty-two men who enlisted from No. 9 Platoon, C Company, 3rd Battalion, forty had been killed, wounded, listed as missing or hospitalised due to sickness within twenty-seven days of fighting. Only 150 men were left to fight out of the 15th Battalion's original strength of 1000, according to Private Robson. The 7th Battalion mustered 480 out of a roll call, and one of its colonels, Ernest Herrod, reflected that it was a wonder any of them had come through. 'It would have been impossible to have kept it up—as it was one officer went mad, and several had to be sent away, nervous breakdowns'.[21]

Some of the wounded and sick theorised about what had happened, or what had not. As he lay nursing his bullet wound through the jaw, Sergeant Newson postulated that 'the Turks wanted them [the Anzacs] to land and then drew them into the hills [on the day of the landings]'.[22] While resting at Lemnos, Lieutenant Austin Laughlin wrote to his father that 'if we had 20 000 more troops instead of the miserable 15 000 we started with, we would have, in all probability reached Maidos' within a week. And now at the rate the Allies were going, it would take 'ten years to open the Dardanelles, or to reach Maidos'.[23]

A 'spell' in a hospital bed was always appreciated, especially if one had not been maimed, but a culture of stoic resilience in every tier of the army deemed it unacceptable for men to be on their backs for inordinately long periods, if at all, when there was fighting to be done. When Lieutenant Henry Molony presented himself as ill at a sick parade in July, the examining doctor told him to 'have a shave and take only light food once more'.[24] Corporal Lewis told his mother that he felt 'ashamed' with only a 'flea bite' when all of his mates were gone, and he was now surrounded by all 'these poor chaps so knocked about'.[25] Lewis had actually been hit by shrapnel while sitting in his trench reading a letter from his mother.

The high casualty rate ensured an equally high rate of promotion in the ranks. The Australian knew an extra stripe was as much to do with some poor beggar's bad luck as his own good fortune. Some, no doubt, also saw promotion and the responsibilities that it entailed as a step closer to one's own demise in battle, and perhaps that is why some promotions were knocked back. They believed individual initiative was as vital as the chain of command, and were suspicious of any-one who, like most British officers, adopted the cultivated airs of privilege or breeding. Consequently, a healthy vein of self-mockery ran through the AIF's officer system. It was a way of keeping everyone equal.

'Dick Casey who was at Trinity [College] with me in 1909 amused me by his superiority in telling me to get down from my post, calling me "boy",'[26] wrote Private Cooke.

Corporal Aitken would later chortle: 'I'm commander of No 3 Platoon & Chris Prout is a Lance Corporal in it; you ought to hear him call me Sir'.[27]

The summer of June and July brought a relative calm at Gallipoli. While dan-ger always loomed, opposing commanders seemed content, for the time being, to contain the slaughter, and put their troops to work on improving tracks and trenches, while tunnellers drove chambers closer to one another's front lines in a separate underground war. Passing the weeks became an exercise in adaptation and invention, a test to keep oneself together in body and mind and, in moments of rare abandon, an opportunity to match wits with an adversary. It was then clear that the men in the opposing trenches were ordinary fighters who, like the Australians, enjoyed a joke and who saw the futility of the mess they were in. Once it was seen that Australian bullets did as much damage as Turkish bullets, and that the average Red Crescent soldier was an honourable fighter, not a butcher, an unwritten camaraderie knitted them—strange as war's nuances are. Snipers duelled, bombs and insults were hurled back and forth. Some humorous but lethal exchanges occurred when slouch hats marked with the name of an Australian's home town or city came into the possession of the enemy after skir-mishes. Private Henry Pepper wrote: 'The Turks used to get hold of them. They [the Australians] would call out anyone from Mordialloc or some place & if some-one [from an opposing trench] said "Yes" they would say: "Then take that you cows" & throw a bomb'.[28]

Private William Callinan of the 6th Field Ambulance recalled the sad demise of a Turk whose antics had commanded an Australian following: '... every morn-ing in a certain Turkish trench, "Fatty" a cook, would hop up + greet our boys with "Good morning", until one morning a new rein. [reinforcement] man spot-ted him + Fatty was no more'.[29]

But these diversions did little to alleviate the monotony and heat. The onset of scorching weather and plagues of flies spread dysentery and other illnesses that debilitated thousands, particularly those exhausted and malnourished from battle. To escape the oppressive conditions, soldiers swam at Anzac Cove, heed-less of the danger of sniper and shell attack and the theory that the beach was contributing to the dysentery outbreak. Even General Birdwood would risk his life for a swim (see photograph page 125) and, on one occasion, a protective Australian soldier yelled for old 'Birdie' to duck as a shell screamed down—the silver-haired general bobbed up a few seconds later, smiling. Others were not so lucky.

Private Gerald Cochrane heard the buzz of a sniper's bullet, and a soldier who was taking his clothes off near by suddenly lurched forward—'before we could get him out of the water, the poor lad was dead'.[30] A 24th Battalion soldier (identity unknown) was knocked flying by a shell that killed a bather next to him. 'The force of the explosion knocked me over. I rolled in to cover + out of the road of the next one. I am quite used to it now we take no notice of it'.[31]

Towards the end of July the 'beach-goers' observed signs that their summer idyll was coming to a close. Several Allied hospital ships appeared off the coast and large consignments of ammunition began arriving daily. General Hamilton and his staff had been working on a plan to break the deadlock. Anzac troops were to contest the worst terrain of the peninsula as they had done on the day of the landings. They were to secure the heights above them—Lone Pine, Baby 700, and beyond that, Chunuk Bair and Hill 971—then link up with British forces to their north flank, coming from Suvla Bay, and their south flank, from Cape Helles. It was a protracted, last-ditch stunt weighted with as much faith in providence as logistical calculation. Its failure would lead to heavy casualties and fresh calls for an evacuation.

Although many soldiers were still ill, Anzac sick parades diminished significantly in anticipation of the push. The first Australians went in at sunset on 6 August, to win back the coveted and well-fortified Lone Pine. Lieutenant John Merivale, 4th Battalion, watched, overcome by tears. 'They went like a pack of forwards charging down a field after a football, and in an instant hundreds of rifles turned upon them and shell...they fell in tens but the remainder dashed on.'[32]

After half an hour of hand-to-hand fighting, Lone Pine was in the hands of the 1st Brigade. Merivale's moment then came. Communication wires had been cut, and Merivale, with his batman already gone, chose to run a vital message.

> The trenches were smashed about terribly, and one had to crawl half cocked along them, often as not crawling over some poor beggar, who had passed his marble in. I raced as hard as I could lick across an open space, and a man alongside me dropped like a stone, his head had been half carried away by a flying shell case, and 50 yards further on another chap who was waiting for a second, got a shrapnel bullet in his wrist, which miraculously just missed me.[33]

When the din had briefly subsided, Merivale saw a 3rd Battalion soldier, whose leg had been blown off, being stretchered along a trench towards him. '[He] put out his hand and I shook it hard. He never said a word, but his slight pressure on my hand spoke volumes.'[34]

Merivale, like any other man, did what he could to steel his constitution as a three-day barrage of Turkish counter-attacks was repelled. 'In our possie in the

Lone Pine, I always hum to myself that last bit of *La Tosca* when they are shelling us, you know the piece I mean, just as Mario is shot'.[35] Merivale, 28, died at Lone Pine later that month. He was one of 368 AIF officers killed at Gallipoli.

Sunrise on the second day (7 August) of the August offensive saw New Zealand troops push gamely towards the summit of Chunuk Bair. General Monash's 4th Brigade was becoming split up amid heavy sniper fire in the precipitous approach to Hill 971, while two regiments of the 3rd Light Horse assembled (without their mounts) near an oddly named verge called the Nek. It was their mission to somehow break past a tier of Turkish machine-gunners and take Baby 700, which had been let slip from the grasp of the Anzacs on 25 April. In the space of half an hour, 372 Victorians and Western Australians lay dead or wounded in an area the size of a bowling green. So suicidal and devastating was the charge (depicted in Peter Weir's *Gallipoli*) that none of the Australians made it into the Turkish trenches. It was thought by most war writers including Charles Bean that none of them inflicted a single Turkish casualty with the rifle; none, that is, until the story of David McGarvie, the Victorian dairy farmer with the hare-lip, came to light.

> I was lying on the ground [in a natural fold] and I could see about [illegible] yards back the Turkish trench, and one fellow stood up about waist high, looking down in that direction. I got a good shot at him and I put in another clip of cartridges, and I had 4 or 5 shots. I don't know just how many I fired. Heads and shoulders at 10 or 12 yards was just easy shooting. Every time I fired a man went down. Well, after this chap [a fellow light horseman] had thrown the bomb, he put several men out of action, the other bayonets were coming along to fill up the vacancies. Well then the fellow next door to me on this side, he said 'I got one in the ear...' This (other) fellow got one in the chest—fellow named Truin, and he stood up and staggered way back. Well then after I'd fired a few shots, I got this crack on the foot. It came from way over [t]here at Lone Pine.[36]

McGarvie waited till dark and while attempting to crawl back to his trench, he was mistaken for a Turk by Australian sentries but, thankfully, one of them recognised his voice as belonging to 'that bloke with the hare-lip'.[37] Bleeding and nearing exhaustion, McGarvie was oblivious to the fact he would one day attach a missing entry to Australian war annals.

The following day, 8 August, a group of New Zealand Wellingtons took the crest of Chunuk Bair and were there long enough to glimpse the Dardanelles at sunrise before fighting to the last man against waves of Turkish reinforcements. Near by, the remnants of the 4th Brigade were cut down in the shadow of Hill 971, hamstrung because of the failure of British troops from Suvla Bay to link up to their left flank. Some of the Australians had ventured far enough into enemy territory to be taken prisoner. Some of the unluckier ones were clubbed to death and stripped of their uniforms, before the arrival of a few Turkish and German officers put a stop to it. A few dozen of them, including a badly wounded Corporal George Kerr, whose story is told in *Lost Anzacs: The Story of Two Brothers*, were among seventy Australians captured by the Turks at Gallipoli. They reached Constantinople not as triumphant raiders but as forgotten POWs. With the August offensive in tatters, the dejected Allied survivors retreated, knowing that Gallipoli was lost.

The troops who remained were dispirited by their failure, exhausted and increasingly aware of privations like lack of water and food. By September it was estimated that three quarters of the Anzacs were totally unfit for active service.[38] Sergeant George Hill, of the 7th Battalion, had been active in the line of fire almost continually for more than 100 days. 'I wish it was over now for I have had a long time here and been under fire all the time, for out of the 17 weeks, the Machine Gun Section has been in the trenches 15 of them, so you can imagine what we feel like by now',[39] he complained to his brother on 22 August. The lot of the Gallipoli servicemen seemed almost superhuman when measured against the experience of troops in other wars.[40] Yet they continued.

The fighting went on at a gradually lessening frequency, and opposing commanders seemed content to forget the idea of set-piece attacks. Tunnellers penetrated further underground, mining and counter-mining opposing trenches, while those above ground continued their spats. A section of 24th Battalion reinforcements was locked in combat with Turks in a trench just six metres away one September morning. They fought hard, true to their battalion 'elephant' motto: 'No surrender'. Bullets from snipers punched the dust on the parapet inches above their heads, so Corporal Pat Lynch and his mates tried throwing fuse bombs. But their tactic went horribly wrong when one of them fumbled a lighted bomb. 'He got dumfounded or something and dropped it. Corp Geddes made a grab to throw it out, when it exploded, blowing his arm & shoulder to bits, it got Willy Turnbull in the eyes and stomach',[41] wrote an unidentified 24th Battalion soldier. Lynch was killed instantly, Geddes and Turnbull died from their wounds, and several other men were badly wounded. Hugh McNidder, a corporal mindful of the shame and embarrassment the incident would cause his section, wrote, 'while one (not Pat) was throwing a bomb it exploded'.[42]

Storms and snowfalls lashed the peninsula in the months of October and November, causing dozens of fatal cases of frostbite and exposure, and reducing the fighting further. However, Anzac tunnellers were getting the upper hand in underground skirmishes with the Turks, and were steadily advancing their galleries to beneath Turkish entrenchments including the Nek. Lieutenant Ross was given a tour of the system in early December. 'I was then 60 feet below the surface of the earth and 50 or 60 yards behind the Turks trenches.' Ross was sworn to secrecy about his visit, but was assured that, by the time the engineers and miners had finished, 'they would alter the geography of the place'.[43]

Tired as they were, a view held among the Anzac lines that the best way of getting one last crack at the Turks was to charge their positions after the detonation of the underground mines, which was not such a secret, contrary to Ross' letter. But, for two months at least, Allied commanders had been secretly planning for an evacuation. They had run out of key moves, a long winter promised more misery for men waiting idly in trenches, and the rate of attrition in France increased the need for reinforcements at the Western Front. In October the new chief commander of Gallipoli, Sir Charles Munro, recommended the withdrawing of the Gallipoli expedition, but added that the Anzacs were the only troops equal to a sustained effort on the peninsula. His predecessor, General Hamilton, who had been recalled over the failure of the August offensive, was of the view that at least half the total Allied force would be lost during an evacuation.

When news of the evacuation finally came on 8 December, the Anzacs were devastated at the thought of walking away from their first big contest, and to be leaving so many of their mates behind. The only consolation for many was that their immediate destiny was in the grasp of an Australian tactician, General Brudenell White, who devised the withdrawal plan. Anzac troops were instructed to gradually decrease their firepower, but otherwise create a semblance of normality in the lines. They were evacuated on waiting boats over the nights of 18 and 19 December with just two Australian casualties.

Private Makeham, of the 7th Battalion, recalled the tension.

> All the men had their boots padded to prevent the Turks hearing the tramp of their feet as they moved about. We tried all sorts of dodges to puzzle Abdul and thank goodness they were successful, for it only needed a slight hitch…and he would have been after us like flies.[44]

As the last of a skeleton line of Australians sailed away, the mines left by Anzac tunnellers were detonated, causing hundreds of Turkish casualties and lighting the night sky with a blinding inferno. The baptism was over.

An Australian troopship about to sail from Alexandria for the Dardanelles

Australian troopships draw level for unloading at Mudros Harbour, Lemnos

'Good-bye Egypt. I hope I am not invalided back to you at any rate',[19] wrote Corporal Hedley Kitchin, 6th Battalion, as the 1st Contingent sailed from the port of Alexandria for the Dardanelles on 8 April. Two days later, Kitchin's transport, the *Galeka*, drew level with another ship for unloading at Mudros Harbour, Lemnos, where Anzac forces drilled for the Gallipoli landings. The photographs were from the last roll of film taken by Kitchin, a 20-year-old electrician from East Melbourne. He was killed in action at Lone Pine on 25 April.

3RD BRIGADE *soldiers practise landing drills at Lemnos*

This photograph by Lieutenant Edwin Dollery shows a group of 3rd Brigade soldiers in a practice landing at Lemnos. The 3rd Brigade, consisting of soldiers mostly from Queensland, Tasmania, South Australia and Western Australia, had been chosen as the initial strike force for the invasion. Dollery, a 21-year-old electrical engineer from Hobart, went on to win the Military Cross. He was repatriated in 1919.

PRIVATE JOHN SIMPSON KIRKPATRICK *and fellow members of the*
3RD FIELD AMBULANCE

Private John Simpson Kirkpatrick, reclining bottom right, soaks in the Aegean sun during a field ambulance drill near Lemnos, in the weeks before the Gallipoli invasion. The maverick fireman with the likeable smile used a donkey to ferry the wounded at Gallipoli, and was admired for his courage under fire. He was killed within a month of the landings.

Among those who attended Simpson's funeral was the man who took this photograph, Colonel Alfred Sutton, 3rd Field Ambulance.

2ND DIVISION *soldiers approaching Gallipoli*

Soldiers of the 2nd AIF Division intently check their packs and rifles as the RMS *Arcadian* nears Gallipoli. A group of officers and NCOs, standing to the left of the first funnel, appears to be holding a tactical briefing over maps. This photograph is from a collection by Lieutenant Thomas McCormack of the 5th Field Company Engineers.

1ST BATTALION *soldiers await transfer to rowboats on 25 April 1915*

Judgement hour awaits these 1st Battalion soldiers just after sunrise on 25 April. They are waiting to be transferred from a destroyer into rowboats which would take them the rest of the way into shore. A small number of rowboats, or lighters, have already made it to Ari Burnu (Anzac Cove) in the background. These men are wearing British Regular Army caps as directed, although some men insisted on wearing slouch hats.

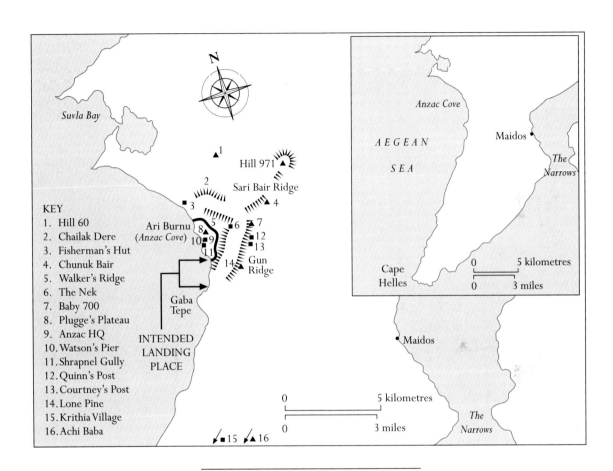

KEY
1. Hill 60
2. Chailak Dere
3. Fisherman's Hut
4. Chunuk Bair
5. Walker's Ridge
6. The Nek
7. Baby 700
8. Plugge's Plateau
9. Anzac HQ
10. Watson's Pier
11. Shrapnel Gully
12. Quinn's Post
13. Courtney's Post
14. Lone Pine
15. Krithia Village
16. Achi Baba

AIF *operations at Gallipoli*

Troops from the ROYAL AUSTRALIAN ENGINEERS *land at Anzac Cove*

These soldiers scrambling ashore at 6.30 a.m. on 25 April are from No. 2 Field Company, Royal Australian Engineers. One company of engineers was attached to each brigade at Gallipoli where their work was crucial in constructing mines beneath Turkish positions, sinking wells and building jetties. Like most other service corps units, their work was carried out at risk of incurring enemy fire.

Landing scene at Anzac Cove

The man who took this spontaneous snap-shot, Lieutenant John McIntyre, probably shot it from the hip, as his 1st Battalion landed. McIntyre, an ironmonger from Dulwich Hill, New South Wales, was wounded twice at Gallipoli then killed in action the following year in France. This over-exposed photograph was located during a search of the Australian War Memorial's collections.

Casualties from the first few hours of fighting at Gallipoli

Casualties from the first hours of fighting at Gallipoli are being assembled in front of a temporary hospital at Anzac Cove. Soldiers who have succumbed to their wounds, centre, have been covered with sheets, their boots removed. By about midday on 25 April, the initial Turkish defences had been pushed back inland, but the men moving about freely in this scene still risked incoming shells and sniper fire.

A stretcher bearer

A stretcher bearer from the 1st Australian Field Ambulance is set for a long day having come ashore at Anzac Cove at 8.30 a.m. on 25 April. Some stretcher bearers did not enlist in combat units because they were ideologically opposed to the war or because they were too small to fight; others were 'hard cases' who would not conform to regular military discipline. To a man, they were remembered for their grit and bravery.

Stretcher bearers

Despite official forecasts that casualties would be high, medical facilities at Gallipoli were grossly inadequate. The wounded who could be retrieved from the battlefield were rowed to crowded hospital ships. Amputations were carried out on open decks and many of the injured died before they could receive treatment.

Going up the line

Gallipoli

Topography at Gallipoli

Anzac forces rarely, if ever, were in a position to face the enemy on level ground at Gallipoli, a factor which made Allied victory improbable. The rugged topography of the peninsula is illustrated in this sequence of photographs taken by an unknown soldier.

A panorama north of the main ANZAC *position towards Suvla Bay*

'Looking towards Suvla Bay from Anzac': this photograph by Lieutenant Ross, of the 27th Battalion, illustrates a focal point in the August offensive. Two fresh British divisions were to land at Suvla Bay, centre, then link up with Australian and Indian troops around Gallipoli's highest peak, Hill 971, about five kilometres inland. The poorly led and inexperienced British barely penetrated the foothills, however, allowing Turkish reinforcements to easily win back Allied gains.

AIF SOLDIERS *camped at White's Valley*

'It is rather funny to see the dash for cover on the arrival of a big one, just like a lot of rabbits making for their burrows',[20] wrote Lieutenant John Merivale in a letter to his father. He might well have been describing this encampment of Australian soldiers at White's Valley, photographed by an unknown soldier. Merivale was killed in action at Lone Pine in August 1915.

PRIVATE JOHN GOODER

Looking more like a bush mercenary than a regular soldier, Private John Gooder, 22, of the 14th Battalion, rests in a dug-out behind Courtney's Post. A souvenired Turkish knife is in a sheath around Gooder's waist, a bandolier for holding cartridges around his left shoulder. His uniform has been adapted to bare essentials for the approach of summer. The 14th Battalion was employed in the early days of the campaign to defend Courtney's Post and several other hotly contested posts above Monash Gully.

A densely populated Australian trench at Gallipoli

'How long, how long O Lord. We are only chocolate soldiers, non-combatants + cannot stand this much longer. If I am hit I hope + pray I may be killed, these experiences are too awful.'[21] Colonel Sutton, 3rd Field Ambulance, diary, 4 May 1915.

Sutton, who survived the war, was an exceptional photographer. He donated an album, which included this photograph of a Gallipoli trench, to the Australian War Memorial. Judging by the absence of rifles, the trench was probably occupied by Sutton's field ambulancemen.

PRIVATE CLIFFORD MCCONNACHY *and*
PRIVATE PETER MCCONNACHY *(inset) in studio, Egypt*

Private Peter Bert McConnachy, 10th Battalion, whose apparition hovers in the inset of this studio portrait, was fatally wounded on 25 April. This is what his mate Private Tom Leahy saw:

> Tough men of Broken Hill were in our lot. Big Bill Montgomery, Darky Stewart, Alf Crother and Chris Christopherson. Little Lieut Byrne was striding up and down, as proud as punch. The sun was warm, the sky was blue, and there was no sound of war, but larks were singing. Everyone was now digging except Peter McConnachy, swarthy and contented, who still sat smoking. 'Dig in, Peter,' I urged, 'they'll counter attack'.
>
> 'Dig in be———', he said. 'I'll finish my fag first'.
>
> He didn't finish his fag. He died in the roaring blast that suddenly swept across the valley to us…Peter was first shot through the head and would not fall back—possibly he would have been alright had he done so. The lad was too game, stayed on and got another hit, this time in the stomach below the heart and lungs.
>
> I crawled over to talk to and try to assist Lieut. Burns when Peter heard and recognised my voice and called out 'Is that you Tom?' I answered 'Yes Peter. What can I do for you?'
>
> 'Where are the stretcher bearers,' he said. I said they will be here in a few minutes— this I said to comfort him (he was dying) well knowing at the time that they (the stretcher bearers) could not get up to us for hours.
>
> A little later on I crept back to them again. Lieut. Burns was still suffering terribly and did not die until some time next day. Peter was dead. He could not have lived long. I took his small khaki handkerchief from his tunic pocket, wiped the blood off his face, had a last look at the face of a good game pal, then covered the face up with the handkerchief…
>
> I cannot say where or how he was buried. There was such a mix up and every man (there were thousands) laid where he fell. It is impossible for me to attempt to describe or for you to try to imagine the terrible and ghastly scene. Little help could be given to the wounded on that first day, we were all fighting desperately for our lives.[22]

Peter McConnachy had a brother, Private Clifford McConnachy (shown here), who served in the 11th Light Horse and survived the war. Clifford sits pensively, wearing shorts and his riding spurs. The cigarette in his hand is a morbid, if not ironic, tribute to his brother.

PRIVATE ROY OLDROYD

'When we got ashore we had a hill 90ft high to climb and the Turks were entrenched on the top, we fixed our bayonets and charged them, they mowed us down pretty fast. When we reached them most of them run. those that didn't we drag them out with bayonets through them, it is bosher sport shooting them over. Thas it all the news this time, hoping you and all at home are well',[23] wrote 1st Battalion Private Roy Oldroyd to his younger brother Will.

Oldroyd, a 19-year-old sugar refinery worker from Abbotsford, New South Wales, was hit five times in the lower right leg by machine-gun fire at Gallipoli on 28 April. It was amputated a month later, despite assurances from surgeons in Manchester that they would 'fix it up again'.

The next letter he wrote home was dated 11 June 1915 and addressed to his mother. 'I went under an operation and had one of my legs off about a week ago and it is doing fine in about another fortnight I will be better.' And a month later: 'Tell Tom to tell them down the sugar house to keep my job for me cause I will get a wooden leg on and will be as good as new'.[24]

Oldroyd spent time at a small private convalescent home for amputees in the English countryside where, amazingly, he met a fellow amputee whom he had carried from the line of fire before his own injury. 'When he saw me he nearly went mad to see me with my leg off. On the first Sunday we landed he was shot about four times through the leg, one bullet went through his knee, I saw him lying nearly bled to death so I picked him up and carried him down to the doctors about two miles away and that was the last I seen him till I come out here.'[25]

In early 1916 Oldroyd was transferred to Weymouth Army Base Depot where he had trouble re-adapting to the discipline and boredom of a military encampment. He was detained intermittently for a string of minor offences including disobeying orders and being absent without leave. He was discharged in May 1916, and returned to his job as a 'bag-grader' at the Colonial Sugar Refinery, in Pyrmont, New South Wales. He married and raised five children but, like so many returned soldiers, the mark of war never left him.

A daughter, Bertha Moran, later said: 'When Dad was sober he was great, but when he drank he was terrible, never violent to us kids but gave poor Mum a bad time. Finally when I was 15 they legally separated, never divorced & I never doubt that they loved each other'.[26] Roy Oldroyd was never known to miss a day's work despite his wooden leg and the pain that it caused him. He died in 1949 at the age of 53.

Soldiers resting in a Gallipoli trench

Soldier diarists complained of not sleeping for up to a week at a time, particularly when relieving troops were scarce in the early stages of fighting. Many behind the front lines also had trouble sleeping because of cramped trenches, random shell blasts and the threat of snipers' bullets. Although soldiers adapted, tiredness contributed to casualties on both sides. Some diarists also said fatigue, rather than machismo, was the reason why many Australians were nonchalant about incoming shellfire.

Casually attired Australians in a well-fortified trench

The soldier standing in the back of this well constructed trench passes time sharpening his bayonet before fitting it to a .303 rifle. Australians reportedly wrought havoc with the bayonet on the day of the landings and used the weapon to psychological advantage throughout the war. In reality, though, bayonets accounted for less than one per cent of the casualties in World War I. Soldiers just as soon used them to kill snakes and rats in trenches, and to open tins of bully beef.

SAPPER AUSTIN LAUGHLIN

'And now your letter dated the 26th, in which you ask some no. of questions. 1. Did Australians toss Turks over their head with their bayonets? I don't believe they did. I haven't seen it done because all the Turks I have seen are too fat. Any one of them would break the bayonets…'[27] This excerpt is from a letter written by Austin Laughlin, of 6th Battalion, written to his father on 25 November 1915.

A contemplative Laughlin sits in this well-constructed dug-out, an improvised chess board to his right. He was serving as a sapper with the 1st Division Signals Company at the time this photograph was taken.

A Gallipoli observation post

The soldier smoking the cigarette, top left, appears to be relaying details of his observations from a periscope to the man below holding the notebook. While sand-bagged trenches of this kind protected occupants from snipers' bullets they presented little resistance to Turkish shells and bombs.

*A soldier turns his rifle upside down
in a duel with a Turkish sniper*

Unsound as his method appears to be, this soldier is taking no chances in a duel with a Turkish sniper. Turkish sharpshooters inflicted many casualties early on in the campaign but Australians, whose training had not allowed for sniping, matched their opponents in time.

Troopers KEN HAMILTON *and*
ALAN DUKE *in a 5*TH LIGHT HORSE
position at Gallipoli

'Ken Hamilton (with rifle) Alan Duke sitting': a photograph taken by Trooper George Millar, of the 5th Light Horse. The three men were among thousands of light horsemen assigned to Gallipoli as infantry. Trooper Hamilton's left hand is bandaged, possibly wounded by an enemy sniper who picked the gap through the narrow peephole beneath the parapet of the trench. Hamilton, a station hand, survived the war; Duke, a motor mechanic, was badly wounded in France in 1916 and was repatriated. Millar, a pastoralist, was promoted to lieutenant in the British Army in December 1915.

Burial armistice at Gallipoli

The stench from rotting corpses in no man's land became so appalling that opposing forces agreed to a burial armistice on 24 May, five days after the Turks suffered an estimated 10 000 casualties in a suicidal charge against strong Australian entrenchments. Some of the dead are visible at Quinn's Post to the right of the soldier hunched over in the foreground. This photograph was lent to the Australian War Memorial by Captain Duncan Maxwell who was awarded the Military Cross for defending a trench against enemy attack in France.

Soldiers bathing at Anzac Cove

While the Turks in the hills had abundant supplies of fresh water to drink, the 'Bronzed Australians' had the Aegean in which to bathe. They did so, however, at risk of being sniped. It did not stop Anzac Cove resembling a surf club in the warmer months.

General Birdwood returns from a swim at Anzac Cove

At first glance this photograph seems like any one of hundreds of incidental scenes captured behind the front line. It shows General Birdwood, Anzac commander at Gallipoli, returning from one of his regular swims. Birdwood (the balding man, top centre) was a man of 50 and somewhat effeminate in his ways, yet immensely pop-ular among Australian troops despite their distrust of British generals. They saw him as one of them, a self-effacing leader who got into the thick of it. And the man who took this photograph, Colonel Sutton, was on the scene in May 1915 when the general put his head up too high in a trench and received a scalp wound from a sniper's bullet.[28]

Horses killed in an artillery attack on Anzac Cove

Animals, too, fell victim to artillery and sniper attacks at Anzac Cove. Many donkeys and some horses were killed while tethered on the beach or being unloaded off barges to shore. Donkeys were used primarily to carry munitions, while some horses were ridden by messengers. The irregular topography of the peninsula prevented horses being taken into combat.

An Australian 18-pounder gun discharging at Gallipoli

This blur of men, earth and steel is caused by the discharge of an Australian 18-pounder gun. Allied artillery and battleship guns had difficulty with range and trajectory at Gallipoli, and caused minimal damage to the Turks' superior trench systems.

Chaplain William Stevens conducts a church service at Chailak Dere

Wounded men are among the congregation at this church service conducted by Chaplain William Stevens at Chailak Dere in September 1915. Wartime sermons explored themes such as predestination and sacrifice, and had to contend with interruptions from artillery and the occasional bullet buzzing overhead. Stevens, who was attached to the 5th Infantry Brigade, died of wounds in France in 1917. The photograph is from Lieutenant Ross' collection.

PRIVATE HARRY SMITH

When the Turks stormed the Australian lines on 19 May, three of Lance Corporal Harry Smith's 3rd Battalion mates were killed beside him, and after the din he took off his cap and realised that it had three bullet holes in it. Although his writings do not convey it, Smith, a deeply religious man, must have wondered if he too was about to meet his maker. In his last diary entry on 12 June he wrote: 'Twenty today. Spent birthday in trenches…Good tucker but no clean socks or clothes'.[29] He died from a gunshot wound to the head eleven days later.

PRIVATE EDWIN HARMER *with unidentified soldier, Egypt*

'Dear Jessie,

I am now writing you the few lines, trusting that you and our baby are quite well...I am very pleased to say I am having the best of treatment and everything I wish. I got injured on the 25th of April. I can't give you much information as all these letters are strictly censored but I might add that I shall not forget our first battle. I remembered the 23rd of May, Sylvia's birthday, I was sorry I was unable to be there. With a little luck I might have the pleasure of reaching Australia at some future date. Well dear you will see that I am unable to write at present, as I said before we can get anything that we want. Well dear Jessie I think this is all that I have to say at present, so must now close this letter hoping to hear from you shortly, with fond love from Ted. Love to Sylvia.'[30]

Private Edwin Harmer, 5th Battalion, letter, Valletta Military Hospital, Malta, 29 June 1915. Harmer, wearing the slouch hat on the right, dictated this letter to a nurse the day before he died of his wounds.

The unknown British soldier in the photograph has Boer War ribbons on his tunic.

Launching a 'jam-tin' bomb from a Gallipoli trench

Photographs of soldiers in the act of fighting are rare because they exposed the cameraman to risk of injury. This shot shows an Australian hurling what is probably a jam-tin bomb towards a nearby Turkish trench. Small but destructive, the bombs were packed with iron fragments and nails and set with a fuse in gunpowder. They were an improvisation of the Australians to compensate for the lack of factory-produced bombs at Gallipoli. This snap was taken by Lance Corporal Gornall.

A sentry guards a vulnerable point in an Australian trench system

This sentry knows the way to Constantinople (signposted), the ultimate objective of the Gallipoli invasion. Whether the Allies would ever get there was the question that remained.

Severed foot at Gallipoli

Gruesome objects like this foot inside a victim's boot were common sights at Gallipoli. A boot similar to this is displayed in the war museum at the entrance to the peninsula, as well as a skull of a Turkish 'martyr' with a bullet embedded in the forehead, and two bullets that joined upon colliding in mid-air. This photograph, by an unknown soldier, was located at the Melbourne headquarters of the Returned and Services League.

The bodies of 11TH BATTALION *soldiers after the battle for Leane's Trench*

The bodies of thirty-six 11th Battalion soldiers lie waiting for burial after the battle for Leane's Trench. The trench was successfully taken on 31 July but a Turkish counter-attack five days later resulted in heavy casualties to both sides. Anzac strategists regarded the trench as crucial because it afforded a vantage from which the Turks could have obstructed the 6 August Lone Pine charge.

CHAPLAIN ANDREW GILLISON *conducts a church service*
for men of the 14TH BATTALION

This 6 August photograph shows men of the 14th Battalion at an outdoor service a few hours before attempting to conquer Hill 971. The service is being conducted by Chaplain Andrew Gillison, who was one of 216 members of the 14th to die in the month of August, 100 of them in one day (8 August) alone. Gillison, seen standing above the small altar, was a figure-head of the 4th Brigade, remembered for his willingness to risk all to help wounded men. The photograph was taken by Private Gooder.

Australian soldiers in a captured Turkish trench at Lone Pine

1st Battalion soldiers in a newly captured Turkish fortification at Lone Pine. The photograph was probably taken on 6 August after the first waves of Australians broke through the timbered roofing of the Turkish systems, and skirmished with the enemy at close quarters.

Trench scene, Lone Pine

An Australian soldier is about to provide covering fire as his mate, top right, bounds out of a Lone Pine trench. Several bodies lie among kits scattered on the trench floor. The Turks counter-attacked Lone Pine repeatedly over three days, leading to some of the most fierce hand-to-hand fighting and bomb duels in the campaign. Lone Pine was held by the Australians at a cost of 2000 casualties.

AUSTRALIAN *troops gather for the August offensive*

Zero hour, 7 August: Australian soldiers mass in the foothills left of the Anzac position for the attack on Hill 971. A cluster of troops receives instructions from an officer in the depression below, while the soldier in the foreground appears to have already been given his orders. The participants are wearing white arm bands and white back patches to avoid being mistaken for the enemy. Even so, dozens of Australians were cut down by 'friendly' fire from Allied battleships and Anzac guns as they attempted to take the heights of Gallipoli.

1ST LIGHT HORSE *roll-call after the assault on Dead Man's Ridge*

This photograph was taken during a roll-call of the 1st Light Horse after its assault on Dead Man's Ridge. The attack took place at dawn on 7 August—the same time as the Nek charge, and, like the Nek, was orchestrated to weaken the Turks' grasp on Baby 700. While the Nek has been enshrined in war histories because of its suicidal futility and heroism, its casualty rate was proportionately less than 1st Light Horse losses at Dead Man's Ridge. At the Nek, 372 out of 600 light horsemen were either killed or wounded (62 per cent), whereas 152 out of 200 men became casualties at Dead Man's (77 per cent). While four successive waves from the 8th and 10th Light Horse were cut down at the Nek, the 1st Light Horse succeeded in penetrating three enemy trenches with the aid of jam-tin and stick bombs. They suffered heavy casualties, however, and were forced to withdraw when finally outnumbered and outbombed.

Five Australian soldiers at Hell Spit

'Hell Spit, Damn Good luck to us all', says the caption on this portrait. Its five subjects, Sapper Jim Campbell, Lieutenant Herb Morris, Private Hamie Read, Private Griff Stevenson and Sergeant Arthur Smith (from left to right) pose at risk of being targeted by Turkish sniper and artillery fire. It was from a knoll above Hell Spit that Australian troops first came under fire on the morning of the 25 April landings. Because the photograph contained no other supporting details, only one of the men, Herb Morris, could be traced in records (see Biographies).

The undated portrait may have been taken on 21 October 1915, the anniversary of the 1st AIF Contingent's departure from Melbourne. The occasion prompted a holiday among some battalions who used the respite to clean up dug-outs, write letters, cook special meals and have photographs taken. Lieutenant Henry Molony, 5th Battalion, remarked however, that 'most of us feel pretty sad at remembrance of all the good fellows missing'.[31]

LIEUTENANT HORACE WALKER

More of Lieutenant Ross' portraits appear in this book than any other soldier's photographs. Ross' easygoing character and his eye for subtlety helped him compile a unique profile of men at war. He was an attaché, it seemed, secretly assigned to study the map of the human face. His camera was guided by an understanding of the ways of men—it could see how dignity and optimism prevailed in spite of the sadness and the danger. Ross' subjects open themselves to his lens and become known through his photographs. They are sometimes animated; vulnerable yet trusting or expressing a quiet grace.

His attitude to war might be explained by a prefatory remark he wrote in 1932 to a collection of his war letters: '…throughout it all we tried to be optimists, and we tried to cheer up those at home who were often needlessly worrying about us'.[32]

In this photograph Lieutenant Horace Walker, of the 27th Battalion, poses casually for Ross in a reserve position at Gallipoli.

The Lieutenant Ross collection is held at the State Library of Victoria. Other examples of his work appear on pages 34, 53, 76, and 249.

PRIVATE WILLIAM McELWEE

Private William McElwee joined the 8th Light Horse in June 1915, but was on his way to the battlefield when his regiment was annihilated in the futile charge at the Nek. McElwee, a 25-year-old tailor from Middle Park, Melbourne, went on to serve in the Middle East and made it through the war. Like nine out of ten other Australian soldiers, he was single when he enlisted.

TROOPER GEORGE SIMPSON MILLAR

'GSM' stands for George Simpson Millar, the light horseman from Clayfield in Queensland. Trooper Millar is catching up on news from home during a respite from battle.

*Lieutenant May and other 22nd
Battalion soldiers*

*Three Australian soldiers man
a trench post at Gallipoli*

Lieutenant May poses with a group of 22nd Battalion soldiers—in the company of a dead mate. The timber crucifix behind them marks the spot where their comrade died, perhaps from a sniper's bullet. May is believed to be sitting middle front, with his hands clasped between his knees. He is a far slimmer version of the Lieutenant May on pages 59 and 60.

Fatigue and the stress of battle are clearly imprinted into the faces of these men occupying a trench post. This photograph, by an anonymous soldier, was probably taken in October or November 1915, and shows a telescope, used to assist in sniping, protruding from the sandbags. By then, generals on opposing sides were reluctant to sacrifice more men in futile frontal assaults, and so the drudgery of trench life—in increasingly cold conditions—set in.

After a blizzard

Bitterly cold conditions produced several blizzards at Gallipoli in November. It was the first time many Australians had seen snow, but the novelty wore off when there was a high incidence of frostbite and fatalities resulting from exposure. The men holding the snowballs are captioned as 'Captain Webster' and 'George Watson' on the back of their photograph. Their details are not known.

Disconsolate troops after the Gallipoli evacuation

Although the evacuation of the peninsula was a master stroke of military planning, Anzac troops were devastated to be leaving dead mates behind, and to be sailing away from an unfinished fight. This forlorn-looking group of Australians was photographed by Lance Corporal Gornall, the unofficial photographer of the 23rd Battalion, days after the December withdrawal. They are destined for Egypt where Anzac forces were restructured in preparation for the Western Front.

4

THE WESTERN FRONT

The Australians hated the Germans well in advance. They were the territorial plunderers who had started the thing in the first place: they had raped Belgian nuns, murdered Nurse Cavell and sunk the passenger liner *Lusitania*; they would leave notes in Australian trenches, promising to bathe the soil of France with Australian blood. Spurned on by propaganda, the AIF was braced for a war of attrition against the force of darkness itself.

Before embarking from Egypt, the base camp of the AIF after Gallipoli, Lieutenant Molony, of the 5th Battalion, attended a church parade in which the chaplain had 'the audacity to preach Fatalism & Predestination'.[1] Private McInerney, a 10th Battalion reinforcement, said: 'The parsons over here are very colourless specimens…One poor fellow told us last Sunday that it was not so very dangerous fighting. That there were almost as many dangers in times of peace with trains, cars and orange peels of all things'.[2]

A new mood of sombre restraint beset the restructured Australian units[3] as they sailed to Marseilles, each man wearing a life belt and his boot laces undone in case of German submarine attack. French authorities had been warned to expect trouble but the Australians landed virtually without incident, a fact ensured by the heavy presence of military police at the port. While disembarking from their boats a day later, to the tunes of the *Marseillaise* and *Australia Will Be There*, the Anzacs glimpsed their first sight of Germans working as prisoners along the wharves. Tall and broad almost to a man, the sight of them made the new arrivals think they were up against a tough opponent, though some diarists saw the lighter side of it and noted that they presented bigger targets.

The subsequent train journey up the Rhone valley towards the front, 200 kilometres north of Paris, was idyllic in contrast to the tortured slopes of Gallipoli and the sands of Egypt, but there were ominous signs: trainloads of wounded French soldiers came the other way from the carnage at Verdun, farms and vineyards were worked almost entirely by women in the absence of their menfolk, children lining the railway tracks made 'cut-throat motions', which some soldiers mistakingly interpreted as meaning 'go give it to the Hun'. But diarists and letter writers kept their observations positive. Private McInerney said: 'It is a really beautiful country and well worth fighting for'.[4] Sergeant Major Gilbert Mulcahy announced that he had seen 'first decent looking girls'[5] since leaving Australia; the port of Marseilles reminded Lieutenant Molony of Sydney Harbour,[6] the landscape 'for all the world like Walhalla [an old Victorian mining township]'[7] to Private George Weatheritt. After passing through one of several long railway tunnels, one card next to Private William Callinan remarked: 'Well this is [a] waste. All this dark tunnel & all boys in the carriage'.[8]

Many of the soldiers were hopeful of a stopover in Paris on the way but the nearest they got was an outlying suburb that afforded a distant view of the Eiffel Tower. Wherever they stopped, they were lauded as crusaders. Private Douglas Westwood, a field ambulanceman who arrived with the 2nd Anzac Corps in June, could not contain his excitement.

> Passed through Lyon about 7.30. bonza big place. Get a great reception all along the line had breakfast or dinner or whatever it was at Macon at 11.30…Passed plenty of old Chateaus and ruined castles and monuments right on top of big cliffs. Land marks I suppose, also some bonza water falls and streams. The roads look A1, chalk white, winding in and out among the hills. Passed train load of French soldiers at St Germain Au Mon d'or one of them gave me a drink of wine, good oh![9]

As Anzac troops were detrained around the town of Hazebrouck in mid-March, they could hear the report of artillery guns from the front. They were put into training camps at Etaples and Erquingham, among others, then filtered into the front line near Armentières, a 'nursery' area where opposing sides seemed to have developed a mutual agreement to keep hostilities to a minimum for the sake of untried or resting troops.

The Australians' induction to fighting in these early months was tame in comparison to the close-quartered dustiness of Gallipoli. They were far better equipped with weapons and supplies, and they had been trained more thoroughly. Their trenches were well constructed and the nearest enemy trenches were hundreds of metres away, and estaminets (a type of rural cafe) were in close proximity. It did not take Corporal Aitken long to develop an association behind the lines. He told his mother in an April 1916 letter: 'I've been kidding to one of the girls here, pretty too, + I told her I'd marry her at three o'clock today; when I asked if she were ready she said "But I've to wash my underclothing first". Or was she kidding me?'[10]

By the end of April 40 000 Australians were among 1.2 million Allied troops manning trench systems which snaked 800 kilometres from the North Sea through Ypres, to the Swiss/French border. A total of 120 German divisions faced them.

The front had been established in November 1914 when retreating British forces made a stand against the invading Germans in front of the ancient Belgian town of Ypres, about 35 kilometres south of the coast. While the British dug in and formed a salient jutting out from the moats of Ypres, the Germans took control of the surrounding ridges and hills. The British had to hold Ypres at all costs; to lose it would enable the Germans to sweep through to Paris and the key channel ports; for this reason it was equally coveted by the Germans.

To the newly arrived Australians, the German was an invisible enemy but one who observed with calculating precision. Lieutenant Ross was probably joking in an April 1916 letter when he told his mother 'We all wear steel helmets—the Germans can't hurt us'.[11] But Hun marksmen were ever ready to capitalise on a moment of carelessness in a trench and, in fact, the introduction of the helmet in World War I aroused a deeper sense of hostility between the opposing sides, and made soldiers more inclined to aim directly at the head of a man wearing one.[12] Meanwhile, German artillery observed the movements of Anzac billets to farmhouses and barns, and targeted them with lethal consequences.

Quartermaster Sergeant Ernest Jones explained to his family in a May 1916 letter that 'if you keep your head well down you are quite safe'.[13] He was killed instantly when shot in the head at Fleurbaix a month later. Around the same time Private Fred Mitchell of the 24th Battalion was walking along a 'safe' zone with his twin brother Hawton, when he was mortally wounded by machine-gun fire.

Claude Ewart, an artillery driver, found the going warm on the open supply roads.

> 9th July [1916]. More shells to the Bty, had another narrow shave. Today a piece of shrapnel hit my horse on the back it gave him a nasty wound. You ought to have seen him when he was hit he stopped and looked round at me as much as to say 'who done that'.[14]

Ewart was blown off his horse three times in separate shelling attacks in 1916.

Lieutenant Ross saw a lighter side to it as he wandered through a ruined town in April: 'Just opposite a little railway station there is a brick building smashed up with shell fire. Some wag has printed in chalk across it Melbourne Mansions. Young & Jacksons…Young & Jacksons is the pub opposite Flinders St Railway Station'.[15]

Lieutenant Aitken was unlucky enough to be caught in a German artillery attack around that time. '…I had just started the men on digging & remarked to George that we'd be shelled to hell at daybreak when over I went; a high explosive shell blew me clean on to my head in a shell hole + wounded me slightly in the throat…George was killed.' An eight-hour barrage followed. 'Mother, it's quite indescribable…men were being buried and blown to pieces all around…D Coy went into the line with 176 strong + came out with 38, I could have cried'.[16]

The Germans also demonstrated willingness to fight at close quarters, and in May they launched two overwhelming infantry raids on separate positions on the

Australian line. The Australians were humbled. Their trenches had been smashed, casualties were high and in the first foray at Bridoux the Germans plundered two 'secret' Stokes mortars.

Plans for retaliation began in earnest. One of the first rejoinders was led by the former captain of the Melbourne University and Victorian lacrosse teams, Lieutenant Laughlin of the 6th Battalion. The assault involved fifty men selected from 400 volunteers crawling across 210 metres of no man's land at 1 a.m. on 13 June at Fleurbaix. Laughlin's party crawled behind an accompanying artillery barrage. They were obstructed by an unexpectedly wide barbed wire entanglement forty metres from the trench.

Laughlin momentarily panicked.

> And then there flashed through my mind, probably what flashed through everyone else's mind also: exactly how the whole division was watching us, how the Battalion was watching us and how indecision and lack of forcefulness loses every time…In 15 seconds from the time I got to the parapet, all of the men, not one was missing, had taken up their positions…And then I saw a German about 5 yards away against a traverse. We fired together, but he was probably more startled than I was, for his bullet went through my leg and mine caught him fair in the stomach and as our revolver bullets are thick, softnosed bullets, you can imagine he was about done.

> I dropped down in the trench and called to the men and they came pouring on, in their correct positions and started on round the trench. At this time I didn't realize I was wounded. My leg felt just as if someone had banged it with an axe handle. It was stiffening but I limped along the trench alright…the results were 6 prisoners, 12 Germans killed, and occupied dug-outs bombed but results unknown. Probably 24 killed, but we definitely counted 12…Altogether the raid was most successful as we had only 2 wounded—Private McKenzie and myself.[17]

Laughlin's raiders were the toast of their division. After he recovered from his wound, Laughlin was awarded the Military Cross and he was courted by English nobility while on leave. But his methods that night at Fleurbaix were brought into question. Captain Bean, the official correspondent, judged the attack less a raid, more a brutal *coup de grâce*. In his official history Bean singled out the execution of two Germans in the raid: one who was shot repeatedly at close range until he 'sank helpless to the side of the trench'; another who was 'found brained by the knobkerry of some soldier whose lust for blood was not yet satisfied'.[18]

After the war Laughlin wrote an annotation in Bean's book beneath the reference to the executions: 'This occurred in 6th Bn. raid. Wounded German (bald) would not stop struggling thus preventing scouts from searching him for papers and documents and identifications. Accordingly, I gave order to a scout who appealed[?] to me to bash his head in with a knobkerry, which was done. A.L.'

The trench raid became the main instrument of Allied intimidation on the front throughout the rest of June. The brutality that Bean readily condemned in Laughlin's attack became the calling card of nearly every raiding party, Allied and German alike. Australian raiders, and presumably raiders from other armies, used the forays as an excuse to pillage and souvenir. Some like Driver Ewart 'went exploring' through the 'underground palaces' of the Germans well after they had been attacked. A 17 July diary entry records what he came across in one dugout.

> We found eight dead germans & would you believe it there was a dead woman with them. My God it made my blood boil what I saw. I suppose they took her from one of the towns they captured. Well I could not help kicking one of them. She did have a sorrowful look on her face. We carried her out and gave her a decent burial. We found nothing on the Germans we left them where they were…My word the day of reckoning will come for Kaiser Bill. He will have to pay for it all.[19]

The trench raids of June and early July were a precursor to Australia's first major battle near the France/Belgium border. The newly arrived Australian 5th Division was thrown in to attack the Sugar Loaf salient, near the village of Fromelles, to ease pressure on the British and French at the main fighting front to the south. With only five days to prepare, the Australians were rushed to the battle zone and exhausted by the time they got there. The Australian Brigadier General 'Pompey' Elliott tried to convince commander-in-chief General Haig's staff that the attack across 400 metres of no man's land, under a curtain of Allied artillery, would be disastrous, but he was overruled. Later, Elliott roused his men by telling them not a German would be left alive by the time the artillery had finished, but privately he and his operatives knew it was suicide. On the night of the battle, one of Elliott's subordinates, Major Geoff McCrae who had been wounded three times at Gallipoli, closed his last letter to his family with the words: 'Farewell dear people, the hour approacheth. Love from GEOFF'.[20]

While the Allied artillery was effective to a degree, machine-gun and rifle fire whipped out from the German lines, particularly from the area earmarked by the 15th Brigade. Wave after wave of Australians crumpled; the British 61st Division to the right suffered badly.

When the whistle sounded for McCrae's company to attack, he was first over the parapet, a pistol in his hand. The 26-year-old fell in no man's land with a fatal bullet wound to the neck; his last mortal instinct being to outstretch his arm and aim his pistol at the enemy.

A shell-shocked survivor who charged with McCrae, Private George Blair, wrote:

> From the moment we were over the parapet Fritz started his machine guns and mowed us down. I got about 150 yards towards the German trenches when my leg got a bullet and I could go no further. Then a shell burst near and I was laid out for some time. I came to myself and it was dark, then I began to crawl back to our own line...The sight in our trenches was sickening, men were lying about dead and shattered to pieces.[21]

As the survivors of the 15th Brigade limped back to Australian trenches, Pompey Elliott wept as he shook their hands. 'It was the 8th Light Horse Charge at Walker's Ridge [the Nek] over again—on a tenfold scale...Geoff's regiment was practically annihilated', wrote Elliott in a letter of condolence to Major McCrae's father. 'One of these [recovery parties] found Geoff's body. He was quite dead, kneeling on one knee, with his pistol pointing towards the enemy'.[22]

The roll call for McCrae's 60th Battalion was sixty-five.

Although some sections of the Sugar Loaf line were captured by Australians, the Germans realised the attack was merely a demonstration, and did not divert troops away from the Somme as Allied strategists had hoped. Almost half (5500) of the 5th Australian Division became casualties for little gain.

There was worse to come. The 1st, 2nd and 4th Divisions had been seconded to the Somme where the Germans had been stubborn in the face of British and French offensives. The Australians knew that the fighting would be bad—20 000 British troops were killed there on the 1 July opening alone, and the region was as vital to the German Army's defences as Ypres was to the British Army. Their objective was the town of Pozières which had been ruined during four previous attempts by British infantry to capture it.

'We camped on a hill near Albert for two days and before leaving we had a Bde church parade and our Padre told us that probably many of us wouldn't attend the next service', wrote Private Weatheritt. What they saw on the way to the battle zone impressed on them the padre's forecast of doom. They filed through the town of Albert and saw a statue of the Virgin leaning from a half-wrecked cathedral; later they walked along a cobble-stoned Roman road through shell-torn valleys. 'Here we saw the most horrible of sights', Weatheritt wrote. 'A shell had evidently caught a batch of men and there were arms and legs and pieces of men scattered everywhere.' Another 5.9" shell then struck a section of one dozen men in front of Weatheritt, killing or wounding all but one of them. The remnants of the company bolted for cover in the depression known as the 'Chalk Pit'. The bodies of dead men lay scattered around the perimeter, and Weatheritt watched disbelievingly as more shells hit the rim of the pit, sending showers of chalk and body fragments everywhere. 'One of the dead men on which the shell landed had been hurled 40 yards, the other was missing altogether'.[23]

Shortly after midnight on 23 July, 1st Division troops smashed outlying German trenches, clearing the way for an assault on the centre of the town which was eventually taken the following night, despite heavy repulses. Weatheritt described one of the counter attacks:

> …we saw the Germans coming from all directions. Our Captain gave the order to charge but as soon as he saw that we were being mown down, he gave the order to get down and then the sniping began. We hopped in to shell holes and began firing for our lives when suddenly the Fritzes were seen to throw up their hands in surrender. There were about 150 of them coming with their hands up to be taken prisoner…We would have taken them alright, but the 4th Battalion machine Gunners sighted them and turned their guns on to them and cut hell out of them.[24]

Several days later, Weatheritt was hit by a machine-gun bullet that was deflected by a button on the back of his trousers, and lodged below his heart.

It was the first time since the commencement of the Somme offensive that Allied troops had made a significant incursion into enemy territory, and the Germans wanted it back. They trained all available artillery on the village they had just lost, and commenced a relentless three-day bombardment which tested even hardened Gallipoli veterans. The ground swayed and churned, men were blown to pieces, buried and driven mad; others shot themselves.[25] Private Fred Russell predicted he would die in it—and did. Private Edward Edwards, who had joined up to avenge the death of a school mate, died there too.

But the Australians clung on, and on 27 July what was left of the 1st Division was withdrawn and replaced by the 2nd Division which was then ordered to attack German garrisons in the ridges above the village. They failed the first time but succeeded six days later, suffering heavy losses roughly equivalent to half their manpower on both occasions. The crest was secured with the arrival of the 4th Division on 4 August, but the bombing and skirmishing continued for weeks as the Germans, who were now shelling on a virtual 360-degree axis, tried to win back both the village and the heights.

Lieutenant Aitken's company was caught up in it.

> Mother dear, You should see the Germans run, they can go some too; but its great to see them drop their rifle on their toes, shove their hands up & yell for 'Mercy, Kamarade'—they got it too sometimes. In our first trench, bodies were every-where & twisted into all shapes; one German was buried alive & my attention was drawn to him. I said to the man 'You can shoot him or dig him out; please your-self'…They call it Pozières village & wood; it may have been once but, by Jing's, now there's scarcely two bricks together or a tree standing.[26]

And a few days later: '…I do hate the trenches; one does get a run for ones money in the open + the excitement in an advance is great, but I'm sick of it all, my Mother + just want to get to you'.[27]

Despite the severe losses of personnel, British generals wanted to extend control of the ridge behind Pozières to Mouquet Farm, about 2 kilometres to the north-west, in an attempt to lever their own corridor behind a German salient at Thiepval. The depleted Australians now suspected they were being put in every time a British general hatched up a near-impossible objective on a map. General Birdwood, the avuncular figure they so loved at Gallipoli, lost some of his polish around then because there was a feeling he could have lobbied harder for British troops to share more of the hard, dirty work, even though the British had suffered similar casualties. 'Everyone is fed up with trench fighting. Especially the infantry. When our boys start bombarding we in the trenches have to suffer when Fritz retaliates', wrote Private Edwin Smith, 22nd Battalion.[28]

But pride stopped the Australians baulking when the moment came to go over the top again. Sergeant Allan Tongs, of the 12th Battalion, recalled: 'It was a grand yet awful sight to see them the last few moments before the Whistle blew [at Mouquet Farm], at last it went, many were cool as cucumbers, one man was sharpening his razor…'[29]

Thousands including Private Smith were cut down and blown up in much the same way as at Pozières village, but this time there was no firm gain of territory. The battle raged from 8 August to 3 September, costing three Australian divisions 11 000 officers and men before the Australians were withdrawn from the Somme. Some of the losses were attributed to the incompetence of inexperienced officers and NCOs—'yobs' who 'lose their heads',[30] is how Private Makeham described them—from training schools in England and Australia. At the end of seven weeks fighting, the Australians had lost 23 300 men around Pozières—comparable to the 26 000 Australians lost in eight months at Gallipoli.

A group of 2nd Division soldiers who had taken part in the Pozières fighting tried to forget about what they had seen. 'We had what I call "A Sentimental Bloke night", wrote Lieutenant Aitken, '…met a chap named Doug Walsh from the 10th; my word, Mother, he was good & gave us songs & C.J. Dennis all night'.[31]

Four days after landing at Gallipoli, Lieutenant Aitken had pondered that 'a man expiates all his sins'[32] in going through the 'hell' of war. Now it seemed that ultimate 'redemption' was beckoning for all, and the savagery of the battlefield had trampled any illusions about fighting for noble causes.

'The more I think it over', reflected Sergeant Tongs, 'the more I marvel we are not all mad. May be we are, only all alike and so there is no one to distinguish the ranks'.[33]

No song so sweet, no estaminet wine so heady allowed them to erase war's actuality from their minds, and its impact was compounded by the numbing impact of death repeated hundreds of times over. Death became so grotesquely familiar that its magnitude could not be absorbed in a reasonable time frame, nor could one articulate its import when clouded by fatigue, fear and sensory numbness. To grieve openly, as one might in peace-time, was to concede defeat and permit a vulnerability that might prove fatal in battle. Diarists and letter writers spoke of disbelief, muted sadness, and a sense of loss, but rarely extrapolated on what it meant or how it felt to lose a mate. A typical registration of a soldier's response to death was to record the fact that it had happened.

After stretcher bearer Private Alex McGoldrick saw four of his mates blown away next to him, it seemed apt for him to write: 'Ypres—Mercer, Ballard, Doyle, Murray killed 26.9.17. Myself slightly wounded'.[34] After the war, McGoldrick told friends that the only traces left of three of the victims were their newly issued leather boots.[35]

A 1916 entry from Driver Ewart's diary read: 'I heard today that one of my mates that I went to school with had been killed. Charlie Hargraeves he was with the 21st Bty his head was blown right off he was from Tasmania. It rained today again it came down allright but I do not think it will last'.[36]

A school of thought reasoned that the best one could do was to pay a dead soldier your respects, think well of the man you once knew, and, above all, survive. A deceased was considered to have been given a decent 'send-off' if his body was located then buried in the same shell hole he died in while someone recited a prayer. If time and safety permitted, the dead man might have been transported to a nearby military cemetery.

At home, AIF telegrams were the initial means of official notification that a soldier had been 'killed in action' or that he had 'died of wounds', or been listed 'missing in action'—a term often used by authorities as a euphemism for death when it had not been established that death was certain. In some cases, however, relatives first found out while reading newspaper casualty lists. The telegrams were prefaced by statements like 'Regretfully advise' and were usually dispensed by military authorities to parishes, from where the clergy would personally deliver the news, upon which the drawing of one's blinds customarily marked the commencement of a period of mourning. Beyond this grim ritual, there was little to console grieving parents, siblings, wives and lovers. Over time, there might be a chain of official correspondence relating to pension details and the personal effects of a soldier, Red Cross statements verifying the details of the victim's fate and a certificate from King George to say that he whom this scroll commemorates has 'finally passed out of the sight of men by the path of duty and self-sacrifice'.

If a loved one was lucky, a few letters arrived from a senior officer, an army chaplain or servicemen who either witnessed the death of a man or partook in his burial. Those letters were almost always consoling and often the most meaningful form of succour for the bereaved. The deceased might have been remembered as *a 'white man' who was always looking out for someone to help*; *we called him 'Mul', the best liked man in the Battery* and that *he did his duty to the end*. Death, or one's *departure from the ranks*, was rarely slow and brutal: *his end was entirely painless* and sacrificed during the attainment of an important objective. If death came slowly, the way he went was honourable.

To soften the blow among the relatives of servicemen who had no known grave soldiers and army chaplains would say things like the enemy *had a great respect for our dead* or *we buried him in a beautiful little cemetery*. Some provided map co-ordinates of a burial site where relatives would find a neat wooden cross and some poppies growing. Most of these letters ended with the expression that a soldier made the *supreme sacrifice*; some ventured to imply that a dead soldier was in the company of an elite Valhalla, and that torn hearts should be troubled no longer for one day the bereaved will be reunited with the deceased.

When Private Callinan was laid to rest in 1916, having been fatally wounded while stretchering a wounded man out of Pozières, seven of his best mates co-signed a letter and sent it to Callinan's parents. It contained a transcription of an epitaph inscribed on a wooden cross above his grave:

> Killed while carrying a wounded comrade.
> At the foot
> Only a private soldier,
> Only a Mother's son
> On the field of battle
> His duty nobly done.[37]

ॐ

The Christmas of 1916 was a season of reflection for troops, and a time to prepare for the most bitter northern winter in forty years. The rain which had prevailed since October, turning much of the front into a bog, abated in December but then troops had to contend with frosts and snow. Generals devised some small-scale attacks in diabolical conditions to keep the pressure on the Germans, while thousands of cases of frostbite and trench-foot were treated. Energies focused on improving conditions in the trenches, communication lines and access routes. In areas where the ground had frozen, soldiers tunnelled beneath the hard surfaces then smashed open layers of ice.

Some efforts were made to improve the lot of soldiers by issuing them with more rations, gumboots (that proved ineffective) and sheepskin jackets from

Australia. Others were sent socks, jumpers, canned foods and the usual quantity of mail from Australia. Seventeen-year-old Private Harry Devine, who had been court-martialled for refusing to pick up a shovel, received a letter from his old headmaster saying that boys like him were the 'backbone of the British Empire'. When he read it to his mates he was drowned out in hoots of derisive laughter.[38]

The respite from hostilities enabled leave to be given more liberally, although a growing percentage of soldiers had begun to go absent without leave since the fighting at Pozières. Those within walking distance of towns packed around the warm fireplaces of estaminets. These informal country cafés ran to a formula which suited the soldier: they served Belgian beer and French wine, fried eggs and chips as a staple, and were run by women. In these venues troops relived battles, defamed superiors, argued about conscription, entertained rumours of a German retreat, and bequeathed themselves to barmaids they had known not more than an hour.

Private Clarence Williams, a 19-year-old farmer of the 10th Battalion, remembered:

> There were four lovely girls running the show [the estaminet]; the youngest being about 18. Somehow she took a fancy to me and I had a job to shake her off. Being a shy sort of fellow I was very embarrassed. Before going back to the billet we discovered that it was my part gold tooth that she was so interested in.[39]

The genial fug of the estaminet was a fleeting glow in an otherwise dreadful 1916–17 winter. By the time the snow began to melt in late January, conditions had become almost unbearable in areas without built-up roads or timber 'duck-board' tracks; trenches had become havens for rats, some reportedly the size of cats. Horses and men sank in quagmires, and it could take a man on foot an hour to travel a few kilometres. George Weatheritt, now a lieutenant, wrote: 'The mud had just about broken our hearts. On many occasions men were too weak to pull their legs out of the mud and the others would help to pull them out. I have seen as many as 6 men required to pull another out of the mud'.[40] Driver Ewart said, 'it was nothing to see our men and horses floundering in the shell holes. We had to shoot a few of the horses, we could not get them out...'[41]

While the mud had introduced a new kind of 'deadlock' at the battle front, the conscription issue had gathered momentum on the home front. Reinforcement levels had been dwindling since mid-1916 and pressure was being placed to bolster units with convalescents who had not fully recovered from wounds or illness. This practice had a negative bearing on the morale of troops, particularly when thousands of able-bodied men continued to 'shirk' the call-up at home. More than this, it ground weakened men through the grindstone of attrition, making them more susceptible to injury, disease and shell shock.

The New Zealanders gave in to pressure from the British Government and introduced conscription in June 1916, and Australia's Prime Minister Billy Hughes was determined the AIF should follow suit. At home, Australians became openly divided about the war. The debate led to heated public meetings, punch-ups, invective from the pulpit and hysterical media coverage. The pro-conscription movement, which consisted mostly of women and the families of volunteers, argued it was time for shirkers to pull their weight in an hour of dire need. Anyone who was seen to oppose the war in some way—German emigrants, striking workers, conscientious objectors—were lumped together as 'disloyalists'.

Sergeant Murray Knight expressed a common gripe in a 1917 letter to his brother: 'I think a lot of the boys are going to vote "Yes" just in the hope of getting some of the strikers across here. They will then have a chance of doing some striking but of a different kind'.[42] Although a slight majority of Australian soldiers favoured compulsory enlistment, two conscription referendums attracted significantly more 'No' votes in October 1916 and December 1917.[43] The defeat of conscription embittered some soldiers, but over time morale eventually benefited from it because AIF members retained their unique status of being the only volunteer force at the Western Front.

It was intended that the Australians play no part in the major offensives at the front in 1917. They would be used to plug holes, to mop up when required. Their first experience of combat since the Somme offensive was in March 1917 when some divisions harassed the German army as it retreated to a shorter line, 50 kilometres to the rear of its old trench system. The Australians were checked by strong rearguard units and fighting broke out for the control of several towns outlying the new Hindenburg system.

To smash the Hindenburg Line, a major offensive was hurriedly orchestrated for Bullecourt, a town fortified by German garrisons. An attack by the 62nd British Division at the town of Arras, south along the Hindenburg Line, had earlier failed. Again an attack involving the Australians had been organised at short notice for a seemingly untenable gain. But this time the British had a trump card, tanks, which might do the job of the thousands who had been sacrificed against artillery guns and machine-guns blasting out 600 rounds per minute. But the debut of the Mark 1 tanks was a spectacular failure. Initally, they were slowed down in a snow storm and had failed to arrive in time, forcing the attack to be put back one day, and when the dawn manoeuvre was re-launched on 11 April, the machines struggled in the mud and snow, leaving thousands of men stranded out in front. And one tank that did make it as far as an outlying village mistakenly opened fire on Australians in the confusion.

The infantry achieved the near impossible by advancing into the second line of Hindenburg entrenchments without covering artillery and tank fire. But the system went back further still, and the Australians were overcome by waves of German troops who emerged from rear bunkers. Almost 3300 men from the 4th and 12th Brigades were killed or wounded; a further 1200 were taken prisoner. Such was their induction to the attrition of 1917.

In a second attempt on Bullecourt on 3 May, Australian 2nd Division soldiers (without tanks) seized a vital section of the Hindenburg Line and repulsed heavy counter-attacks. More Australians and later some British troops were brought in as relief during two weeks of furious fighting in what had become the focus of the whole British front. Lieutenant Laughlin, who had just returned to his 6th Battalion after his wounding in the Fleurbaix trench raid, was struck down with bullet wounds to the head and groin. Half way through it, Private McInerney, of the 10th Battalion, wrote: 'Probably before this letter reaches you George I will have a medal or a commission, a wooden leg or a wooden cross. Maybe it is much the same whatever happens for all is changed nowadays and the world is upside down'.[44]

Private Williams, also of the 10th, wrote:

> …unfortunately one man's nerves went on him and he cried and said Corporal 'I can't go back'. 'You'll have to,' says the Corporal 'or I'll be in trouble.'…we decided that he would be useless in the front line and that he would only get himself killed; so the Corporal sent him back to a dressing station.[45]

General Gough, commander of the British Fifth Army, was blamed for Bullecourt, as he had instigated it, while his junior staff, including Australian tacticians, had failed to allow for the complexities of such an offensive. The AIF casualty toll of 7500 severely depleted three divisions and deepened the lines of estrangement back home. One of the victims, Private Edward White of the 24th Battalion, died in a tangle of wire on the first morning of the battle. His body was never recovered and when Mrs Annie White received official confirmation that her 29-year-old husband was dead, she refused to believe it. She placed 'Soldiers' Whereabouts' notices in Melbourne newspapers, asking any returned diggers who knew anything of Edward White to contact her at her Melbourne address. Her searching would go on for more than a decade after the war.

In June, Australian troops were marched in for the battle of Messines, which was aimed at getting a step closer to routing the Germans from their hold around Ypres, near the Belgian coast. To that end, mines containing one million pounds of TNT beneath German positions on an outlying ridge at Messines would be detonated, paving the way for an infantry attack.

So devastating were the 7 June mine blasts that Australian, New Zealand and British troops had secured the Messines–Wytschaete Ridge in two hours. But a segment of the Australian 3rd Division ran into trouble beforehand as it was pounded with gas shells in Ploegsteert Wood. There were many more casualties around the ridges later as some Australian troops were mistaken by their own artillery as Germans. Hundreds more were hit in retaliatory German barrages or cut down by machine-guns set in squat concrete forts known as 'pill-boxes' which the Germans were using for the first time in the war. Messines was regarded as a great success, but as usual the casualties were high: the 3rd and 4th Australian Divisions lost 6800 men between them; about 500 of the victims had been gassed in Ploegsteert Wood.

One of the abiding fears of the latter part of the war was the insidious use of gas, which was used openly by both sides. Sometimes it smelt like candy and stripped the lining of your lungs; other times it reeked of mustard, blistered your skin and blinded you. Sometimes fatal, its residual effects reduced the fighting capacities of soldiers and debilitated many of them after the war: '... it [tear gas] makes your eyes run worse than onions and if it was not for the seriousness of the whole concern it would be quite amusing to see hundreds of men weeping their eyes out',[46] wrote Private Makeham.

Major Donald Coutts, of the 6th Field Ambulance, treated many gas victims.

Friday, March 22nd [1917]. Another gas bombardment...there were more than 200 gassed men...many of them were vomiting and coughing, and all of them had red eyes, with tears running down their faces. We lined them up as well as we could outside the R.A.P. [Regimental Aid Post], and I went along and had a look at each man. I evacuated most of them. We sent them off in parties of 5 and 6— walking behind the other, with their hands on the shoulder of the man in front, and a stretcher bearer leading the way. Many of them could not see at all.[47]

Attacks like this engendered a deeper hatred of the Hun war machine, and Australian soldiers entered into the spirit of retribution. A 1917 letter by Sergeant Albert Goodsir of the 33rd Battalion was typical of this mood:

We have had several hand to hand goes with the enemy in raids but soon as we get in close quarters with him, he turns and runs...one party of Germans were on a machine gun and when we were getting close to them their gun failed and they were doing their best to fire at us with one hand and holding the other up singing out Mercie (they got it, not very much though, about four or five inches of our bayonets, Napoo Finish).[48]

Sergeant Tongs wrote that when an Australian stretcher bearer became the twentieth victim of a German sniper at Pozières, an officer finally located the sniper's position and instructed a fusillade of 20 rifles to fire into it.

Private Makeham said:

I had no idea that Fritz was such a despicable creature...he has left nothing but ruin in his wake. He has even cut down all the fruit trees and gone into the cemeteries and blown up the vaults and village after village has been blown up till there is nothing left but heaps of debris'.[49]

Some Australians wrote more favourably of the Germans after personal dealings with them, and began to see they were not the spike-helmeted monsters depicted in propaganda cartoons. A wounded Private Allan Hislop was given cigars by 'big useless Germans'[50] then carried to a dressing station after they found him lying in a shell hole in 1916. Lieutenant Ross spoke to a German POW who had farmed 16 hectares of land in Renmark, South Australia, and who was 'grabbed' by the German military upon returning to his native land to marry his sweetheart. Another prisoner captured by Ross' 27th Battalion produced reference letters, evidently written by Allied POWs whom the German had once guarded. 'Lads. Treat this man well as he has treated us', one of them read. 'He is a white man and for our sake look after him'.[51]

Driver Ewart once kicked the corpse of a German soldier whose body he found next to a dead woman, but later expressed compassion for some Germans who had been subjected to an Allied bombardment: '...some of the Germans came running into our lines crying like babies, well we could not help pitying them, they are half starved they said they had nothing to eat for four days'.[52]

❧

The Belgian front was again dumped by rains in August/September, reducing much of the battle grounds to mud. Logic deemed it sensible to cease fighting, but General Gough continued to push his army for futile gains in quagmires. The commander-in-chief General Haig intervened, and put the more even-minded Plumer in charge of offensive operations. Plumer would wait for the weather to settle before he called for new troops, which prompted orders for I Anzac Corps to enter the Third Battle of Ypres.

The aim of this offensive was to capture Gheluvelt Plateau, another height from which German artillery pounded Ypres. Plumer had reasoned that a series of short thrusts supported by artillery into fortified German zones would be the best way of getting the plateau. The first of these thrusts for Menin Road (20 September) was a success with the 1st and 2nd Australian Divisions suffering comparatively few casualties, despite heavy fighting around pill-boxes. The second attack at Polygon Wood (26 September) was equally effective, thanks largely to a side-stepping manoeuvre by Pompey Elliott's troops which captured an objective originally assigned to the British, but the 4th and 5th Divisions lost 5770 men.

At Broodseinde (4 October) I and II Anzac Corps fought alongside each other for the first time. The conditions were atrociously wet and muddy, and it was thought that the pounding of artillery had caused ancient swamp systems to re-emerge. Invading forces were at an obvious disadvantage even before considering the effect of machine-gun fire and increasing concentrations of German artillery. The Australians took Broodseinde Ridge in spite of the difficulties, 6500 of them becoming casualties.

Two more thrusts in deteriorating weather conditions failed. At Poelcappelle (9 October), 1250 Australians were either killed or wounded; Passchendaele (12 October) cost Australian divisions another 4000 men in bogs that made it near impossible to walk, let alone hold a rifle. In the midst of it, Driver Ewart, a 2nd Division artilleryman wrote:

> Well I would like a nice Blighty [wound] myself now ... I would like to get my Photo taken to show you what it is like over here. I don't think I will be able to stick it out much longer. My nerves are in a terrible state. The rain and mud is something awful. I lost my poor horse last night. He was wounded again. He was sent away to hospital.[53]

Eventually, the Canadian Corps took the heights of Passchendaele on 10 November, by which time the Australians had been withdrawn from the battle zone. But hundreds remained there under mounds of raw earth, in bogs and shell holes. Lance-Corporal Errol Davis, who won the Military Medal at Bullecourt, was among them, killed by a shrapnel blast as he and his brother Clifford retreated from Passchendaele; Private John Wilder, a Lewis machine-gunner of the 58th Battalion, lay there too. Seven months later his father E. A. Wilder, of West Wyalong, received a Red Cross letter, telling him what had happened. 'He was killed alongside me at Polygon Wood. We were crossing an open space...he was shot [in the neck] and killed outright. He did not speak after being hit. I saw his dead body but know nothing as to burial'.[54]

After their battering at Ypres, the Australians entered a period of recuperation at Flanders in the relatively quiet Messines sector. It also heralded the beginning of complete autonomy in the command structure of Australian troops. This passing of the baton from Commander Haig to General Birdwood in November 1917 was the symbolic seal of the Australian army's coming of age. The effeminate general with the quaver in his voice had seen the diggers evolve from the days of Cairo where they stole his car one new year's eve and dumped it in the desert.

They saw Birdwood as a man of great wisdom, a charmer who seemed to see through the stiffness of the English class system and who had the trick of spinning his monocle into the air and catching it between his eyebrow and cheekbone.[55] They saw him as a warlord who took advantage of his camaraderie with them, who at times overestimated their morale, and who inculcated the view that the only way to beat the Germans was to fight harder. Before the 1916 battle of Mouquet Farm, Sergeant Tongs, the 50-year-old farmer from Tasmania, wrote: 'General Birdwood who gave us a brief outline of our position we were to take in a few days time also told us it was fight & fight again—no peace'.[56]

After being awarded the Military Medal by Birdwood in 1918, a somewhat more cynical Sergeant James McPhee of the 4th Field Ambulance concluded: 'Altho lavish with the soft soap, he must be an efficient man'.[57]

Perhaps it was Birdwood's confidence in the Australians—and the way he pushed them—that prompted them to overcome any inferiority complexes they might have had, and to rise to greatness in battle. As the war progressed, the AIF's reputation in battle grew, particularly in the estimation of some of its own members.

'We are always having rows with the Tommies [English],' wrote Driver Ewart,

> they try and knock us back all they can but they find their mistake each time...if there is any hard fighting to be done it's the Australians & Scots called upon to do it, we get on very well with the Scots, they think a lot of the Australians.[58]

While the Australians had been crucial to the outcome of some strategically important battles, it is debatable whether they were any tougher, more skilful or braver than the New Zealanders or the Scots, or whether they were imbued with any more singularly distinguishing features than the British. Every participating country had its heroes of whom to speak, an *esprit de corps* said to be unique, improvisations to uniforms, morale problems, flamboyance, cowardice, black days, battle locations etched on their maps of glory, and sacrifices over which to grieve.

Off the battlefield, the Australian soldier projected his self-esteem and stature as a sportsman—some romantic writers believed the Australian was a sportsman on it, too. Captain Bean embraced the view that the Australian attitude to war was inexorably linked to its national obsession with sport. Although Saturday football in Victoria and South Australia was blamed for a large absentee rate from compulsory cadet drills, Bean believed that a large proportion of Australia's sportsmen did not hesitate to enlist because they understood the nature of a 'contest', and they quickly adapted to the rigours of the army because of their fitness, self-discipline and sense of teamwork.

At Gallipoli, the prospect of playing sport presented certain danger because of the ever-present threat of sniper and shrapnel fire, and most of the time soldiers were too exhausted anyway. Sometimes, though, a football would be seen spiralling over a reserve position, while intrepid cricketers occasionally chanced their arm on a natural sporting amphitheatre at Shell Green.

It was not until the AIF arrived at the far more expansive Western Front that Australia's fanaticism for sport flourished, in relatively safe environs. Football games, cricket, boxing and athletic meetings were seen as a tonic for improving morale and fitness, and a means for fiercely competitive Anzac units to test their mettle against one another. In June 1916, football was mixed with bayonet training and revolver practice in preparation for the 14th Battalion's first trench raid at Bois Grenier.[59]

The nature of the contest depended on the season, the availability of venues and the egos and proclivities of commanders. Contestants would play, some still sore from battle, on 'ovals' that were occasionally frozen and strewn with shrapnel and barbed wire, and within firing range of enemy shelling positions. Spectators ranged from German Taube pilots, men in trenches with telescopes, to the Prince of Wales at one celebrated 3rd Division match at the Queen's Club in London.[60]

Gunner Sydney Cockburn, a Military Medal winner, played in an Australian Rules match on Saturday 29 September 1917, staged to commemorate Grand Final day in Melbourne. 'Played Rollestone 6th I. Btn on their ground and won after a strenuous game by three points. Scores 5 – 8 to their 5 – 5. It was a splendid ground, and a good game. We had three association and several league players playing. I played a good game, showing form'.[61]

Some contests presented the opportunity to settle an old score. 'Holding boxing lessons and contests, under instructions of Alf Morey the W. Aust. champion…Two men got 18 months each for punching the Sgt Major & breaking his nose',[62] Cockburn wrote in 1918. Three days earlier, Cockburn had participated in a similar incident. 'Fought the bully of the Bty. and gave him a severe thrashing. Broke his nose bone penetrated his eye, blackened both his eyes, and bruised his face which nececcatated him going to hospital. Got complemented from all'.[63]

A flash of brilliance in a pack or a commanding opening spell gave a previously unnoticed soldier a chance to shine, a disgraced reinforcement a chance to wipe his slate clean. 'It was through football that Dannie McArthy came under my notice as a hard working forward,'[64] wrote Lieutenant John Barton. 'He had lost his paybook due to it having too much red ink in it. In this case red ink was brought about by drunkness. Some men are misunderstood and wrongly crimed.'

The likes of Danny McArthy were prone to boredom and trouble when their energies were not properly harnessed during rest periods. Venting one's spleen in a publicly demonstrative fashion was seen as a privilege (among some sections of the AIF, at least) that had carried over from the Wazzer riots in Cairo. When 8th Battalion soldiers paid in advance for a 'no-show' at the 'Blood House' theatre near Sutton Veny camp, retribution was automatic. Corporal George Bailey was there as 'the troops started to pull it down & eventually set fire to it. They pulled the piano out & played Keep The Home Fires Burning & Will The Blood House Be Forgot'.[65]

In quieter moments, soldiers hoped that the war might be over soon, a grow-ing number being severely fatigued and debilitated from the lingering effects of shell-shock. AIF medical authorities believed that waves of shell-shock from the 1916 Somme offensive subsided by the time most of the victims reached casualty depots. The problem, which at its worst manifested itself by violent physical tremors, dementia and protrusion of the eyes, was not addressed in any concerted fashion until 1918, and not at an institutional level until 1919, partly because of an attendant stigma of weakness or shirking. Soldiers in past wars had not exhibited this 'nervous condition' to any notable degree. Were the soldiers of World War I of any lesser constitution?

It seemed some commanders bent on minimal strategic gain through attri-tion had overlooked a fundamental difference between the localised impact of nineteenth-century cannon balls and the annihilating tendencies of high explo-sive shells—the mostly deadly technical innovation of World War I. British commanders had been embarrassed by the high rates of shell-shock treatments among its officers, while a view persisted among Australia's high command that malingerers exploited the syndrome as an 'open sesame to the Base',[66] although the statistic of 205 1st Division cases in one day alone during the Germans' 70-hour shelling barrage of Pozières would suggest that was not the case.

The thought of another year in battle was too much for many, leading to a dramatic increase in officially recorded incidences of self-inflicted wounds: 388 soldiers wounded themselves in 1918 to try to ensure a passage out of the battlefield, as opposed to 126 in 1916.[67]

Even the optimists among those who stayed to tough it out could see no immediate end to the war. Some major developments ensured it. The Red Army had disintegrated following the Russian Revolution of 1917, releasing streams of German divisions to boost efforts at the Western Front. So the German Army which had begun to lose its hold on the front in early 1917 was suddenly in a position of awesome power by the end of the year. Commander Haig's grave concerns were compounded by the fact that British troops were depleted from the fighting at Ypres and that the French Army was in the throes of mutiny.

Australians would soon be ordered to assist General Gough's army which was being pushed back by the Germans in the Somme area. Private McInerney rea-soned to his brother George that he probably would not have 'any brother at all at the end of the second act…They go, all the good men go, but it's little use wailing'.[68] Private Percy Smith's mother, meanwhile, thought that sending a steel vest might improve her son's chances of survival. He wrote back to her from Sutton Veny in February, saying he would be 'mentally deficient' to wear it in action. 'I will see if I can sell it to some officer…the company that would advertise them as suitable for an infantryman…should be had up by the govern-ment for trading in such things'.[69]

Some Australian units went to the Somme for skirmishes against General Ludendorff's army which was advancing steadily through the weakened British line. Seeing some British troops falling back, an infuriated Pompey Elliott demanded the execution of any stragglers who refused to be rallied. Fortunately for those troops (and probably for Elliott) the order was immediately repudiated by higher command.[70]

The fighting involving the Australians around towns like Dernancourt and Morlancourt was small in scale yet bitter. Gunner Cockburn was among a group of Australians at Morlancourt targeted by shells captured from British artillery positions.

> 29-3-18. Good Friday but was Bad Friday for the battery. 5 o'clock in the morning Fritz shelled the battery and played havoc, killing thirteen and wounding and gassed fifteen with one gas shell—28 casualties with one shell, takes some beating. The gas was deadly, some of the lads not living a quarter of an hour, our little dog mascot died in a few minutes.

A day later, Cockburn wrote: 'I was sent to HQrs with a sample of the gas, an analyses [sic] was ordered through it being so deadly. We heard nothing official but it was surmised that it was one of our own shells sent back'.[71]

The major offensive involving the AIF for that period was fought at Villers-Bretonneux, which overlooked the Somme River and linked up to the strategically important railway junction town of Amiens. Australians had captured the town earlier in April, suffering heavily from German gas attacks, but the relieving British forces lost it on 23 April; the Australians returned to recapture it the next night. During the fighting, Lieutenant Barton questioned his ability to hold his own. 'Our Company was badly shaken and a most horrible feeling of fear and failure came over me…and my prayer to Almighty God was "save me from cowardice" '. Later, while catching a few hours sleep in readiness for a German repulse, the 30-year-old grazier had a vision of his deceased father. 'He was mute, his face was placid, but the message that passed to me was "if you are crossing over to me let me be proud to shake your hand" '.[72]

After one night of fierce attacking (24–25 April) by Pompey Elliott's 15th Brigade and the 14th Brigade, Villers-Bretonneux was retaken at a cost of 1500 AIF casualties. The victory was a huge morale booster for the Australian Corps after the lingering tinge of the Passchendaele defeat, and some firmly believed that they were the key to saving the Western Front. 'The Hun seems to leave us fairly well alone. He does not attack us, as he does the Tommys. Fully half the number of times the Tommys take over a position from us, the Hun is in it a few days later, which speaks for the Aust. as a fighter',[73] Corporal Bailey wrote after the battle.

By then, however, the frenetic German advance had lost some of its vigour, and French troops—not the Australians—had taken the lion's share of the defence from the British who had suffered huge casualties while Australian divisions rested through most of the winter. Other crucial developments had come into play by mid-1918. British artillery emerged as being not only numerically superior but technologically better than the Germans, with the development of sound detection systems which could quickly locate and knock out enemy batteries. Allied tanks had been improved vastly since the dismal debut of the Mark 1 in 1917, and troops by then were better equipped with new supplies of weapons produced in Britain's munitions industry. These improvements, together with the entry of American forces, became the decisive factors of 1918.

After Villers-Bretonneux, Australian forces were employed to harass the enemy back across the Somme. The Australians had developed platoon tactics to a cunning science, and set upon the enemy in groups of forty, each platoon comprising a section of Lewis machine-gunners, a group of rifle bombers and two sections of riflemen. The Australians were victorious in almost every instance, taking control of towns and hamlets, secretly patrolling and knocking out posts and demoralising the Germans with trench raids. 'I got our first prisoner that night', Private Devine, of the 37th Battalion, wrote after one raid, '...went down a dug-out, candle in left hand, revolver in right. German officer wounded, called for stretcher bearers, one of the boys hopped down and took Fritz's revolver and watch, I then hopped in for my cut, and took his dagger'.[74]

German regiments were reportedly relieved when their 'bloody tour' of the region had ended. Around this time a British officer wrote that the Australian Corps had gained a 'mastery over the enemy'[75] that was not equalled by the British.

The attacks further consolidated confidence among the Australians who by then had effectively liberated dozens of villages. Gunner Aubrey McCallum of the 8th Field Artillery Brigade reported to his family in an April 1918 letter:

> As the infantry were coming on the march behind, the french girls + women would run out with jugs of beer + pat them on the back. 'Tres bon Aus'. Of course, the boys were black from the din of motors etc + looked quite hard types + they would chip all the french people in their own language screaming 'Fritz was coming Weren't they frightened' + they could see they were joking. You may think it funny but this is a fact. Some of the civilians are there as soon as they hear we are shifting from one front to another they pack and follow us.[76]

Letters and diaries from this part of the war record stories of intimidation and thuggery in towns previously occupied by German forces: an escaped British prisoner being clubbed to death in front of townsfolk; a French woman ordered by Germans to shine a lamp on to her captured son as he faced a firing squad. Isolated incidents, such as the murder of Nurse Cavell, the execution of Allied prisoners and the mutilation of London school children in zeppelin raids were sometimes taken to represent the inhumanity of every German. The stories got worse, and those who reported them seemed to forget that many were simply acts of war. 'Incidents' that descended to new depths of cruelty, such as a German soldier giving a French girl a box of chocolates containing an explosive device, never seemed to be witnessed first hand. While the veracity of such accounts was to be doubted, an ideological zeal among soldiers ensured they were not forgotten as they continued their crusade against the forces of Teutonic oppression. Yet some accounts, as told to the Australians by their French hosts, also paint German soldiers as gentlemen who were courteous and could be trusted not to steal anything.

While moving through the ruins of these towns, the minds of soldiers locked on to the bizarre and surreal: 'I believe a well dressed woman was seen walking through the ruined streets [of Villers-Bretonneux]. The only thing that was wrong was the pair of issue military boots which gave the show away',[77] wrote Lieutenant Ross. And from Corporal Bailey's diary: 'The Battn Q. M. [Quartermaster] salvaged a fine piano last night, it has been lying by the roadside for two or three days. The lads used to have a little rag time on it every time they went passed it while on ration fatigue'.[78]

The Australians were glad that war had not visited their home country, yet they saw how life could go on in spite of war's suffering. Soldiers curiously noted how French boys no older than 10 would imitate their dead fathers by smoking cigarettes and drinking wine, how an elderly lady obstinately risked sniper fire by walking through part of no man's land to retrieve valuables from her house, how women dressed in black would tend farms to which husbands would never return. Private Williams and some mates happily volunteered to stack hay on one farm.

> About 10 o'clock the Frenchman's wife and daughter turned up with morning coffee made with milk. Hot scones and cake. Did we rubbish the rest of the Company when we got back at lunchtime. It was a picnic for us and we really enjoyed it. I don't think Frenchman realized the danger his daughter had been in.[79]

Others like Major George Robinson, MC, regimental medical officer of the 11th Battalion, longed for a future beyond war. 'Well dear', he wrote to his lover, an Australian nurse, in London, 'I have been thinking it over hard—and truly I am just longing to be married just to feel I really have you—your heart your thoughts your sympathy and your troubles as part of my own'.[80]

The AIF's next big engagement was the battle of Hamel which was staged on 4 July in honour of the newly arrived Americans. Although small in scale, it had been meticulously planned by the new commander of the Anzac Corps Lieutenant General John Monash, following Birdwood's secondment to the British 5th Army in place of Gough. Monash, an engineer in civilian life, left nothing to chance. Three brigades of Australians would fight alongside the inexperienced Americans for the first time, and their advance would be preceded by the usual artillery guns and aircraft to mask the sound of sixty British tanks. Everything went to plan, and Hamel was taken in 93 minutes with relatively few casualties. It became a logistical model for generals elsewhere on the front.

The following month British and Canadian forces descended on the Somme where 'peaceful penetration' raids by the Australians had prevented the Germans from fortifying their front. Tacticians planned attacks on several key towns, but the object was not to seize these towns, rather, to drive the Germans further away from the railway systems that connected them. For the 8 August attack on Amiens, the British were to form the main attack, with the Australians and Canadians in support. It was launched just before dawn with perhaps the most damaging Allied artillery barrage in the war. The growl of advancing tanks was again silenced by preceding aircraft, repeating Monash's tactic at Hamel. But the artillery inflicted the initial damage by silencing most machine-gun emplacements and rival batteries. The Australian infantry took the front trench systems with relative impunity, but some pockets later met strong resistance after British troops on their left flank had fallen behind, leaving the Australians exposed. By nightfall the Allies had reached their objectives and secured probably the biggest bounty of the war. They captured 450 guns and seized most of the old Amiens line while inflicting 27 000 German casualties, which included 16 000 prisoners. Allied casualties were again minimal. The German army was on the way to defeat and its commanders knew it. General Ludendorff described 8 August as 'the blackest day' of the German Army in the war.[81]

In the ensuing days Australian divisions supported British and Canadian troops in a wave of continual motion against the retreating Germans. But the arrival of élite 'shock' troops from the Kaiser's army allowed Germans to put up stiffening resistance, and several thousand more Australians became casualties. One of them, Lieutenant Aitken, whose letters revealed the graduation of a sentimental young accountant into a hardened soldier, died near the ruins of Lihons. Corporal George Smith, MM, of the 16th Battalion, was shot in the chest and abdomen during the push but survived. A letter written by Smith's sister Dolly arrived while he was recovering: 'As you say this war is up the putty, every day the boys who are returning [with long-term wounds] give me spasms down my spine, they either take to drink or anything else procurable to drown memory, I suppose, or pain'.[82]

General Monash masterminded the next big AIF triumph at Mont St Quentin, the last bastion of German defence on the Somme line. The three-day attack was preceded by an awesome artillery barrage which took nothing away from the skill of 600 members of the 5th Brigade who silenced outflank positions then cleared the summit. A crude tactic was used to deceive the enemy—Australians yelled like demons to hide the fact they were undermanned—and as they charged the top of the hill, bewildered German guards surrendered in droves or fled down the other side. But the Germans re-mustered for a counterattack and pushed the outnumbered Australians to just below the summit. German glory was brief. The 6th Australian Brigade mounted an attack, securing Mont St Quentin, and enabling the 7th and 15th Brigades to storm through some outlying woods and take the nearby town of Péronne on 2 September. In doing so, a vastly outnumbered mix of Australians from four brigades had put five German divisions out of action (at a cost of 3000 Australian casualties) and forced the rest of the German army in that region back to the Hindenburg Line.

The Allies now had the Germans pinned, but they were not yet done for. The defence system they had retreated to had been vastly improved since the fighting at Bullecourt in 1917. Its six-kilometre defensive zone, east of St Quentin Canal, was marked with deep pits, machine-gun posts, mines and paddocks of barbed wire. The Australian 1st and 4th Divisions were given the job of attacking the centre of the outpost line on 18 September, and they took it easily in drizzling rain, while British troops lagged either side of the Australians. But this action blemished the AIF's record as an unrelenting fighting army. About 120 men from the 1st Battalion decided they would not go back in to fight, citing exhaustion and an unfair burden of battle commitments.[83]

With all element of surprise gone after the outpost attack, on 26 September, Allied artillery commenced a two-day pounding of the main Hindenburg Line with a barrage of 750 000 shells, including mustard gas. Most of the shells fell wide, however, making the job of the infantry difficult, and tanks that were supposed to be supporting the Allies were knocked out. Two newly arrived American divisions, which had been bolstered by some experienced Australian officers and soldiers, suffered heavily from machine-gun fire on 27 September and failed to take the first part of the line. The 3rd Australian Division entered the fray two days later, and skirmished using Lewis guns and rifle grenades for three days. Slowly, the offensive gained headway thanks to the persistence of the Americans to the south, which allowed the 5th Australian Division to capture the village of Bellicourt at the mouth of the canal. Victory was sealed by a brilliant flanking manoeuvre by the British 9th Corps which breached the final section of the Hindenburg Line to the north.

The final assault on the line—and Australia's last battle of the war—took place at Montbrehain. The Anzac Corps was in the midst of a manpower crisis: eleven of its sixty battalions had been disbanded in 1918, and most of the surviving battalions were down to a fighting strength of 300 or 400 men, compared with an original strength of 1000. Many of those soldiers left standing were near the point of exhaustion, so Monash took the radical move of attaching a non-combat unit, the 2nd Pioneer Battalion, to the battle.

Separate attacks by 2nd Division troops as well as British troops had failed to secure the town in early October, but the 6th Brigade finally took it triumphantly on 5 October, in the face of heavy machine-gun and sniper fire, with the help of the 2nd Pioneer Battalion. It was the AIF's deepest penetration into German territory. The Australians were withdrawn from the line, having suffered another 400 casualties. Some soldiers who took part in the 25 April landings at Gallipoli three and a half years earlier were among fifty-five Australians to die at Montbrehain.

The Australian Corps was scheduled for a return by the line in November but by then emphatic victories by the British Army, the French and the Canadians had crushed the last of Germany's fighting spirit. On 11 November Germany effectively surrendered on Allied terms by agreeing to an armistice.

A machine-gunner on board the NORTHLAND

German submarine activity in the Atlantic Ocean and North Sea prompted the fitting of guns on Allied ships transporting troops to France. In this photograph taken on board the *Northland* by Lieutenant Ross, an Australian machine-gunner is on the look-out for submarines. Small calibre guns like this Vickers .303, although effective on the battlefield, were inadequate in the event of torpedo attack.

LIEUTENANT DONALD BAIN *on board the* NORTHLAND

'Donald Stuart Bain has his throat painted'. This photograph, also by Lieutenant Ross on board the *Northland*, shows a gentler side to the stereotype of the tough, flinty soldier. Bain is probably being treated with medicine to cure a sore throat. He is holding a camera, believed to be the Kodak pocket model popular among soldiers. Captain Bain, who operated as a stock and station agent from Collins Street, Melbourne, was repatriated about six months after this photograph was taken.

Commonwealth troops on board a transport ship near Plymouth

This undated photograph was taken of troops, who had probably been convalescing or on leave in London, before being transported to France for battle. The soldiers, an assortment of English, Scottish, Australians and New Zealanders, are enjoying a variation on an old nursery game as their ship sails near the English Channel port of Plymouth.

Troops aboard the ULYSSES

'Every evening our choir collects outside & sings the same class of songs, and a good many hymns. One of the officers wanted to know if the men formed a fighting army or a Salvation Army',[33] wrote Lieutenant Ross in a 1915 letter. The men pictured singing hymns in this scene were reinforcements travelling on the *Ulysses* to France in November 1916. They are wearing baggy fatigue hats, an AIF innovation later worn as 'giggle hats' by Australian soldiers in the Vietnam War.

A soldier with two monkeys

*Australian soldiers exercise on
the deck of a transport ship*

'A study in expressions. Two of the ships' pets; and their "Dad"—an AMC orderly', wrote the anonymous soldier who took this snapshot. The monkeys were probably purchased in a Cairo market and smuggled on board for the AIF voyage to Marseilles in 1916. Many battalion mascots including dogs and kangaroos were taken on board the first transport ships to leave Australia for Egypt in 1914. While authorities handed most of the animals over to the Cairo Zoo, a number of dogs, including Gunner, a 14th Battalion mascot, 'saw action' at Gallipoli.

The same soldier took the snapshot on the right. 'Cheering up a little. Much more vigorous "Jerks" on our Foward Deck', said the caption.

Playing cricket on an AIF transport ship

An unstable pitch and a wet outfield did not prevent these Australians from pursuing their love of cricket en route to the Western Front. A net has been erected to prevent on-side players from losing the ball. The photograph was taken by Eric Dewar who enlisted in the 2nd Field Artillery Brigade in 1916 as a 22-year-old lieutenant.

Cape Town during AIF shore leave

Transport ships carrying AIF reinforcements bound direct for France sailed via the South African coastline to minimise the danger of enemy submarine attack, and to take advantage of coaling facilities. This photograph by Lieutenant Dewar was probably taken while on shore leave in Cape Town in 1916.

Practising musketry at Etaples, France, 1916

This anonymous snapshot of troops practising musketry procedures was scrawled with a caption that read: 'Etaples France 1916'. The odd-sounding location on the North Sea coast was promptly renamed 'Eat-apples' by Australians. Thousands of newly arrived AIF soldiers were drilled into near submission by fanatical instructors in the notorious Etaples 'Bull Ring' before being sent into battle.

26TH BATTALION *troops, Belgium*

Morale is buoyant among these 26th Battalion men as they march into battle. Some of the soldiers at the rear of the column appear to be barely out of their teens; their faces reflect the yearning for adventure which motivated many to enlist. The photograph was taken at Dickebusch, Belgium, in 1917.

An Australian ammunition limber

'Well we had a parson with us one day [at Albert] we were giving him a ride and we were getting shelled the boys started swearing he only laughed but my word he got a rough ride while it lasted in shell holes and over tree stumps.'[34] This 1916 diary account of Driver Claude Ewart could well have been written around this snapshot of an Australian ammunition limber galloping through a dangerous cross roads. Ewart, of the 4th Field Artillery Brigade, survived the war despite many close shaves with death. He was blown off his horse three times in 1916 alone.

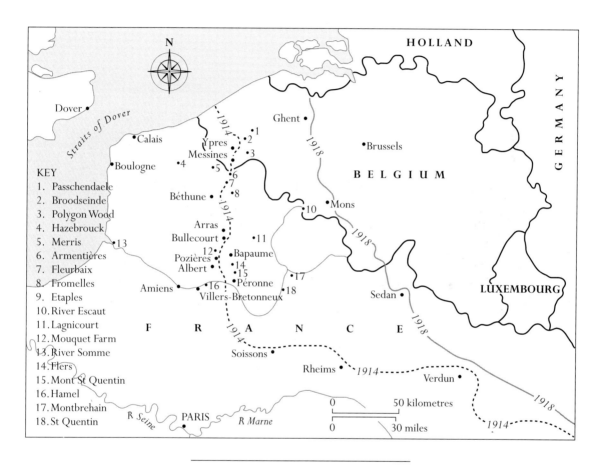

KEY
1. Passchendaele
2. Broodseinde
3. Polygon Wood
4. Hazebrouck
5. Merris
6. Armentières
7. Fleurbaix
8. Fromelles
9. Etaples
10. River Escaut
11. Lagnicourt
12. Mouquet Farm
13. River Somme
14. Flers
15. Mont St Quentin
16. Hamel
17. Montbrehain
18. St Quentin

AIF *operations on the Western Front*

A meal break at Ypres

Ypres salient 1916. The Australians enjoy a meal outdoors at a time when trees were still a feature of the landscape. The photograph illustrates the three common types of head-gear worn by AIF troops at the Western Front: the soldier to the right has retained the traditional slouch hat, the man at the back of the group wears the new oval-shaped tin helmet modelled on the British design, while the soldier on the left favours the British Regular Army cap which was phased out by the AIF in 1917.

The devastation of the Western Front

22ND BATTALION *soldiers*

22ND BATTALION *position*

Private Aneese Jaboor, a reinforcement to the 22nd Battalion, had a love of trees that began in his native Syria. The 33-year-old clerk, seen smiling at the back of the trench, bottom left, took photographs of forests whenever he could. But soon there were no more trees left, and Jaboor's camera focused on what remained: surreal landscapes spun with mangled root systems, shattered trunks, shell-torn villages, vacant stares on men in bare trenches.

Dead German soldiers

'We found some more dug outs today, there were some more dead Huns in them if you touched them they would fall to pieces, one of them had his head blown right off. I got a pair of boots off one of them. I am wearing them now, they are good ones.'[35] Driver Ewart, diary, 1916, France.

This photograph by an anonymous soldier was taken of an annihilated German position at the Western Front.

LIEUTENANT AUSTIN LAUGHLIN *and* CAPTAIN J. D. ROGERS *with French billets*

'No-one was to be left wounded. The wounded had to be killed… It is gruesome and rotten to have to do it but it is war',[36] wrote Lieutenant Laughlin of a trench raid at Fleurbaix in June 1916. The official war correspondent Charles Bean singled out the 6th Battalion raid—one of the first staged by the AIF—as being excessively brutal. After the raid, Laughlin, left, and Captain J. D. Rogers, right, pose in a studio with a couple who billeted them in France. Laughlin and Rogers were both awarded the Military Cross for leading the Fleurbaix assault.

QUARTERMASTER SERGEANT ERNEST JONES *and his father* VICKERY*, studio portrait*

Quartermaster Sergeant Ernest Jones, of the 10th Battalion, was reportedly killed outright when struck in the head by a rifle grenade at Fleurbaix on 26 June 1916. In this 1915 photograph, Jones, a draper by occupation, is standing beside his father Vickery, before going off to war at the age of 42, which was considerably older than the AIF average of 23. (In February 1915, the AIF began signing up volunteers as old as 45.) A few months after this photograph was taken, Jones, of Alberton in South Australia, sent a postcard to his daughter Phylis. It read: 'Good bye my dear little girl I am leaving for the front in a day or two Be a good girl & help Mother all you can With best love from Father'.[37]

SERGEANT ALEX BLAIR *and* PRIVATE GEORGE BLAIR, *during convalescence*

Unlike most brothers who enlisted in the AIF, George and Alex Blair joined up separately in the 60th and the 22nd battalions respectively. It seemed unlikely their paths would cross but the two were injured in the fighting in 1916, and met up while recovering in England where this studio photograph was taken for old times' sake. Older brother George, a 25-year-old private, who was shot in the leg and shell-shocked at Fromelles, is seated; Alex, a 23-year-old sergeant, is standing.

A while later, George sent a copy of the photograh to Alex back in the front line. On the back of it, he wrote: 'To my loving brother Alex, Trusting that we may be spared to meet again on earth should it be God's will. From George (JG Blair) in hospital England'.[38]

They saw one another again but George was not the same man his brother knew. George was admitted to hospital in March 1917, suffering from a relapse of shell-shock, though George himself saw it as not much more than 'loss of memory'[39] (diary, 15 March 1917). His field medical card read:

16/3/17 On admission patient was quite dazed and very shaky on being spoken to became very emotional and broke out into crying. No statement obtainable.

17/3/17 Remains very nervous and shaky and is still dazed. Cannot answer questions properly.

20/3/17 Patient chatters much. Very dazed and wandering in speech.[40]

George was discharged from the army in February 1918 and took up work as a timber contractor in the Dandenongs, east of Melbourne, but was classified as having an 'apparently permanent' disability that entitled him to a pension. He married in 1919 and raised four children with his wife Ellen at Sassafras, but according to granddaughter Lyn Gibbs, the marriage suffered and the rest of the family moved to South Melbourne in 1936: 'My mother recalls that George was often absent from the house due to his health and drinking problems'.[41]

George Blair died in 1941 aged 50. Alex Blair survived the war, worked as a gardener and died in 1952, aged 59. The brothers saw little of one another after the war.

PRIVATE HAWTON MITCHELL, TROOPER MATTHEW MORRISON *and*
Private Fred Mitchell, enlistment portrait

Trooper Matthew Morrison, seated, and his first cousins Private Hawton Mitchell and Private Fred Mitchell, standing left and right respectively, were childhood mates. They came from border country Wodonga, worked as graziers on their family farms, and learned to ride and hunt together. So it was natural that they would want to be in it, but they had to wait till they were old enough to join up. All three enlisted on the day of the twins' 18th birthday, 3 August 1915, but not before getting written permission from their parents. Morrison, who was older by a few months, joined the 7th Reinforcements to the 13th Light Horse, and the Mitchells the 8th Reinforcements to the 24th Battalion.

Before leaving for France, they met to have this enlistment portrait taken at the Pall Mall studio in Bendigo. They were proud and excited, but the puff of the camera flash seemed to penetrate some subtle resonances. Their faces are partially masked by uncertain, solemn shadows; their eyes are composed yet tentative, perhaps sadness in recognition of being together for the last time. Their postures are resolute and upright, true to classic formal poses of that era, yet there is a certain awkwardness about the way they fill their uniforms.

The twins did not hold it against their lanky cousin for wanting to join the Light Horse—he was a superior horseman and a damned good shot, even though his slender hands seemed more suited to a piano than a rifle. Whatever way their paths went, the cousins would keep in touch by writing to each other at the front, and hoped to meet up again from time to time.

The triumvirate was broken before the AIF entered its first battle at the Western Front. 'On June 30th [1916] Fred was hit in the right side,' Hawton Mitchell wrote to his cousin two days later. 'We were both walking along the open, Fred was behind me, when the machine gun let go and caught him. Fred was attended to at once, and taken straight away. I don't know how he is getting on.'[42]

Fred died from his wounds on 1 July. His surviving twin articulated a kind of muted grief in a subsequent letter written while he was recovering from a middle ear infection: 'Now that Fred is gone,' he told his cousin, 'I don't care for France any more'. Indeed, in the same letter from Lord Derby War Hospital in England, he confessed that his parents were placing pressure on him to return home. And yet while the smoke of Warrington's factories darkened the sky outside his window, there was a flourish of black humour. 'There is an Australian sister in my ward—she is a little thing but well built. I like her the best, but some of them say she is rough dressing wounds. They say she is used to an operating theatre, chucking the piece about that the doctor cuts off.'[43]

Hawton Mitchell's estimation of his survival had dwindled since the death of his brother, and in July 1917 he composed a will, bequeathing all his assets to his mother. Nonetheless, he got through the rest of the year unscathed and was promoted to lance-corporal, which, at that time, had as much to do with factors of attrition as one's soldiering abilities.

Meanwhile, Morrison kept a diary of experiences. '17 Jan [1917] six inches of snow everywhere—plenty of snow fights & snowballing.'[44] And on '21 March [1917] put in the day sniping at 1,000 yards & fired 80 rounds…'[45]

The following year, 1918, held mixed fortunes for both men. Morrison recorded his war experiences in the usual desultory way. On 22 March 1918 'heavy fighting on the Somme—our troops driven back'. And the very next day: 'played Cycle Corp football & got beaten'.[46] He was also mentioned in despatches for 'bravery and devotion to duty' during the advance of the Anzac Corps through the Hindenburg Line and the Somme from September to November 1918.

Mitchell, meanwhile, had his pay forfeited for being absent without leave, redeemed himself and was later promoted to corporal. But his luck ran out on 24 August when he was hit by a sniper near Chuignes, France. 'Suppose you are wondering where I am, not looking you up, but I have got the Blighty', he wrote to Morrison a few days later. 'Have a pretty big gash in my leg…It hurts some, I tell you.'[47]

Mitchell's wounded leg haemorrhaged twice, forcing an amputation. He recovered briefly after the operation, but collapsed and died the following day, 1 September. To compound the family's tragedy, Braddon Mitchell, father of the twins, died in December from diabetes, though relatives believe his death was exacerbated by the trauma of losing his sons. Mr Mitchell's passing ended an era of family grazing on the banks of the Murray.

When Private Morrison learned of Hawton Mitchell's death he recorded the event as a statement of fact in his diary. Perhaps his grieving was withheld until a day, well after the fighting, when he rode quietly along the Murray and reminisced about days he and his cousins could call their own.

Matthew Morrison got through the war without being wounded. He was discharged in August 1919 at the age of 22.

CAPTAIN GEOFF MCCRAE

Geoff McCrae, an architect's apprentice from Hawthorn, was 25 when he was made 2nd in command of the 7th Battalion in Egypt. Captain McCrae came from a Melbourne family with links to the establishment and the arts: father George was a Collins Street-based architect and brother Hugh was an emerging actor and poet. McCrae, who had attained his rank in the citizen forces, was a product of a promotion system that put flair and youth before experience. Some observers noted that the Australians had a surfeit of 'baby-faced' officers, and it was hardly surprising in a corps so young in military tradition. While for the most part the policy worked spectacularly, questions hung over the mettle of some officers on account of their 'greenness' alone, and, for a time, it seemed McCrae was not cut out for the real thing.

On the way to the front, he nearly drowned when he fell overboard at Port Said, broke his leg in another boating mishap then collapsed after leading a desert march near Mena in March 1915 (see page 55). He was wounded three times at Gallipoli, once when a gunshot to the arm almost warranted amputation, later when the periscope he was using was shattered by a sniper's bullet—'It gave me rather a shock'[48]—and on another occasion when a shell burst fragments from a sandbag into his face.

After sailing back to Egypt, he was promoted to major during the reorganisation of the Anzac forces, but was soon in hospital again with a six-week spell of typhoid. A senior doctor advised that it was time young McCrae went home, but General Birdwood visited the hospital and asked him to stay on because there was a shortage of officers in the AIF. McCrae was back in uniform in time to leave for France with the 60th Battalion, but bad luck shadowed him almost as soon as he arrived. In a 13 July letter home he confessed, somewhat sheepishly, to being overcome by 'hay fever' and to being 'fearfully homesick'.[49]

McCrae, then 26, was given command of the 60th Battalion for the battle of Fromelles. 'Farewell, dear people, the hour approacheth. Love from GEOFF';[50] he wrote on 19 July, hours before going in to fight.

He was shot through the neck while leading the fourth wave of the battalion towards German trenches later that evening. When a recovery party found Major McCrae's body, his hand was clasping a pistol aimed at the enemy.

McCrae's brother Hugh was moved to write: 'So he remains still to me the little brother; and even as I think of him now in Pozières he has a child's figure, a child's eyes, and a child's small, sensitive hand—a boy too bright, too brave and beautiful to ever miss the road to Heaven.'[51] (While this quote suggests McCrae was killed at Pozières, in fact he died at Fromelles.)

A dead Australian soldier at Fleurbaix

As if asleep, this dead Australian soldier lies behind breastworks in the German 2nd line held by the 5th AIF Division during fighting around Fleurbaix on 19/20 July. The photograph was brought back from the war by Captain Charles Mills of the 31st Battalion, who was awarded the OBE in 1920 for services rendered while interned as a prisoner of the Germans.

Ruined church, Somme region

'There are a lot of shrines round here, images of the crucfiction I dont know how to spell it & the virgin mary, with everything around them shelled to peices I have never seen one broken yet.'[52] Lance-Corporal Henry Pepper, 7th Battalion, letter, France.

Battlefield folklore held that religious icons, like this figure of Christ in the ruins of a French church, were beyond destruction. This photograph is believed to have been taken by a member of the French Army. Its caption reads: 'Turteueur de l'église de Marquivillers Somme, le christ', translated to mean 'Christ, Guardian of the Church of Marquivillers on the Somme'.

GERMAN SOLDIERS *in the remains of a church*

Australian troops went to France with a hatred of the 'evil' Hun, whom they saw as perpetrator of European aggression, a military regime who fashioned stealth and cruelty into twentieth-century warfare. But, like the Allies, the Germans had their righteous cause, their honour, their God. In this photograph, possibly souvenired by an Australian in a trench raid, German troops defer to the figure of crucified Christ suspended precariously over the remains of a bomb-torn church.

23RD BATTALION *soldiers*

'Some types': the measured eye of Lance-Corporal Gornall is evident in another of his photographs. The 23rd Battalion digger to the right is wearing a souvenired German belt inscribed with the motto 'Gott Mit Uns' (God is with Us). A pair of wire cutters and a club ('knobkerry') used in trench raids appear to be leaning against the wall of the trench, bottom right.

PRIVATE FREDERICK RUSSELL

For every Canadian elm planted in honour of Bacchus Marsh's 281 war dead, there is a story to be told. Sadly, most of these have faded from memory or were never told in the first place. Even the stories that can be recounted are tinged with unresolved grief generations later, gnawing questions, irony and a yearning as constant as the trees themselves. At the base of elm number 225 is the name Private Frederick Robertson Russell.

Russell was born illegitimately in 1891 to Miss Agnes Russell, and was told as a boy that his parents were dead. He was brought up by his grandparents, believing his real mother to be his sister.

He enlisted in July 1915; aged 23, his occupation was chauffeur. He was described as being 'about 5ft 8" or 9", fair, slight and single'. It is said that as he was about to leave for the front, a 'kind relative' informed Russell of his true parentage, a revelation which drastically altered his outlook on life and probably explained why he did not write home.

'I do not know what is the matter. We have not received a letter from you since the 13th Feby', wrote Agnes Russell on 7 July 1916.

> I wish the war was over. It is terrible. I wish you were all back, it would be the happiest day of my life. It was very sad about Lord Kitchener, he was a great man but I do hope he will be avenged by the fall of Germany...I think this is all. Trusting you get it all right, please answer as soon as you can and relieve our minds. I remain your ever loving and affectionate sister. Lilly Agnes Russell (write soon dear Fred).[53]

The family has no record of a reply.

When a clergyman holding a telegram appeared at Miss Russell's front door in August 1916, she knew the worst had happened. Although she had dreamed vividly that Russell had been killed, she hoped vainly that he might have survived.

A letter arrived the following year. 'Dear Miss Russell, In answer to your letter of the 1/10/17 inquiring if I knew anything of your brother I have asked some boys in B. Coy and they told me that your brother was killed on the 10 August at Pozieres. He was buried by a shell and was dead when dug out...I myself was in B Coy at that time but had been wounded on the 7 Aug. also at Pozieres. Will you kindly accept my deep sympathy in your great loss...Yours sincerely, Bert Jacka.'[54]

Another letter arrived, from 14th Battalion Sergeant William Groves in October 1919. 'Now I remember quite distinctly a conversation between Fred and me', Groves recalled. 'I had been congratulating those who had pulled through the previous stunt, when poor old Freddy said that the next would be his last. Light-heartedly we laughed him to scorn, but he persisted, a premonition seemed to have beset him.' And later...

> We excavated the one man whose thigh was badly broken—Roghurst was his name. Two more were dug out in turn...The 3rd was poor dear old Fred. I looked at his head and recognised him. And now you have asked me for the truth, you ask a question which is really difficult to answer. But I've duly weighed it over in my mind and decided that nothing will be gained by concealment. Fred's hair was matted with blood! (God this is hard to write; I hope I'm not doing wrong. I never intended telling you) and his scalp or skull was raised—split across the forehead so badly that the interior could be seen. Your dream was correct. Death must have been instantaneous...
>
> There is so much I can tell you about Fred. You loved him, so did I. He was in my tent in Egypt and was always what is uncommon amongst soldiers—a man proud of his king, proud of his folk, proud of his regiment, but above all in face of all tempters or taunters, proud of his God! I can say of him the best one soldier has said of another—'He was a dinkum man'...[55]

In 1920 Miss Agnes Russell was interviewed by Bacchus Marsh police over the fact that she had been claiming a pension as Fred Russell's 'mother', when his enlistment papers had stated that both his parents were dead. Miss Russell confessed to her true identity and laid to rest a terrible family secret, officially, at least. In 1997 a descendant, Dianne Quinert, travelled to northern France to try to locate Russell's grave but was unable to find it. Russell had a brother Ivan, a labourer, who served in the 9th Battalion and survived the war.

Stretcher bearers carry a wounded man

Almost 23 000 men from three Australian divisions were killed or wounded at Pozières, making the lot of the stretcher bearer difficult and dangerous. This team attached to the 6th Brigade is passing the remains of the old Pozières cemetery. The man on the stretcher was wounded as the fighting progressed to Mouquet Farm in mid-August. The man at the head of the group holds aloft the Red Cross flag for immunity from fire, a gesture generally respected by the enemy. Even so, casualties were high among the men known as the 'body-snatchers'—624 field ambulance and regimental stretcher bearers became casualties between 19 July and 5 September 1916 alone.[56]

Snow fight at an AIF *camp*

'More willing snow fights. Had some great joy tobogganning down the hills on sheets of galvanized iron. Doing fully twenty miles an hour in places & snow flying everywhere.'[57] Gunner Sydney Cockburn, 4th Field Artillery Brigade, diary, 9 March 1917, Larkhill Camp, England.

The photograph was taken by an anonymous soldier at an AIF base camp.

Australian soldiers at Mametz

Marching from a year of terrible loss to a gloomy future, these Australian soldiers cross over a trench bridge near Willow Siding, at Mametz, in January 1917. A British official photographer recorded the moment.

A RAILWAY CORPS *member near Hill 63*

The unparalleled winter of 1916–17 placed intolerable strain on opposing armies, exhausted after the first battle of the Somme. While generals devised small-scale attacks to keep pressure on the Germans, energies focused on making life more bearable behind the lines. In this photograph taken by a 23rd Battalion soldier near Hill 63, a light rail corps member pulls a trolley for repair works along the line.

Martinpuich

Where roses once grew and children played, these soldiers form alien figures on a street in the deserted town of Martinpuich, France. This scene was taken by Lieutenant Thomas McCormack, whose grandson Matthew Darby, a photographer by profession, lent the photograph.

A captured German pill-box

Victory was swift and decisive, but 6800 Australians were killed or wounded on one day's fighting for the Messines–Wytschaete Ridge. Some of the victims lay around this concrete fortress, or 'pill-box', occupied by German machine-gunners. It was the first time AIF troops had encountered the virtually indestructible pill-boxes, which could only be put out of action by underground detonations or by being outflanked by exceedingly brave men under intense covering fire. This photograph was taken by Captain Daniel Aarons of the 16th Battalion.

"a 15inch shell-hole."

"a bath in a shell-hole."

"Swaynes Farm."

"Battery staff at dinner."

The Messines–Wytschaete Ridge

Sergeant Norman Martin of the 8th Field Artillery Brigade took these snapshots using a Vest Pocket Kodak. Invented in 1912, the camera produced a number of small negative formats—Martin's 1⅝ by 2½ inch being the smallest—and enabled Great War servicemen to be the first soldiers to photograph the battlefield. Martin's photographs were believed to have been taken after the conquest of the Messines–Wytschaete Ridge in 1917.

Hyde Park Corner, Messines

An unexploded shell

These photographs were taken after the battle for Messines. The scene on the left overlooks a cemetery near Hyde Park Corner, where some of the victims of the battle were buried. Hill 63, where AIF strategists devised tactics for the battle, rises gently in the background. To the right, an unexploded German shell has lodged into the trunk of a tree on the Messines road.

PRIVATE HENRY HERROD *and mates*

'Could you kindly let me know if there would be any possible hope of getting my son 718 Private H R Herrod home for a health trip',[58] wrote Mrs Elizabeth Herrod to the Defence Department in March 1916. Her son Henry, a 21-year-old timber mill worker from Yarra Junction, Victoria, was recuperating in Cairo at the time from a mild dose of scabies, but scars on his body told of other traumas.

At Gallipoli he had been wounded on three occasions, defying the odds he set for himself when he composed a will on 25 April 1915, assigning all his personal effects and money to his mother. Within a week, he suffered a gunshot wound to the scalp; in August he was shot in the right buttock and suffered a shrapnel wound to the ankle.

A smallish man with blue eyes and a tattoo on his right forearm, Herrod transferred from the 14th Battalion to the 4th Pioneers Battalion in May 1916. The transfer brought him no change in fortune;

if anything the trench repair work and tunnelling missions of the Pioneers exposed him to new dangers. Less than three months later, he was shot in the neck and jaw, being one of 230 4th Pioneer casualties in ten days at Pozières. Although he could open his jaw only half an inch, he was discharged from hospital and ordered to rejoin his unit. He was killed in action by a high explosive shell near Messines on 11 July 1917.

A mate, Eric Hansford, tried to console Herrod's mother in a letter dated 18 July 1917. 'It will comfort you greatly to know that he was spared any pain… He was just the same old Henry, with the same sweet smile. Not a mark on his face to show where he was hit last August at Pozières.'[59]

In his last known photograph, Herrod is standing back right with a group of 14th Battalion mates at an AIF training camp in 1916. He appears in two other photographs on page 26.

Wytschaete, Belgium

Communication breastworks like this one occupied by Australian troops at Wytschaete were constructed above ground level because of the swampy nature of the country, to avoid filling with water and to minimise the damage of incoming fire. The soldier in the foreground appears to be having his morning wash. The wooden duckboards beneath him enabled foot traffic to pass along muddy trench systems.

'Hellfire Corner', Menin Road, Belgium

A section of men followed by mounted troops risk the same fate as an earlier convoy, foreground, as they pass through 'Hellfire Corner' in 1917. Even though this dangerous section of Menin Road exposed Allies to German artillery fire, it was considered a crucial route from Ypres to outlying sectors of the battlefield.

3RD DIVISION AIF *headquarters, Ypres*

This shell-scarred building became the headquarters for the 3rd Australian Division at Ypres, Belgium, during the Broodseinde, Poelcappelle and Passchendaele operations in October 1917. A field ambulance parked out the front might have been an omen for the terrible Australian casualties in the rain-drenched battles to follow.

13TH BATTALION SOLDIERS *at base camp*

During a respite from battle, these 13th Battalion soldiers enjoy some light-hearted moments at an AIF training camp. The picture is from an album of Sergeant Charles Lewis' photographs. Lewis died of wounds received while manning an observation post in the 1918 battle of Hamel.

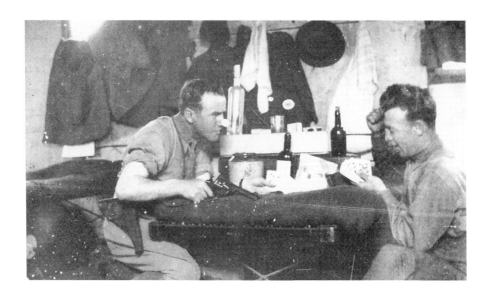

Card game between two AUSTRALIAN OFFICERS

Who has the upper hand? Two Australian officers engage in a spirited game of cards, observed by Lieutenant Ross who took this photograph.

AUSTRALIANS *play two-up*

Gambling assumed fanatical proportions among Australian troops. On the way to the front, bookmakers took bets on the Melbourne Cups in Egypt and soldiers could lay a few piastres on the outcome of a cock-fight; at Gallipoli, they gambled on which way beetles crawled along trenches and on which side two coins flung into the air would land. A two-up school at Simpson's Gap attracted crowds of 100 even when Turkish shells landed near, and the game thrived behind the lines at the Western Front. This photograph of a two-up school was taken by Captain Aarons.

Two-up players being 'struck' by a German shell

This remarkable photograph shows an Australian two-up game at the precise moment an enemy shell has landed. A caption on the back of the picture says 'Shell burst in centre of Swy [two-up] and all men were killed'. Or were they? Closer inspection reveals that the shot is a well-constructed piece of chicanery. According to Ian Affleck, head of the Australian War Memorial's picture collection, two images—one of soldiers in their 'death throes', another of what is probably a grenade harmlessly exploding in the dirt—have been overlaid to create this impression.[60] The contrivance might have been a lampoon of unsubstantiated tales of overzealous soldier-gamblers being killed in this way.

LANCE-CORPORAL PERCY WHITEOAK

Percy Whiteoak was a plasterer from the Melbourne suburb of Preston. He did not answer the call-up till March 1916 when he joined the 6th Field Ambulance at the age of 23. What stopped him from volunteering earlier? Perhaps he shared the view of many other non-combat enlistees who did not want to bear arms on ideological grounds, but wanted to help out all the same. But there was no doubting their courage and sacrifice, a fact testified by the heavy casualties suffered by service corps units. Whiteoak's courage showed while he assisted the wounded under fire in the third battle of Ypres in 1917. Lance-Corporal Whiteoak, who was later awarded the Military Medal, survived the war.

Medal presentation ceremony

'This is Newton J. Moore decorating Sgt J. O'Beirne of the 22 Btn with the Military Medal. That is me with the Bugle. I'm not receiving a medal. Please contradict all rumors saying I have received a medal',[61] wrote Private Harry Devine, the author's maternal grandfather, on the back of this photograph in which he appears, facing camera with a cross marked over his head. Critics of the medal system argued that honours were as much to do with luck as courage, and how well one fitted into the grooves of AIF hierarchy. O'Beirne was decorated with the medal in early 1917.

GEORGE WOODINGS *before enlistment*

Private George Woodings, a farm labourer from Coromandel Valley, South Australia, joined the 10th Battalion in August 1915 and was killed in action at Bullecourt in May 1917, one of 7500 AIF casualties in the battle behind the Hindenburg Line. The 25-year-old's body was never recovered.

PRIVATE
ERROL DAVIS

PRIVATE
CLIFFORD DAVIS

PRIVATE
RAY DAVIS

PRIVATE
VERNON DAVIS

How Bill Davis, a Victorian farmer, coped with his four sons away at war is a story best told in statistics and bald facts. Three of his boys, Errol, Ray and Vernon, worked on the family farm at Stewarton, Victoria; a fourth son, Clifford, was a carpenter. They were all single and strong; they liked the outdoors and knew how to shoot. There was never any question of stopping them from going to fight, particularly when all four decided to join.

Errol, 19, and Cliff, 20, joined up in the 14th Battalion, and stuck together through everything: Pozières, Bullecourt (where Errol was awarded the Military Medal), Messines. They fought through the diabolical mud of Passchendaele too, but on 13 October 1917, as the 14th Battalion was being withdrawn from the attack, a German shell burst near them, killing Errol, yet leaving Cliff unscathed.

Ray, 23, the oldest, last and perhaps wisest of the Davis boys to enlist, joined the 2nd Pioneers Battalion in March 1916. Although the Pioneers were not a combat unit, they were exposed to regular danger in their line as the 'fix-its' of the AIF. But in September 1918 General Monash took the unprecedented step of asking the 2nd Pioneers to fight in Australia's last battle at Montbrehain to make up a deficit in manpower. The Pioneers fought bravely; Ray Davis was awarded the Military Medal.

But Vernon, who had put up his age to qualify for enlistment in 1915, had no such glory. He was seriously wounded while serving as a private in the 23rd Battalion, and returned to Australia in 1918 as a 20-year-old amputee. He could not re-adapt to farming, and he had the added burden of making do with only one leg. Depressed and alienated, he never married and died from alcohol-related poisoning.

The graves of two Australian machine-gunners

A soldier wearing a trenchcoat pays his respects at the graves of two Australian machine gunners who died in fighting for the control of a railway.

A dud shell

Most of the soldiers who died at the Western Front were killed by artillery fire. Shells varied in shape and in the type of havoc they inflicted: there were 'pineapple bombs' cased in segments which left a trail of sparks, the 'flying pig' which took two men to lift and which rotated through the sky, 'the minnie', fired in rapid succession and with a noiseless descent that gave the victim no chance to find cover. When a dud like this 15-inch shell landed intact, soldiers were curious to inspect them and sometimes remove the nose caps at risk of detonation. Soldiers also chalked them with slogans like: 'Thank God you're a dud'.

This photograph was taken by Captain Aarons.

A wounded CAPTAIN DANIEL AARONS

After being wounded in France in 1917, Captain Aarons manages a stoic pose while being stretchered to an aid post. Aarons, an oil company manager from Fremantle, was awarded the Military Cross and bar for bravery at the Western Front, and returned to Australia in 1919.

Convalescing Australian soldiers in London

These two convalescing Australians light up cigarettes while on leave in London. One of the men is believed to be Lieutenant John Lorimer, 23rd Battalion, whose photograph album was obtained by the Australian War Memorial. Lorimer, an accountant in civilian life, survived the war.

Street scene, London

Public square, London

Lieutenant Cedric Lowden of the 36th Battalion took these snapshots while on leave in London. He returned to the battlefield and died of wounds in July 1917 after the fighting at Messines. He was 20 years old.

Australian soldiers and their female company, North Wales

'During a "smoke-oh"': although their boots are polished to a sheen, the khaki uniforms of these two Australians are humbled by the elegant attire of their Welsh company. This undated photograph taken during a leave excursion in North Wales is from the Lieutenant McCormack collection.

LIEUTENANT HENRY BARTLEY, *London*

This officer appears well and truly bored with his uniform, and has opted for more carefree apparel during a visit to a friend's apartment in London. The officer is believed to be Lieutenant Henry Bartley, of the 1st Division Artillery, who was probably recuperating in London after being wounded. The photograph was chosen from Lieutenant Lorimer's album. Photographs on adjoining pages suggest that Bartley was a guest at a fancy dress party.

Although it was common for some theatrically inclined soldiers to play the part of women during concerts at AIF camps, incidences of cross-dressing were rare at the battlefront, although one soldier-writer, Lieutenant Ross, described an incident in which a soldier in women's clothes walked through the rubble of Villers-Bretonneux (see page 168). And in the absence of proper underclothing of their own, some 24th Battalion soldiers reportedly made use of women's lingerie found in deserted houses at the town of Morlancourt.[62]

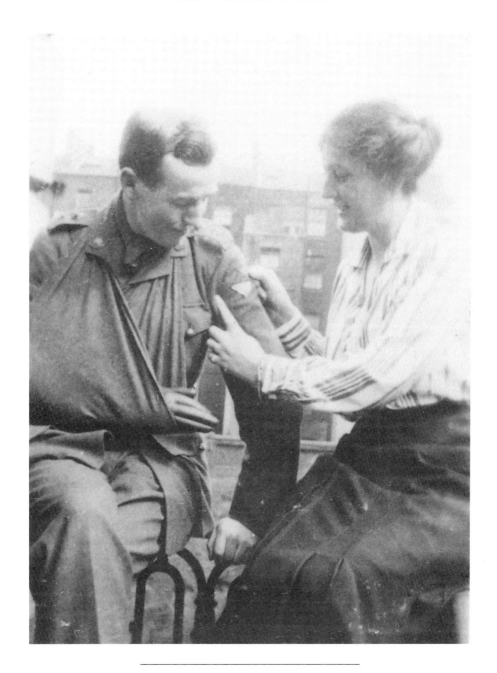

LIEUTENANT ROSS, *London*

'I was just thinking that it's almost "great" to be wounded—that is if it is a nice little one like mine',[63] wrote Lieutenant Ross, of the 'Blighty' wound that earned him a spell in hospital and a visit to 'Mrs C's' flat in London. Ross' May 1916 letter to his mother was written in erratic lines with his left, non-writing hand. His wound was more serious than he admitted, and he returned to Australia to recover before rejoining his battalion in 1917. He used part of his recovery period in South Australia to campaign at rallies for the introduction of conscription.

Convalescing Australian soldiers

This group of convalescing Australians seems to have formed a close attachment to the young nurse with them. Courtship between soldiers and nurses was officially condoned on the provision that it did not interfere with duties. Some nurses were asked to leave the nursing corps after marrying soldiers, while others kept their romances a secret.

PRIME MINISTER BILLY HUGHES *among wounded Australians, England*

Prime Minister Billy Hughes, remembered for his tireless conscription campaign, poses, cigarette in hand, with this group of convalescents at Dartford Military Hospital, England. Hughes believed the only way to win the war was to bolster Allied forces with conscripts, but two referendums on the issue in October 1916 and December 1917 carried majority 'No' votes. Troops seemed to like Hughes for his passion and endearing diminutiveness more than anything else. He was popularly known as the 'Little Digger' but also had his face chalked on the top of dud shells following the defeat of the conscription campaign.

Blinded soldiers at St Dunstan's Hospital, England

Soldiers blinded at the Western Front gather on the steps of St Dunstan's Hospital, England, for this forlorn 1918 portrait. A number of patients wearing Australian uniforms are standing beneath the column on the right. Most of these men were victims of shrapnel blasts and gas. This photograph was donated to the State Library of Victoria, the name William George Clifton on the back of it. Private Clifton served with the 26th Battalion in France, and was probably a patient at St Dunstan's.

Dead German soldier

The body of a German lies in what looks to be a shell crater. Many of the dead never had the dignity of a decent burial; others were obliterated by shells. Mostly, their graves became the spot where fate and the laws of attrition conspired to end their existence. This photograph was taken by Lance Corporal Gornall, of the 23rd Battalion. While some soldiers brought home photographs of enemy victims, it was considered disrespectful to photograph their own dead.

The 13TH LIGHT HORSE *football team*

Australian Rules Football was, to many, a metaphorical conduit of war. Its tendency to lift morale and promote healthy rivalry within the corps was never underestimated by generals. The game, which boasted ex-league and association players, was encouraged despite obstacles like battle fatigue, shell holes, snow and enemy observer planes. This 13th Australian Light Horse team went to the trouble of having jumpers made for a game at Tidworth, England, in 1917.

Football match, WESTERN FRONT

This spirited game of football was staged on a stubbled field; the players wore army boots. Judging by the shape of the hat worn by the soldier in the rear, the group may have been New Zealanders, playing rugby.

A dog handler at work

Sapper George Flanagan, a 4th Division signaller, looks on as a dog handler fits messages inside the collars of two dogs during a training drill. Messenger dogs were used in some major battles, particularly mid-way through the campaign, when heavy bombardments made it impossible for the delivery of normal communications. Good canine runners did their job six times faster than a human, knew how to dodge shells and often carried on while wounded. But even the best dogs were vulnerable to the enemy ploy of allowing bitches on heat to stray into the front line.

War refugees

Coming from a land where a working dog's lot was to round up livestock, Australians at the Western Front were surprised to see dogs supplanting the role of the cart horse. Two large dogs are harnessed to a cart belonging to this boy and his father—refugees who have left their Belgian town in the hope of better fortune. They were photographed by C. Hithcock, an AIF soldier whose personal details could not be found.

LIEUTENANT ROSS, *France, 1918*

LIEUTENANT ROSS, *Cairo, 1915*

Billets in the French countryside were a common form of accommodation for Australian soldiers, especially officers. But because dwellings and surrounding barns presented easy targets for enemy artillery, many soldiers preferred to camp in open fields rather than take a comfortable bed.

Lieutenant Ross, left, is standing in the yard of a billet which became such a target in 1918. His disconsolate expression and a face clearly worn by battle fatigue contrasts with a 1915 photograph of him in Egypt, captioned 'My beastly eye-glass'.

27TH BATTALION *soldiers, England*

'It is easily the best in the A.I.F.',[64] wrote Lieutenant Ross of his 27th Battalion, pictured here in England towards the end of the war. While Ross' claim would have been doubted by every other Australian unit, perhaps the local children vying for position at the back of the portrait shared the lieutenant's view. Ross is standing middle, second row, of a platoon of D Company soldiers, to the left of the biggest man in the group.

2ND BATTALION *soldiers, France*

Leaving a trail of dust in its wake, a platoon of 2nd Battalion soldiers marches from a successful operation at Harbonnières in August 1918. A cavalry unit follows the platoon, while, to the right, maintenance work is being carried out on an observation balloon. Leading the column is Corporal Bert ('Snowy') Causer, 23, who was promoted to sergeant shortly after this photograph was taken. Causer survived the war and returned to New South Wales where he fathered thirteen children.

28TH BATTALION *soldiers resting in a trench*

With a wounded mate in their care, these 28th Battalion soldiers are on their way to secure a spectacular victory at Mont St Quentin. This photograph was taken at Herbecourt on 31 August 1918. Two days later the depleted battalion, as part of the 7th Brigade, routed the Germans from the summit of Mont St Quentin, allowing, in turn, the taking of the nearby town of Péronne.

American and Australian troops at Péronne

The arrival of the Americans at the Western Front in early to mid-1918 put prospects of Allied victory beyond dispute by weight of their numbers alone. But the Australian foot soldier argued that the hard slog had already been done by him, whereas the British artillery strategist laid claim to outsmarting his enemy counter-part, and the German realist admitted to being a spent force anyway. This scene at Péronne shows 3rd Australian Division soldiers marching past an American division in October. The Americans are on their way to hold Hindenburg Line defences captured by Australians.

German troops

This rare undated photograph of Germans running during an action at 'Belleau Wood' invites intrigue. If the photograph was taken by a German, how did it get into the hands of an Australian soldier? Presumably, it was an Allied soldier who gave this photograph its caption: 'German machine gunners retreating at Belleau'. But were the Germans really pulling out, and if so, who was behind them? 'Belleau Wood' could not be found on battle maps. The photograph is held at the Australian War Memorial.

Dead German soldier

This young German soldier appears to have been impaled against the fractured plate of a battery gun. He was probably thrown back with great force when a shell struck his position on the Hindenburg Line. The photograph was taken by Lance Corporal Gornall as his battalion swept into the line after an Allied artillery barrage.

German POWs

A captured or dead German was considered fair game for war trophies including pistols, boots, daggers, watches and personal photographs. In this photograph, from an official British source, German prisoners from a Hindenburg Line outpost are being searched by Australians for papers and souvenirs at Hargicourt, France.

Australian souvenir hunter

This Australian soldier nursing a kitten on his knee is wearing a German *picklehaube* parade helmet distinguished by its eagle insignia, spike and highly polished black leather. For maximum head protection in battle, the *picklehaube* became an inner to a metallic helmet. It was a forerunner of the steel 'coal scuttle' helmet (see page 235), which afforded better protection against bullets and shrapnel. This photograph appeared in an album by Captain Errol Knox, of the 2nd Battalion. Knox, a journalist, was twice Mentioned in Despatches for bravery at the Western Front.

SERGEANT RALPH WOOLNOUGH

When Ralph Woolnough was 16 he got tired of watching ships leave Port Adelaide where his father worked as a warehouse manager, so he changed his name to Woodmonger and sneaked away to sea like a character from a Conrad novel. But with those reckless days behind him, the 38-year-old father of two had a lot more to lose by joining up in the second year of the war. Yet Woolnough, a warehouseman, knew the lure of a ticket to a big journey and did everything he could, as once before, to hasten his passage away once his mind was made up.

He had tried unsuccessfully to get into Duntroon, and failing that he completed certificate courses in musketry and bomb throwing. But when he realised his promotion to sergeant would delay his departure he demoted himself to private so that he could be on the next available ship with reinforcements to the 27th Battalion. 'I will be embarking for the front soon and Agnes [wife] will feel the parting very much, Helen [daughter] does not want me to go away and Geoffrey [son] is pleased to see me in uniform',[65] he wrote to his sister Gladys in August 1916.

His battalion saw the worst of it: Bullecourt, Lagnicourt, Zonnebeke, and despite a few scrapes with illness and injury, Woolnough made it through to 1918, which, to an ageing soldier, was a milestone in itself. But on 28 March when the 27th was holding Armentières against the Germans' spring offensive, Woolnough, by then a 40-year-old sergeant, was reportedly struck in the head by a shell and killed instantly.

His wife Agnes did not learn of the death until some weeks later when she was on her way to visit relatives and saw the announcement in a newspaper being read by another train passenger.

PRIVATE JOHN ('JACK') McINERNEY

JACK McINERNEY, *brother* GEORGE *and mother* ELIZABETH

Private Jack McInerney was a chemist and secretary to the Rose and Carnation Society of Mt Gambier in civilian days. One third of his 10th Battalion was wiped out in one night at a 'hot corner' of Pozières in 1916, and he was later wounded twice and rushed back to the front before fully recovering. Luck was in, for a while at least, when he was promoted to corporal then lieutenant in 1917 and briefly reunited with his fiancée Olive Deane, a nurse with No. 5 Sea Transport Staff, while on furlough in London.

McInerney was killed instantly in the battle for Merris on 28 June 1918. He was 30 years old.

With their mother in mourning, Jack McInerney, right, and his brother George, left, pose for their first formal portrait, circa 1893. Mrs Elizabeth McInerney was then grieving over the loss of her husband to typhoid after only three years of marriage. The grieving would begin again with the death of her soldier boy Jack in France.

Throughout the war George worked as a station master with the South Australian Railways, which placed him in an 'essential service' category.

PRIVATE MURRAY AITKEN

Such was the bond Murray Aitken had with his mother that barely a week passed without him writing to her in the most tender, sentimental way. His writings are the stuff of the innocent abroad—bathing with his 'close chum' McCallum three times a day on the way to Egypt, and while in Cairo: 'Oh I don't look longingly at the Egyptian beauties, tell Grandma.'[66] He spoke of his loathing of the bayonet as a weapon, the removal of his moustache because it had become a 'blooming nuisance', and, after the Gallipoli landings, hugging the earth closer than he ever hugged a girl.

Private Aitken got through Gallipoli unscathed, and enjoyed a rapid ascent through the ranks, even if his self-effacing narrative style suggested he was out of his depth. His commanders had also overlooked the occasion en route to Egypt when he was put in detention 'like a criminal' for skylarking during a life-belt drill. By March 1916 he was in charge of a company and mixing with important generals like Birdwood. But he was still his mother's boy. 'My word Mother you should hear me giving them lecturettes; I had no idea I could yap so well & tell Jack O. I'm afraid I've got a slight touch of the gift.'[67]

Upon arriving in France with the 11th Battalion, Aitken described the beauty of the countryside, and revelled in the attention afforded to young officers from local inhabitants. 'I collected lots & lots [of kisses] & I only threw them to the prettiest girls, too. Did I tell you I'm going to marry a French woman?'[68] And while on leave in Scotland: 'The Scotch lassies are "perfect bliths"; fresh, rosy cheeks and nice plump figures, no wonder Winks is in love with one; so am I—with the lot'.[69]

Mrs Aitken received letters from her son for another two years. He wrote in much the same vein: another girl to marry, an account of a cuckoo bird's call lilting amid the sound of enemy shells, the horror of another battle. And from the sweet boy she knew before the war so continued the emergence of a man accustomed to killing, until Lieutenant Aitken himself ran out of chances. He was killed in action on 10 August 1918 while Australian troops attempted to seize the ruined village of Lihons. Aitken was awarded the Military Cross posthumously for single-handedly knocking out a German machine-gun post which had been inflicting severe casualties among the 11th Battalion.

5

THE MARK OF WAR

The war was over and, as inevitable as it may have seemed, news of it took some time to sink in. Australian soldiers who were resting at Abbeville were overcome by a mixture of relief, disbelief, emptiness and sadness. Some wept, some sang, some discharged the last of their ammunition, threw away their rifles and joked that they had been made redundant. Men stuck in base camps and smoky estaminets wished they could be celebrating in the big cities; some lucky enough to be on leave in London and Paris wished they could be back with their mates, or everywhere at the same time.

Now that the Western Front was silent, the past and the future came tumbling in. To some who had dreamed of a Homerian passage to glory the whole thing had ended with a thud. To those deeply traumatised by the fighting the fetid stench of rotting corpses clung to their nostrils. Some who had transcended every endurance known to man—and had become a breed apart as a result of it—were gripped by pangs of dread about the transition back to civilian life.

Lieutenant Ross was on leave, touring the Georgetown Munition Factory in Glasgow when the Armistice was announced. When the factory whistle blew, the all-female staff cheered and departed en masse for celebrations in the nearby town of Paisley. But amid cheers and songs, a precursor to the enduring grief of war: 'I believe many of them were crying not because they would lose their jobs, but because their soldier relations would never return with the troops when they came home'.[1]

In the waiting to get home, soldiers fretted around base camps, played football, got the blues and got drunk. 'After lunch, a general shicker up', wrote Major Coutts, on 31 January, in France; 'I managed to keep sober. Started tossing in blanket. Sedgewick fell through blanket, owing to tear, and landed on his head on the floor—unconscious for about 10 minutes. Cut head'.[2]

Some like Private Charles Jackson's 1st Australian Mechanical Transport Company held a stop-work meeting in the village of Châtelet while it snowed, and decided to strike until commanders agreed to let the Gallipoli originals go home first.

Thousands went to London to reclaim their freedom; they found war brides or married ladies in waiting. Major Robinson wed his sweetheart Sister Mary Carey in secret because the code of Australian nursing did not allow its members to be married while on active service. Sister Carey wore her wedding ring on a chain hidden beneath her pinafore till her duties were complete. The couple returned to Australia and raised a family.

Many enrolled in AIF vocational schemes that would help them to find work at home. These schools had limited success other than to fill the days, yet served an unintended secondary function: they became unofficial 'debriefing' centres for fighters who were expected to simply adapt once they returned to Australia. With the exception of counselling facilities for shell-shock victims and asylums for the recuperation and interviewing of POWs, there was no form of trauma therapy or debriefing for the average soldier.

When spare time permitted, some disappeared to parts of the continent they would never have the chance to see again. Others like Corporal Kerr, a former POW by-passed by history, embarked on personal odysseys. He limped into the AIF headquarters in London, got some back pay and travelled across the English Channel to look for the Frenchmen he had been imprisoned with in Turkey, only to find they had not yet been demobilised.

The demobilisation period was particularly harrowing for thousands of light horsemen who chose to shoot their horses in the Middle East rather than leave them in the hands of the Arabs.[3]

Meanwhile, an élite group of AIF soldiers wondered what the hell they were doing still fighting in some dirty sideshow in Russia. 'Gee its bad luck for us who have done our bit for 4 years, to be out in this mix up',[4] wrote Sergeant Bert Perry, MM, while serving with the North Russian Relief Force at Archangel. He had just witnessed Allied machine-guns open fire on a battalion of White Russian soldiers who had refused to fight alongside the Allies against the Bolsheviks.

About 180 000 AIF troops were eventually shipped out on a 'first come, first go' basis, the earliest boatloads sailing down the Mersey in December 1918. Some who stayed on participated in victory marches through London where the 'Little Digger' Billy Hughes was there to eulogise: 'Soldiers! Your deeds have won you a place in the temple of the immortals'.[5]

Lance-Corporal Percy Whiteoak, MM, left for Australia in June on board the *Königin Luise*. The voyage home was punctuated by the usual boxing and wrestling bouts, but troops were as restless on the way home as they were on the way to the Front. 'Trouble over piano, troops got it first but officers wanted it for dance, but troops would not give it up. Things very serious for a time. Officers had to unscrew ship's piano', he wrote on 28 June. A week later: 'Life belt drill during which man fell overboard, afterwards it was found out he jumped over-board. Lived to do so again at night but was caught & locked up'.[6]

Riots and fighting broke out on board the *Friedrichsruh* when diggers found out it was dry of alcohol and that the ship's plumbing had been sabotaged by a German company which previously owned the boat.[7] The passage of the *Persic* was smooth as it neared mainland Australia. Sergeant Makeham had nothing much to say towards the end of his diary. He saw fit to close it with an aberration: 'These birds [albatrosses] seem to glide through the air without any motion of the wings at all and they never seem to stop, backwards and forwards, over the ship all day long…'[8]

Homecoming celebrations were tempered by a kind of hesitancy on the part of many soldiers. Loved ones too were unsure whether to cheer or cry as they noticed afflicted eyes and the faces of hardened men coming down the gangplanks. The AIF had indoctrinated soldiers into the belief that the regiment was everything, yet now the vast home front would see them go it alone and make do quietly, away from the compounded madness and glories of war.

War had possessed them of a common dream to settle back in their old jobs, to start over and get blocks of land, to raise families. But once the homecoming hangovers wore off, diggers saw that the old Australia had sobered up, become more mindful. They realised that not everyone appreciated them going to fight 'England's war', even if they had suffered the worst casualty rate of any Allied country in fighting it. They faced up to the fact that old girlfriends had not waited, that 'scabs' had encroached on jobs.

Of the 270 000 soldiers who came home, about 156 000 had a wound of some kind.[9] There were pensions and Government workshops, but it was felt that the Government was not doing enough to help them after what they had been through. Vivian Flannery had lost two legs and a lung in France but because only one of his legs was taken off above the knee he was good for only half the pension—42 shillings a week. The Government, however, placed him in a bootmaker's job; sharp irony to a soldier with no feet.[10]

About 11 000 Victorian diggers took up soldier-settlement blocks around the state. The Government promoted the scheme as the beginning of a new Australian yeomanry pioneered on the brawn and initiative of returned soldiers, but most 'blockers' could not withstand the enormous physical and financial burdens the scheme imposed on them.

Marriage rates sky-rocketed in the early post-war period, but 90 per cent of the AIF had been single before enlisting, and the war had made it difficult for many to adapt to the passivity of domestic life. Conversely, the privations of the trenches made some appreciate domestic life and the garden as never before, making them better husbands.

Thousands of grieving widows, meanwhile, never remarried.

Some emotionally adrift diggers longed to be back in the trenches where they were understood, where they were driven by a peculiarly exhilarating solidarity that eluded them in civilian life. They turned to drink, quietly went mad or took it out on long-suffering wives. On Anzac Day, 25 April, most of them marched, played two-up, drank too much and sobbed in the intimacy of their own circle. Scarred as they were, they got on with life on farms and in cities and limped into the canvases of peacetime anonymity. Collectively, they represented a new moral force that stood for something better, whatever that was, but as the years passed the mantle of 'ex-AIF' generally accorded no special status to them, except among their own cliques.

They were more worldly for their war days, less trusting of politicians and more inclined to take notice of developments on the international stage. They became dependable husbands and nurturing fathers, and long-serving members of RSL clubs.

David McGarvie, the hare-lipped soldier who got some of his own in at the Nek, went back to dairy farming at Pomborneit. Lindsay Ross, the lieutenant for whom war seemed to be one long absurdity, became a school headmaster then lectured defence force trainees in technical instruction at the outbreak of World War II; while his mate Gordon Beith, who was shell-shocked at Lone Pine, went straight from the army to Mont Park Military Mental Hospital, becoming one of 850 men invalided back to Australia because of 'mental trouble'[11]. Austin Laughlin, the lacrosse star who became a formidable fighting officer, re-enlisted and served as an intelligence commander in the next war. Bill Chave went back to the clean air of Tumut, near the Snowy Mountains, but could not get over the loss of his brother Ted in the war. He committed suicide in 1925 at the age of 32. Meanwhile, Roy Oldroyd, who had lost a leg at Gallipoli, never missed a day's work as a bag-grader at the Colonial Sugar Refinery in Pyrmont.

George Kerr went to Red Cliffs as a soldier-settler, became a citrus industry administrator and settled in Melbourne. His young children wondered why he stopped going to the big Anzac Day marches. It was not his limp that stopped him going, and besides there were far worse cases, even amputees, who marched from the Shrine. They guessed, in time, that it was too painful for him to be reminded of a younger brother killed at Lone Pine and the fact that his 14th Battalion was a column of strange faces.[12]

On a national level, the war and the social upheavals that accompanied it had prised a gulf between the segment of the population who openly supported Australia's involvement in it and those who did not. Antagonisms in the workplace led to industrial strikes, particularly during the recession of 1921, and brawls between returned soldiers and labour unions. It took the intercession of 'Pompey' Elliott to dissuade ex-diggers from further participation in the 1923 police strikes in Melbourne. The divisions reinforced the kind of disunity that prompted Captain Bean to lament that Australia had not made 'the full and real use of the Peace for which our finest Australians fought'.[13]

By 1932 Australia's Great War death toll of 60 000 was repeated among diggers with war-related ailments, and about another 30 000 returned soldiers were in hospital. But Elliott could see it coming sooner and campaigned, mostly unsuccessfully, as a National Party senator for better treatment of ex-soldiers. They walked through walls of fire and lead for him in France, and if he could promise them one thing, it would be to deliver them unto a promised land. While walking down Collins Street one day, Elliott's massive frame was spotted by a soldier who had served under him at the Western Front. 'You promised this would never happen to us Pompey',[14] the broken-looking digger implored. Elliott walked away bearing the anguish of Judas. He would take his own life in 1931.[15]

ॐ

After the war thousands of soldier portraits hung in hallways and above mantel-pieces. The images faded and crumbled and radiated dull auras that reminded lovers, parents and children of lives irrevocably altered or obliterated by war. A generation paid homage to them through decades of muted grief and respectful silence. In some cases the photographs were the only link a family had to its Anzac past but as the Great War receded, some were dumped or sold to collectors or left at RSLs, or consigned along with diaries and letters to drawers where the sour, melancholy whiff of lives past embalmed them.

It was a smell that never went away, keeping the past alive. Well after the war was over, Mrs Annie White still clasped to the illusion that her beloved Edward might one day knock on her door, even though AIF officials had confirmed that he was killed in action at Bullecourt in 1917. Tormented by grief, she tried the 'Soldiers' Whereabouts' columns of Melbourne newspapers and when that did not work she reasoned that her husband might have returned to Australia and been admitted to a mental hospital, perhaps under an alias, without her knowledge. A letter dated 15 January 1930 came back to her from Mont Park Military Mental Hospital, stating that there was 'no news' in response to her inquiry about a Private E. C. V. White. 'You may visit this Hospital on any day, visiting hours, 2.30 pm to 4.30 pm, when every assistance and any information will be gladly given. Yours faithfully, Photo herewith returned'.[16]

Some returned soldiers spoke about the war, or let their scars and their reticences speak for them. Descendants in turn drew on a few poignant anecdotes to try to ascribe what war made of their fathers, and how it impacted on their family lives, long after the event.

George Smith settled in Sydney, married and took up work in a silo, later as a newspaper delivery truck driver and as a mailman. 'He used to tell us when he went to get his "civvies" he stepped out of his uniform & left it lying on the floor of the shop',[17] said his daughter, Mrs Marcia Wordsworth.

'He did not talk about his time at Gallipoli, and only a little of his time in the desert', recalled Mrs Pam Rudgley of her father, Robert Percival Miller. 'Mum couldn't cook haricot beans because he and one of his mates were cooking some in a bully beef tin at Gallipoli, when a sniper's bullet shot his friend's head off and the brains fell into the tin of beans'.[18]

One of Snowy Causer's thirteen children, Mrs Grace Connor, said that her father was troubled by his memories of war, and for years on end, he would vomit every morning, a condition believed to have been brought on by the effects of gas in France, and for which he received no compensation.

> He reckoned that the war took 10 years off him, he used to say that to us... When I asked him to come and see the fire works, he replied he had seen enough fire works to last a life time. They only reminded him of the stench of gunpowder and death of his men and mates with their legs and arms blown off...[19]

Forty years after the war, Alex McGoldrick, who had won the Military Medal as a stretcher bearer in France, visited the Australian War Memorial and was impressed by the vividness of the battlefield dioramas. But the visit brought it all back to him and he had terrible dreams about his mates being blown apart next to him at Ypres in 1917.[20]

Sydney Cockburn occasionally picked up a letter written to him from New York by the young wife of an American soldier who died in Cockburn's arms in 1918. 'You know I never realized there was so much sadness caused by war', she wrote, 'when I heard about my brave husband I thought I could never stand it. I often wonder how we can stand so much pain and still go on...I must not give up although my future looks so lonely (I am only nineteen)'.[21]

And so it went.

Now that Australia's Anzac heritage is fading, a new questioning has taken root, and photographs and diaries that were once regarded as quaint curio items are now arousing excitement over physical similarities perhaps in a nephew, third generation removed, or the fact that a family member has bothered to find out who that great-uncle in the khaki uniform really was. They provoke questions like how they lived and died, what if I were he, and what might or might not have been had the war never happened. War diaries and letters illumine some of these questions, in part at least, but deeper constants like 'why they fought' and 'what war made them' remain.

Occasionally a seemingly incidental line written in a Western Front trench enunciates, in similes that can be universally understood, how war scars the psyche. 'When I get home please never fire a gun, place them in some dark corner where I can never see one', wrote Sergeant Tongs in fractured pencil. 'I am sick sick of the sight of slaughter, sick of the smell of powder, and the sound of screaching, grunting, bursting shells…But what is the use of all this scribble I cannot Explain it to you.'[22]

At times, a subtlety that has been overlooked countless times shines like a gemstone turned over in the mullock. I am reminded of my grandfather's studio enlistment portrait which hung on my bedroom wall for so many years. George Kitchin Kerr's broad stance commands the frame and his earnest gaze pierces the gloom, drawing the observer back to his sepia past. Again I look and I see, for the first time, the backdrop he has chosen for posterity. There, on a ridge behind his midriff is a small tree, a leafy signpost bearing the seeds of a healing beyond war.

27TH BATTALION *officers on the road to Charleroi, Belgium*

With the fighting done and the road to an uncertain future ahead, these 27th Battalion officers pause during a march through Belgium in December 1918. They were destined for the town of Charleroi which became a base for some Australian divisions awaiting demobilisation after the Armistice.

The officers are (left to right) Lieutenant Fred Summerfield, a grocer from Malvern, Victoria; Lieutenant Taylor, whose details could not be traced, and Lieutenant Maurice Cronin, a civil servant from the Melbourne suburb of Richmond. Lieutenant Ross took the photograph.

*Children looked after by AIF soldiers during
the latter part of the war, Charleroi, Belgium*

Lieutenant Ross sent this photograph, taken at Charleroi, home to his mother in early 1919. In an accompanying letter he wrote: 'These poor little children [André and Paulette Gauguier] had been half starved during the war and, altogether had a miserable time and with the coming of the Australians and the few odds and ends we gave them they didn't know whether they were really alive or whether it was only a dream'.[70]

Australian soldiers in Bethune

A semblance of normality is evident as townsfolk of Bethune go about their business in March 1919, but shell-torn buildings and the presence of three Australian soldiers on a once-busy corner are reminders of war not long gone. The slow process of demobilising troops gave soldiers the opportunity to tour France, or what was left of it, although most gravitated to London while on leave.

Scene outside a French café during the Armistice period

Photographs of this kind were rare in France because of a strict ban on the use of cameras by soldiers for security reasons. It was probably taken after the Armistice when the ban had been lifted. The officer second from left is holding a style of folding camera which became popular among Australian soldiers. This photograph is from a collection by Private Charles Jackson (see page 252).

Striking members of the 1ST AUSTRALIAN MECHANICAL TRANSPORT COMPANY

'Meeting last night, Pte Tucker arrested, decided to strike this morning',[71] wrote Private Jackson, of the 1st Australian Mechanical Transport Company, which stopped work over concerns that 1915 AIF originals would not be sent home first. The group waits in falling snow to thrash out the issue with generals on 31 January 1919 at Châtelet, France. The AMTC decided to resume work after it was promised that Private Tucker would be released, and that 1915 enlistees would be on their way back to Australia within a month. Jackson is marked with two crosses, slightly left of centre.

Convalescing soldiers at an Australian military hospital

These men wore light blue suits and red ties, standard AIF attire first issued at the Western Front to distinguish genuine convalescents from malingering soldiers. The group seems beset by a mixture of bemusement and disconsolateness, except perhaps for the man, middle front, with the cigarette in his mouth and the Military Medal riband over his left breast.

13TH LIGHT HORSE *mess hut*

'Saturday 18th [January] Never did much today—wrote home & to Dicks. Sunday 19th Races at Thuin—dance at night—on guard. Monday 20th On guard 8–10—turned horses out in paddock for the day. Tuesday 21st Went to regiment for a ride—no word about going home yet.'[72]

The diary of Trooper Matthew Morrison conveys the restless boredom during the wait to go home. Pictured here with his 13th Light Horse mess group, Morrison is seated, third left, and has marked a cross over his head.

CORPORAL GEORGE KERR

'Tea with the ladies, London, After the Armistice'. The author's paternal grandfather Corporal George Kitchin Kerr reclaims his freedom, having spent more than three years as a prisoner of the Turks. While most soldiers were keen to get home, Kerr used the hiatus to his advantage, vowing to 'improve himself' by attending an art school in Chelsea, catching up on lost time and travelling to France, hoping to visit friends he had made while a POW.

PRIVATE VIVIAN FLANNERY

Vivian Flannery, a 21-year-old tailor from the Melbourne suburb of Northcote, is in the prime of his life in this photograph from France. He has the 'mud & blood' colour patch of the 23rd Battalion on his left shoulder, and his brooding, handsome features are obvious beneath the tilt of his slouch hat. But in time the photograph would only remind Flannery of what war took from him. Fate caught up with him a few months before the Armistice when he was struck by fragments from a high explosive shell. He suffered horrific wounds, losing both legs and the use of one lung. Somehow he survived, and was repatriated back to Australia in January 1919.

He was fitted with artificial legs, got around using a walking stick, and started to go grey by the age of 25. He made the most of a rotten hand, held down several different jobs as well as his injuries would allow, and married his sweetheart who had waited for him to come home. They raised two children in the suburbs of Melbourne. Flannery, whose hobby was to breed and judge gun dogs, died from pneumonia, aged 45.

Flannery's wife Clarice Kitchin was the sister of Corporal Kitchin Kerr who appears in the photograph on page 255.

AIF *victory parade, London*

This photograph of Australian soldiers participating in a victory parade through London in July 1919 was taken in unusual circumstances. Lieutenant Bob Demaine of the 6th Battalion obtained the shot from a soldier friend who was struggling to get a vantage point in the crowd. According to Demaine, a household butler who saw the soldier's predicament invited him to the first-floor window of a nearby apartment. The butler later declared that they were standing in the personal rooms of His Royal Highness the Prince of Wales.

Australian troops on board the NESTOR

Trooper Matthew Morrison's voyage home took forty-two days. It was punctuated by heavy swells, a stop at Cape Town, dancing, boxing, concerts and lectures on topics including armoured cars of Russia and the principles of irrigation. In this scene, troops are listening to an address by an officer of the *Nestor*, dressed in white, standing over the lower rails. Morrison is immediately to the right, leaning on the same rail. The *Nestor* sailed into Port Melbourne on 2 July 1919.

Amputees on an Australian transport ship

About 40 000 convalescents were demobilised back to Australia after the war on ships allocated exclusively for them. The trials of the amputees in this photograph were only just beginning.

Boxing en route to Cape Town

This impressive shot of a boxing match in progress was taken en route to Cape Town in 1919. The fighter wearing the singlet is using the classic Marquess of Queensberry stance, with gloves poised at the midriff.

Throughout the war, boxing was considered good entertainment for spectators, an excuse to lay a quiet wager and a way for the participants to keep fit.

LIEUTENANT JOHN HAMILTON

The shores of their home state are in sight, but these New South Wales officers seem tentative and uncertain about their transition back to civilian life. The officer with his leg hanging over the railing is Lieutenant John Hamilton, of the 3rd Battalion, who was awarded the Victoria Cross for eliminating a number of enemy bombers during fierce fighting at Lone Pine in August 1915. Hamilton, 25, was a butcher in civilian life.

Homecoming for returned soldiers, Wodonga

'3rd July [1919] kissed more girls in 10 mins than I did in all my life before',[73] wrote Trooper Morrison after his homecoming to Wodonga, Victoria. Morrison is in the middle of the group of servicemen in the foreground. Each of them attended Albury High School before the war.

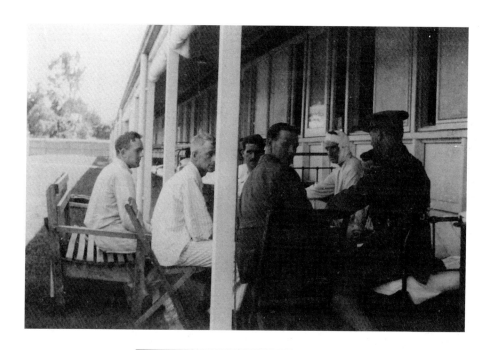

Convalescents at the Caulfield Repatriation Hospital

Of the 156 000 Australian soldiers who were wounded during the war, many bore combat-related ailments and injuries for the rest of their lives. TPIs ('totally and permanently incapacitated' soldiers) were common sights in every Australian city and town. With the exception of the man whose head is bandaged, these patients at the Caulfield Repatriation Hospital, Melbourne, appear to be nursing 'invisible' wounds such as nervous conditions and respiratory disorders.

EDWARD EDWARDS

Private Edward Edwards died at Pozières in 1916. While his father William had to live with the grief, it might have been some compensation if he got Edward's belongings back. He was determined to retrieve Edward's watch, camera and a sum of money believed to have been in his possession when he died. The following year, a package turned up containing a prayer book and a Bible, but none of the other items, which were given up as lost or stolen.

Mr Edwards, of Wangaratta, Victoria, was still quietly fuming well after the war was over. He took umbrage with the Defence Department over another matter, the erroneous issuing of the 1914–15 Star medal to his son. The Star was awarded to all Australian soldiers who entered a theatre of war prior to 31 December 1915, but a bungle arose over the fact that the *Commonwealth*, a comparatively slow troopship, arrived at Suez on 30 December 1915 and did not actually begin to disembark troops until 2 January. The oversight was apparently not noticed until after the Star went into circulation in 1920, and 900 reclamation notices were issued to soldiers or families of deceased soldiers who had sailed to Egypt aboard the *Commonwealth*, stating that unless the Stars were returned, no other medals, clasps or gratuities would be issued. Mr Edwards refused to hand the medal back on principle, even after local police demanded it. In February 1921 the Assistant Defence Minister's office allowed Mr Edwards to keep his son's Star because of 'exceptional circumstances'.

Prayer book of CORPORAL WILLIAM LOWE

In 1917, as war raged in France, William Lowe sat shivering on the deck of an Australia-bound convalescent ship as it entered the sweltering tropics. The 30-year-old corporal was wearing his greatcoat, but his mind was still ashudder over the terror that visited him in the cold muddy trenches of France. In February 1917 he suffered a nervous breakdown from the after effects of shell-shock, and was discharged several months later.

Before he got home, his mother Frances received a torn prayer book in the post. It had been badly damaged when Lowe's trench was shelled in September 1916. The leather-bound book was accompanied by a note:

> I had a bit of good luck the other day in the line [at Hill 60] and think one of your prayers was answered that day as I was the only one of 4 poor mates that escaped being wounded they were lying down half asleep both sides of me in dougouts and two of them got blocked in and while I was digging them out in the dark I took my tunic off and threw it on the ground when another shell came and killed two more and nearly blew my tunic to pieces and pierced your old Prayer book right through your photo just leaving your dear face untouched. Hope you will not worry when I send it home...[74]

William Lowe spent the rest of his life in the Callan Park Psychiatric Hospital, Sydney. He received the occasional visit from his half-brother Hughie Lowe, who had served as an artillery driver in France (see page 29).

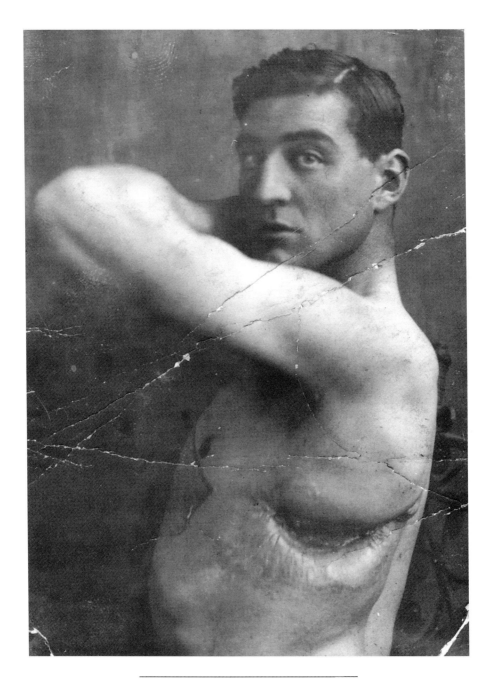

Anonymous soldier reveals war wound

Who was this returned soldier with a midriff still agape, whose stare pierces the conscience, conveying for a moment how war scars a man's soul as well as his body? Who saw things, did things of which he could not speak; whose wounding seeped into the veins of other generations. Who, other than his diminishing gun-wise fraternity, knew what that stare meant?

This anonymous portrait was taken at a studio in Korumburra, Victoria, some time after the war.

Unveiling ceremony at the cenotaph, Yarra Junction

Ex-soldiers from Yarra Junction, Victoria, gather for an unveiling ceremony of the town's new cenatoph in remembrance of those 'who gave their lives' in the Great War. The cenotaph was opened in 1921 by Senator H. E. Elliott, better known among returned soldiers as Brigadier General 'Pompey' Elliott. He is sitting beneath the flag-pole with his head turned.

Forty-one soldiers from the Yarra Junction district were killed out of the 153 who enlisted. The dead included four sets of brothers and Private Henry Herrod whose photographs appear on pages 26 and 204.

Memorials like this one were constructed in virtually every town and city in Australia after the war, as permanent symbols of a nation's mourning.

BIOGRAPHIES

This list contains 163 AIF servicemen whose photographs or written accounts are used in *Private Wars*, or servicemen who emerge as significant characters as a result of what has been said of them, or the fact that they have been identified in photographs. The profiles have been constructed from embarkation rolls, nominal rolls, pay records, battalion histories, diaries and, in some cases, the recollections of soldiers' relatives. Often only scant details were available. Details of wounding, transfers and medal commendations have been included where known. Burial details have been included where available, while servicemen's religious denominations have been generally excluded. The profiles, while thought to be accurate, are not to be regarded as conclusive. Soldiers who could not be positively identified were omitted from the list.

AARONS, Daniel Sydney, MC and bar. A manager of the Vacuum Oil Company in Fremantle, Western Australia, Aarons joined the 16th Battalion in October 1915. Captain Aarons was wounded in 1917; he was also decorated with the Military Cross for conspicuous gallantry in the battle of Bullecourt in May 1917. He earned the bar to his Military Cross for encouraging his men to 'their highest endeavour' during an enemy counter-attack. Aarons returned to Australia in June 1919.

AISBETT, Harold Edward. A labourer from Merino, Victoria, Aisbett sailed to war with the 39th Battalion in March 1916. He arrived in France as a reinforcement and survived the war. Aisbett returned to Australia in January 1919 at the age of 22.

AITKEN, James Murray, MC. An accountant from the Western Australian mining town of Kalgoorlie, Aitken, 23, joined the 11th Battalion in August 1914. Aitken rose quickly through the ranks and was solid in battle. He got through Gallipoli unscathed and was promoted to lieutenant. He was killed in action on 10 August 1918 at Lihons, and was awarded the Military Cross posthumously for knocking out a German machine-gun position that had been inflicting severe casualties among his battalion.

ALLSOP, Thomas Ernest. A horse trainer from Woori Yallock, in Victoria's Yarra Valley, Allsop joined the 11th Battalion in Western Australia in August 1914. Allsop enlisted as a 30-year-old driver, and one of his jobs was to land horses ashore while under fire at Gallipoli. He returned to Australia in December 1918, having attained the rank of sergeant.

BAILEY, George. Bailey, a married man, did not enlist until July 1916. The 26-year-old farmer from Charlton, Victoria, was taken on as a private in the 8th Battalion and served as a Lewis machine-gunner in Belgium and France where he became a corporal. He returned to Australia in September 1919 and became a soldier-settler in the Mallee region. Unlike many soldier-settlers who struggled to make ends meet, Bailey became a successful landholder in the region.

BAIN, Donald Stuart. A 34-year-old stock and station agent who operated from Collins Street, Melbourne, Bain enlisted in the 5th Battalion as a lieutenant in August 1914. Bain, who was married, returned to Australia in August 1916.

BARTLEY, Ernest Henry. A 24-year-old farmer from Esk, Queensland, Bartley sailed with the 11th Light Horse from Sydney in October 1915. He transferred to the 4th Division Artillery (and later the 1st) and held the rank of lieutenant. Bartley was wounded in France, and returned to Australia after the war.

BARTON, John Hampden. A 27-year-old grazier from Homebush, New South Wales, Barton enlisted as a second lieutenant in the 55th Battalion in November 1915. He participated in operations in France and Belgium and was wounded but recovered to serve out the rest of the war. He returned to Australia in April 1919 as a lieutenant.

BEITH, Gordon. Beith's previous stint in the citizen forces saw him taken on as a lieutenant in the 24th Battalion. A 21-year-old single clerk from Ballarat, he enlisted in May 1915 but was wounded and badly shell-shocked during a Turkish artillery barrage on Lone Pine. He suffered a nervous breakdown and was admitted to Mont Park Military Mental Hospital on his return to Australia in mid-1916.

BERTWISTLE, Wilfred Hall. A civil servant from North Adelaide, Bertwistle enlisted in the 27th Battalion at the age of 20 in March 1915. He was attached to the battalion's machine-gun corps and was wounded in France. Lieutenant Bertwistle returned to Australia in February 1917.

BLAIR, Alexander. A gardener from Geelong, Victoria, he joined the 22nd Battalion aged 22 in 1915. Blair, whose older brother George was discharged in 1918, was wounded in 1916, rose to the rank of sergeant and returned to Victoria after the war.

BLAIR, John George. A 24-year-old labourer from Geelong, Victoria, Blair enlisted in the 60th Battalion in July 1915. He was shot in the leg and badly shell-shocked at Fromelles in July 1916. Private Blair never fully recovered and suffered several relapses of shell-shock. He was discharged in February 1918 and was classified as having an 'apparently permanent' disability. Although his war afflictions continued to trouble him, Blair worked as a timber contractor in the Dandenongs, east of Melbourne, and raised four children. He died in 1941 aged 50. Blair's brother Alex served with the 22nd Battalion and survived the war.

BLEZARD, Ivie. A married man who worked as a town clerk at Moama, New South Wales, Blezard, 36, joined the 7th Battalion as a captain in November 1914. He was wounded while leading his troops on the first day of the Gallipoli invasion, and returned to Australia in February 1916 as a major.

BRICE, Charles Christie. Enlisted in the 20th Battalion in January 1916 at the age of 27. Lieutenant Brice, whose other personal details are not known, returned to Australia in November 1918.

BRIDGES, William Throsby. Major General Bridges, a Scot by birth, was given command of Australia's 1st Division at the outbreak of war in August 1914. He gave the force its name, the Australian Imperial Force, and insisted it remained an entity separate from the British Army, but ran the risk of alienating Australian troops because of his determination to uphold stringent military standards. Although Bridges was regarded as an administrator and a vehement proponent of early evacuation from Gallipoli, he did not hesitate to visit Australian troops holding the lines, often exposing himself to danger. He was shot through the thigh by a sniper on 15 May and died three days later from blood loss while on a hospital ship. Bridges, the first Australian officer to become a general, is buried on Mt Pleasant, overlooking Duntroon, the military college he founded in 1911.

CALLINAN, William ('Bill') Lewis. A 23-year-old farmer from Swan Reach, Victoria, Callinan enlisted with the 6th Field Ambulance in May 1915. He participated in the last few months of the Gallipoli campaign and was one of scores of stretcher bearers whose devotion to duty cost them their lives in the fighting around Pozières. He was killed instantly when hit in the head by shrapnel while carrying a wounded soldier out of no man's land on 5 August 1916. Private Callinan is buried at the Pozières British Cemetery, France.

CAUSER, Bert ('Snowy'). Causer, 19, was the youngest of four brothers to enlist from Liverpool, Sydney, on 10 June 1915. A share farmer and carpenter, he was given the rank of corporal in the 8th Battalion but was transferred to the 2nd Battalion in March 1916. He was promoted to sergeant in 1918 at the age of 23. He returned to Australia in 1919, married in 1923 and had thirteen children, raised mostly in Sydney. He died in 1966 at the age of 70, and suffered from the after-effects of gas all his life. He leaves behind eighty-eight direct descendants. All four Causer brothers survived the war.

CHAVE, Edwin ('Ted') George. A 27-year-old farmer labourer from Tumut, New South Wales, Chave enlisted in 1915 with his younger brother Bill in the 13th Reinforcements to the 1st Light Horse. On arriving in Egypt in early 1916, he became a driver with the 5th Division Artillery Brigade. He was killed behind the lines in 1917 when a tree limb fell on him while he was cutting firewood.

CHAVE, William ('Bill') Frederick. A farm labourer from Tumut, New South Wales, Chave enlisted as a reinforcement to the 1st Light Horse in 1915. Arriving in Egypt, the 22-year-old transferred as a driver to the 5th Division Artillery Brigade. He suffered minor leg wounds in 1917 and survived the war, yet was devastated over the death of his older brother Ted, whom he idolised. Bill Chave took his own life in 1925 at the age of 32.

CHUGG, John ('Jack'). An electrician from the Melbourne suburb of Hawthorn, Chugg was 19 when he joined the Australian General Hospital in September 1914. He served at Gallipoli and the Western Front and attained the rank of sergeant by the end of the war. He returned to Australia in November 1918.

CLIFTON, William George. A labourer whose address on enlistment was Bell's Hotel, Charleville, Queensland, Clifton was a reinforcement with the 26th Battalion. The 24-year-old private sailed in December 1916 and fought at the Western Front until he was reportedly blinded in a shell blast in 1917.

COCHRANE, Gerald Walter. A 25-year-old labourer from Casterton, Victoria, Cochrane joined the 5th Battalion as a private in September 1914. He was seriously wounded at Braund's Hill, Gallipoli, in June 1915, and discharged in April 1916 after a lengthy period of convalescence.

COCKBURN, Sydney Percy, MM. A 20-year-old carpenter from Bendigo, Victoria, Cockburn enlisted as a gunner with the 4rd Field Artillery Brigade in September 1916. He later transferred to the 3rd Field Artillery Brigade as a signaller. Cockburn was cited for bravery in the battle of Morlancourt in June 1918, and personally received the Military Medal from the Prince of Wales. He also earned admiration among his peers for beating up the unit 'bully' while in France. He returned to Australia in June 1919.

COOKE, Reginald McKenzie. The son of an Anglican clergyman, Cooke was a Trinity College student from the exclusive Melbourne suburb of Toorak, who enlisted as a private with the 5th Battalion in August 1914. He was wounded at Gallipoli and recovered to serve at the Western Front. He returned to Australia in October 1918 at the age of 28.

COUTTS, Donald Dunbar, DSO. A graduate of Melbourne University, Coutts was a doctor who lived in the Melbourne bayside suburb of Brighton. Captain Coutts enlisted with the 6th Field Ambulance in November 1916 and served in France where he became Regimental Medical Officer with the 24th Battalion. He was lucky to escape with his life in March 1917 when shrapnel from a German shell struck his helmet 'like a kick from a horse'. He was awarded the Distinguished Service Order for assisting the wounded while under shellfire during a 52-hour stint at Mont St Quentin on 1 September 1918. He was also Mentioned in Despatches. Coutts returned to Australia as a major in early 1920.

CRONIN, Maurice Anthony. Cronin enlisted as a 22-year-old private in the No. 2 Australian Casualty Clearing Station in July 1915. A civil servant from the Melbourne suburb of Richmond, he later transferred to the 27th Battalion. He attained the rank of lieutenant and returned to Australia in May 1919.

DAVIS, Clifford. Sailed to war with his brother Errol in the 14th Battalion in December 1914. Private Davis, a 20-year-old carpenter, was only a few metres from Errol when the latter was killed outright by a shell at Passchendaele in October 1917. Davis reached the rank of corporal and returned to Australia in March 1918. Two other Davis brothers enlisted in different units (see below).

DAVIS, Errol John, MM. One of four brothers who enlisted with the AIF, Davis came from a farm in Stewarton, Victoria. He sailed to Egypt with the 14th Battalion in December 1914 as a private, saw action at Gallipoli and fought in France where he was promoted to lance corporal. He was awarded the Military Medal for bravery at Bullecourt on 11 April 1917 but was killed in action when struck by bomb fragments while retreating out of Passchendaele on 13 October 1917. He was 22 years old.

DAVIS, Ray Stuart, MM. The oldest of four brothers to enlist, 23-year-old Private Davis joined the 2nd Pioneers Battalion, a non-combat unit, in March 1916. He was a farmer and like his other three brothers he was single. While his unit was not obliged to bear arms, it entered the fighting at Morlancourt, the AIF's last battle in France, where Davis was awarded the Military Medal for bravery. He returned to the family farm in Stewarton, Victoria, after the war.

DAVIS, Vernon Henderson. Davis put up his age to 18 in order to enlist as a private in the 23rd Battalion in February 1915. Two of his older brothers, Clifford and Errol, had earlier enlisted in the 14th Battalion; another brother, Ray, would later enlist in the 2nd Pioneer Battalion. Vernon Davis was badly wounded in 1918, losing a leg. He returned to the family farm at the age of 20 but could not adapt and eventually died of alcoholic poisoning.

DEMAINE, Robert ('Bob') Snowden. A 20-year-old student from the Melbourne suburb of Canterbury, Demaine joined the 6th Battalion in July 1915. His initial rank was private and by the end of the war he had become a lieutenant.

DEVINE, Harry William. A compositor from the Melbourne suburb of Fitzroy, Devine enlisted as a private in the 22nd Battalion in 1915. He was 15 but convinced recruitment officers that he was 18. He was taken on as a messenger and bugler. Though court-martialled in 1916 for refusing to pick up a shovel, he proved himself a capable soldier and a willing participant in trench raids. He suffered shrapnel wounds in 1916, was gassed twice in August 1918 and buried twice while serving in the 37th Battalion. He returned to Australia in 1919, worked mostly as a compositor at the Herald & Weekly Times and raised three daughters. He died in 1985 aged 86.

DEWAR, Eric Neil. A 22-year-old lieutenant who attained his rank in the citizen forces, Dewar joined the 1st Division Artillery in March 1916. He had been living in Moonee Ponds, an outer Melbourne suburb, and working as a clerk. Dewar served at the Western Front and survived the war.

DOLLERY, Edwin Maxwell, MC. A 20-year-old electrical engineer at the time of enlistment in June 1916, Dollery, of Hobart, joined the 12th Battalion. He was awarded the Military Cross for conspicuous gallantry near Proyart in August 1918 when he led six men through German-occupied woods. Lieutenant Dollery's men knocked out several machine-gun positions, then established a crucial post which commanded the approach to the woods. He returned to Australia in January 1919.

DOYLE, Kathleen ('Lillie'). Sister Doyle, of Singleton, New South Wales, was involved in the care of hundreds of sick Australian servicemen in Cairo, and served with the 3rd Australian General Hospital throughout the war. She enlisted at the age of 35 and was single—rules permitted only single women or widows to join the nursing corps. She returned to Australia in 1919.

DUKE, Allan Duncan. A motor mechanic from Rockhampton, Queensland, Duke enlisted in the 5th Light Horse in November 1914. He fought at Gallipoli then the Middle East where he was seriously wounded at Romani in August 1916. Corporal Duke returned to Australia the following month. He was 21.

EDWARDS, Charles. Enlisted from Wangaratta, Victoria, aged 19 in the 24th Battalion. Edwards, an ironmonger, survived the war. His younger brother, Private Edward Edwards, was killed at Pozières in 1916.

EDWARDS, Edward. An 18-year-old clerk from Wangaratta, Victoria, Edwards enlisted in the 8th Battalion in July 1915. Like the majority of recruits in the early enlistment period, he had served in the citizen forces in his early teens. Edwards was killed in action at Pozières on 26 July 1916. His brother, Private Charles Edwards, 24th Battalion, survived the war.

ELLIOTT, Harold Edward, DCM. Born on a farm in West Charlton, Victoria, in 1878, Elliott fought in the Boer War where he was awarded the Distinguished Conduct Medal. A lawyer by profession, he commanded the 2nd Brigade at Gallipoli where he was wounded on the day of the landings. Elliott returned to the peninsula but a bout of sickness then a sprained ankle saw the campaign by-pass him. He was given command of the 15th Brigade in France, and clashed with British generals over his concerns that Australian troops were being sacrificed needlessly in attrition warfare. Despite his hot temper, 'Pompey' proved an adept commander with the 1918 retaking of Villers-Bretonneux standing among his crowning glories. He returned to Melbourne where he entered the Senate and campaigned for better treatment of returned servicemen. In Elliott's eyes, the Government never did enough to help them. He battled depression and high blood pressure, and took his own life in 1931.

EWART, Claude Harold. A 27-year-old driver from the Melbourne suburb of Richmond, Ewart enlisted as a driver with the 4th Field Artillery Brigade in August 1915. He was blown off his horse on a handful of occasions at the Western Front, but miraculously he survived the war. He returned to Australia a month after the Armistice.

FINDLAY, Arthur William. A farmer from Leitchville, Victoria, Private Findlay enlisted in the 22nd Battalion aged 22 in March 1915. He served at Gallipoli and France where he was wounded in action and returned to Australia in February 1917.

FINLAYSON, Christopher. Finlayson, 33, listed his occupation as 'soldier' when he joined the 7th Battalion in August 1914. The captain from Bendigo, Victoria, was badly wounded at Gallipoli and never fully recovered. He returned to Australia in May 1916.

FLANAGAN, George Downey. A 24-year-old electrical engineer from Ascot Vale, Melbourne, Flanagan enlisted with the 4th Division Signal Company in September 1916. He served as a sapper and signaller at the Western Front for the last two years of the war and returned to Australia in July 1919.

FLANNERY, Vivian John. A 21-year-old tailor from Northcote, Melbourne, Flannery enlisted as a private with the 23rd Battalion in April 1915. He saw action at Gallipoli then the Western Front where he was wounded in 1916. After recuperating he transferred to the Australian Army General Hospital, but suffered horrific wounds near the end of the war when a German shell exploded near him. He lost both legs and a lung as a result of the blast, and returned to Australia in January 1919 whereupon he married and took up a Government-assisted position as a bootmaker. He died from pneumonia at the age of 45.

FLEMING, John Allan. A carpenter by trade, Fleming sailed from Hobart to enlist with the 38th Battalion in Melbourne in January 1916. He was 26 and married. Although he kept fit through boxing, Fleming suffered from malaria and other ailments while in France, and he was gassed in 1918. He returned to Australia in 1919, having attained the rank of lieutenant.

FOOT, Cedric Mervyn. A grazier from Ralston, Queensland, who took his skill as a horseman into the war, Foot enlisted in the 2nd Remount Unit in October 1915. He was promoted to lieutenant in Heliopolis, Egypt, where he was under the command of Major 'Banjo' Paterson. Foot served in the Middle East and returned to Australia in 1919.

FREEMAN, William Ellis, MC. A farmer from Warrnambool, Victoria, Freeman, 21, enlisted as a corporal with the 8th Battalion in June 1915. He rose quickly through the ranks and later served with the 13th Field Artillery Brigade. Lieutenant Freeman was awarded the Military Cross for leading his troops heroically at Broodseinde in October 1917. He died of wounds on 14 December 1917 after the battle of Third Ypres. He is buried at the Trois Arbres Cemetery, France.

GARTSIDE, Robert. A former Boer War serviceman, Gartside ran his own orchard in Harcourt, Victoria, at the outbreak of World War I, and had been serving as an officer with the 66th Infantry in the citizen forces. Gartside was 52 and married when he enlisted in the 8th Battalion in October 1914. The lieutenant colonel was given command of the 7th Battalion for the battle of Krithia, Gallipoli, on 8 May 1915. He was mortally wounded in the battle when struck in the abdomen by machine-gun fire.

GEDDES, James Arthur. One of a minority of servicemen who was married at the time of enlistment, Geddes, 35, worked as a builder in the Victorian town of Ballarat. He joined the 24th Battalion in March 1915 and was thrown into action at Gallipoli. He was killed in action on 20 September 1915 when a lighted fuse bomb meant for a Turkish trench just six metres away was accidentally dropped in his own trench. Quartermaster Sergeant Geddes is buried at Lone Pine Cemetery alongside Private Walter Turnbull and Corporal Pat Lynch who died as a result of the same incident.

GEYER, Henry Sydney. A barman from the Victorian gold-mining town of Bendigo, Geyer joined the 14th Battalion as a private in October 1914. His writings to his family from Egypt voiced disgust at the depravity of the Cairo brothel trade. Geyer, 21, died of wounds received at Gallipoli on 13 May 1915. He is buried at the Chatby War Memorial Cemetery in Alexandria, Egypt.

GILLISON, Andrew. A native of Scotland, Gillison enlisted from East St Kilda, Victoria, and became regimental chaplain to the 14th Battalion. The 48-year-old was given the rank of captain, and stood out on the battlefield for his courage (some would say recklessness) under fire. He died of wounds on 22 August 1915 near Hill 60 when struck by sniper fire; he had been trying to rescue a badly wounded man who was being bitten by ants. Gillison, a Presbyterian, was also remembered for his moving sermons.

GOODER, John. An emigrant from Lancashire, England, Gooder was a rubber worker of no fixed address at the outbreak of war. The 21-year-old private enlisted with the 14th Battalion (a Victorian unit) in September 1914. He fought at Gallipoli where he also took some impressive photographs. He saw out the war with the 14th Battalion and returned to Australia in May 1919.

GOODSIR, Albert Victor. A 27-year-old textiles dealer from Toronto, New South Wales, Goodsir enlisted in the 33rd Battalion in March 1916. He served at the Western Front, attained the rank of sergeant and died of wounds on 29 August 1918. His mortal injuries were sustained after he volunteered to assist in a 'hop-over' near Mont St Quentin.

GORNALL, William Arthur. Gornall, from Mount Hawthorn, Western Australia, was an 18-year-old photographer when war broke out in 1914. He enlisted the following year in the 23rd Battalion as a private. His commanders openly supported him photographing the movements of the 23rd Battalion, but some of his best material was taken in Cairo. Gornall returned to Australia in 1919 as a lance corporal.

GREGORY, Ernest Albert. Major Gregory, 23, from Murchison, Victoria, served as an officer in the Victorian Mounted Regiment and before the outbreak of the Great War was attached to the 13th Hussars in India under a Defence Department training program. In 1914, he joined the 8th Light Horse Regiment. He was killed when struck by shell fragments while assisting stretcher bearers at Gallipoli on 27 June.

HAMILTON, John Patrick, VC. A butcher from Penshurst, New South Wales, Hamilton was 20 when he joined the 3rd Battalion in August 1914. Private Hamilton was awarded the Victoria Cross for exposing himself to fire and knocking out several rival bomb throwers in bitter fighting at Lone Pine on 9 August 1915. He attained the rank of lieutenant at the Western Front and returned to Australia in July 1919.

HAMILTON, Kenneth Macleod. A 22-year-old station hand who enlisted in Sydney with the 5th Light Horse in November 1914, Hamilton was one of thousands of light horsemen seconded to fight at Gallipoli without their mounts. He attained the rank of sergeant by the end of the war and returned to Australia in January 1919.

HARMER, Edwin Frank. A Londoner by birth, Harmer was 30 and married with a child when he joined the 5th Battalion in August 1914. The labourer from Maffra, Victoria, was critically wounded at Gallipoli. He was hospitalised in Malta but his condition deteriorated. On 29 June he dictated his last letter, via a nurse, to his wife and baby. Private Harmer died the following day.

HASKELL, George. A 19-year-old farmer from Carrum, Victoria, Haskell enlisted as a private in the 7th Battalion in January 1915. Later, he transferred as a sapper to the 1st Division Signal Company. Haskell survived the war.

HEIGHWAY, Albert Richard. A 20-year-old bank clerk from Melbourne, Heighway joined the 7th Battalion which suffered terrible casualties on the day of the Gallipoli landings. Lieutenant Heighway was shot through the chest but managed to keep steering his rowboat towards the shore, using his foot to manoeuvre the rudder. He recovered but was not fit for more fighting and returned to Australia in July 1915.

HERROD, Ernest Edward, CMG, DSO. A draper from Parramatta, New South Wales, Herrod, 29, enlisted as a second lieutenant in the 7th Battalion in August 1914. He served with distinction through the war, and was given command of the 7th Battalion in May 1917. His decorations included the Distinguished Service Order, and he was also Mentioned in Despatches on four occasions. He returned to Australia in September 1919.

HERROD, Henry. A timber worker from Yarra Junction, Victoria, Herrod, 20, joined the 14th Battalion in 1914 and fought at Gallipoli where he was wounded three times. In May 1916 he transferred to the 4th Pioneers Battalion and was again put out of action at Pozières in July 1916 when shot in the neck and jaw. He was sent back to join his unit before fully recovering and was killed by a high explosive shell near Messines on 11 July 1917.

HILL, George Albert, Médaille Militaire. A 26-year-old labourer who enlisted in the 7th Battalion from Melbourne in August 1914, Hill was commended for 'meritorious conduct' during the Gallipoli landing. He was attached to the 15th Machine Gun Company and held in the line for up to 100 days at a stretch. At Bullecourt in July 1916 Sergeant Hill was awarded the French Médaille Militaire for two separate acts of heroism: on one occasion, he carried twenty wounded men out of danger, while suffering from the effects of gas himself; two days later he took control of an Australian gun detachment whose gunners had been killed, and knocked out two rival German gun crews. Although he was not given the Australian equivalent of the French MM, Hill was Mentioned in Despatches for his overall bravery. He was wounded in action early in 1917, and returned to Australia in May that year.

HISLOP, Allan Henderson. A 19-year-old tailor's cutter from Brisbane, Hislop joined the 25th Battalion in September 1915. Private Hislop was left wounded in no man's land in 1916 and became one of about 4000 AIF soldiers taken prisoner at the Western Front. He was operated on at a German hospital in Göttingen and had one hand amputated, but he died on 18 October 1916 from complications arising from his wounds. Hislop's last diary accounts speak favourably of the Germans. He is buried at Niederzwehren Cemetery, Germany.

HORNER, Allan. Enlisted in the 6th Battalion in September 1914 at the age of 18. Horner, a grocer from Castlemaine, Victoria, initially served as a private and was promoted to corporal by the end of the war. He returned to Australia a week after the Armistice.

JABOOR, Aneese. A native of Syria, Jaboor emigrated to Melbourne where he enlisted as a reinforcement with the 22nd Battalion in December 1915. A clerk by trade, Jaboor was a keen amateur photographer while in the trenches. He suffered mustard gas burns in August 1918, and later became a sapper with the 2nd Division Signal Company. When the war ended, Jaboor used some of his accumulated leave to visit the city of his birth, Beirut, before returning to Australia in September 1919 at the age of 37.

JACKA, Albert, VC, MC and bar. A former member of the Wedderburn branch of the Australian Natives' Association, Jacka was working as a forester at the outbreak of war. He enlisted in the 14th Battalion and became the first Australian to win the Victoria Cross during World War I when he single-handedly routed up to twenty Turks from a captured Australian trench at Gallipoli on 19 May 1915. The following year he was awarded the Military Cross for liberating a group of Australian prisoners at Pozières. Although his feat was an act of stunning bravery and audacity, Jacka was wounded in seven places. The war took its toll on Jacka—he suffered a nervous breakdown after being badly gassed at Villers-Bretonneux in March 1918. On returning to Melbourne in 1919 as a captain, Jacka campaigned to help the unemployed, many of whom included ex-soldiers, and he became the Mayor of St Kilda in 1930. He died from war-related illnesses and exhaustion in 1932 at the age of 39.

JACKSON, Charles Frederick. A 20-year-old electrician from Sydney, Private Jackson enlisted as a reinforcement in the 4th Battalion in August 1915, and arrived at Gallipoli in time for the evacuation. He was later transferred to the 1st Australian Mechanical Transport Company, which serviced and repaired vehicles at the Western Front. His company went on strike two months after the Armistice over concerns that Anzac originals would not be the first to be repatriated. Jackson founded the first Wollongong Scout Group after the war.

JONES, Ernest Vickery. A 42-year-old draper and father of six, Jones enlisted in the 10th Battalion in 1915. He was almost twice the average enlisted age of 23 and was given the rank of quartermaster sergeant. Jones, from Alberton, South Australia, was among the first waves of fatal AIF casualties in France. He was killed instantly when shot in the head by a rifle grenade at Fleurbaix on 26 June 1916.

JUDE, David Harold. A 23-year-old fireman from Ballarat, Victoria, Jude enlisted as a private in the 8th Battalion in August 1914. He was killed in action somewhere between 1 and 3 May 1915 near Baby 700, Gallipoli. Jude is buried at Lone Pine cemetery.

KENNEDY, Martin ('Snowy') Francis. Kennedy, a 31-year-old driver from St Kilda, Melbourne, enlisted in the 22nd Battalion and became batman to Quartermaster Sergeant William May. His papers also state involvement in the Divisional Train Service Corps. Kennedy was killed in action on the eve of the Third Battle of Ypres on 18 September 1917. He is buried in the Hooge Crater Cemetery at Zilleveke, Belgium.

KERR, George Ernest Kitchin, OBE. An art student and timber miller who enlisted from Orbost, Victoria, Kerr, 22, sailed with the 2nd AIF Contingent in December 1914. Illness prevented him being involved in the Gallipoli invasion, but he arrived in May to take part in some heavy fighting and was promoted to corporal. He was shot and captured by the Turks during the Allied August offensive and became one of only seventy Australians taken alive by the Turks in the entire campaign. He spent the rest of the war in remote Turkish POW camps, including Belemedik, where he worked on the construction of the Berlin to Baghdad Railway, a joint German–Turkish enterprise. After the war, he became a soldier-settler at Red Cliffs, in north-western Victoria, married and raised five children. Kerr became active in the administration of Australia's citrus industry—a sector driven by the efforts of returned-soldier 'blockers'—and was awarded an OBE in 1965, the year he died in a road smash aged 73. His younger brother, Corporal Hedley Kitchin, was killed at Lone Pine on 25 April 1915.

KERR, William McMaster. Among the last few hundred soldiers to enlist, Kerr was 18 when he joined the 26th Battalion in September 1917. A clerk from Bororen, North Queensland, he had to wait six months for enough reinforcements to complement a unit before sailing from Sydney. Kerr saw a few months of action and survived the war. He returned home in July 1919.

KITCHIN, Hedley Vernon George. Younger brother of Corporal George Kitchin Kerr (14th Battalion), Kitchin enlisted in the 6th Battalion from East Melbourne in August 1914. The 20-year-old electrician was promoted to corporal not long before the Gallipoli landings. Kitchin forecast doom for the invasion—his company had been assigned the dangerous job of wire cutting. Kitchin was killed in action, apparently when surrounded by Turks at Lone Pine on 25 April. He was among 14 000 Commonwealth servicemen whose remains were never found at Gallipoli.

KNIGHT, Phillip Murray. One of a few young AIF volunteers who was married at the time of enlistment, Murray, 21, was a draper's assistant from Raymond Terrace, New South Wales. He joined the 1st Battalion in June 1915 and served in the last part of the Gallipoli campaign. He was promoted to sergeant in France where he died of wounds on 18 June 1918 after the battle for Morlancourt. He is buried at the Ebblinghem Military Cemetery, France.

KNOX, Errol Galbraith, MBE. A journalist from Wentworthville, New South Wales, Knox had been working with the *Sunday Times* in London before the outbreak of war. He enlisted as a lieutenant in the 2nd Battalion in December 1915 and transferred to the Australian Flying Corps as a captain in 1916, then joined the air staff of the Royal Air Force. Knox was twice Mentioned in Despatches at the Western Front, and became a Member of the Order of the British Empire in 1919 for his war services.

LANSBERG, Gunstaff. A commercial traveller who operated from Flinders Lane, Melbourne, Lansberg enlisted as a private in the 14th Battalion in October 1914. Arriving in Egypt he fell ill, like hundreds of other Australians. He was wounded at Gallipoli, recovered to serve in France but was discharged in October 1917 at the age of 34.

LAUGHLIN, Austin, MC. A former Melbourne University and Victorian lacrosse star, Laughlin enlisted as a private in the 1st Division Signal Company in 1914. The 21-year-old student fought at Gallipoli where he transferred to the 6th Battalion. He led a trench raid at Fleurbaix in June 1916 which devastated a German entrenchment, and earned him the Military Cross. The lieutenant was wounded three times in action (including a gunshot wound in the Fleurbaix raid) and became an intelligence officer. He returned to Australia on 'Anzac leave' in November 1918. He married and became a career soldier, and was appointed as a lieutenant colonel in World War II, specialising in security and intelligence arrangements in north Queensland. Laughlin died in 1974 aged 81.

LEAHY, Thomas. A barman from the Palace Hotel, Broken Hill, Leahy joined the 10th Battalion in August 1914 as a 27-year-old private. His battalion was part of the 3rd Brigade strike force for the Gallipoli invasion. Leahy survived Gallipoli but returned to Australia in April 1916.

LESNIE, Frank Bernard. A native of Warsaw in Poland, Lesnie spent most of his childhood in London's Norwood Orphanage School, which he captained in his final year. At the age of 17, he emigrated to Darlinghurst, New South Wales, where he became an electrician. He enlisted as a private in the 17th Battalion in May 1915 under the name of 'Frank Bernard'. He was killed in action at Warlencourt, France, on 2 March 1917 at the age of 21.

LESTER, Ernest Alfred. A 20-year-old gold blocker from the inner Melbourne suburb of North Fitzroy, Private Lester joined the 6th Battalion in August 1914. He served at Gallipoli but was discharged in March 1916.

LEVENS, George Hill. Private Levens, an orchardist of Surrey Hills, Melbourne, enlisted in 1914 at the age of 35. He sailed to Egypt as part of the 1st AIF contingent and was reported 'missing in action' when his 7th Battalion suffered heavy casualties on the first day of the Gallipoli landings. A court of inquiry, a year later, found that he had been killed in action. Levens left behind four children and his wife Jane, 40, who died of tuberculosis in 1916, not long after hearing the news. Relatives, however, believe Jane Levens died from a 'broken heart'.

LEWIS, Charles Horace. Born in Bradford, Yorkshire, Lewis, 22, was a seaman by trade who enlisted with the 13th Battalion in Melbourne in September 1914. He served at Gallipoli and the Western Front where he attained the rank of sergeant. He died of wounds received while manning an observation post in the July 1918 battle of Hamel. He is buried at Crouy British Cemetery, France.

LORD, John ('Jack'), MSM. A non-combat serviceman, Lord, a 19-year-old bank clerk from Crystal Brook, South Australia, enlisted as a quartermaster sergeant with the 4th Division headquarters. He transferred to the 1st Australian Stationary Hospital and while serving with the 13th Field Ambulance he was awarded the Meritorious Service Medal. He returned to Australia after the war.

LORIMER, John Archer. A 31-year-old accountant from Canterbury, a wealthy Melbourne suburb, Lorimer joined the 23rd Battalion. A previous stint with the 67th Infantry in Bendigo attained him the rank of lieutenant which he held on enlistment in February 1915. He served at Gallipoli and the Western Front where he was wounded, but not seriously. He embarked for Australia five days before the signing of the Armistice.

LOWDEN, Cedric Lloyd. Enlisted in the 36th Battalion as a second lieutenant in January 1916. The 19-year-old clerk from Hornsby, New South Wales, had previously served in the citizen militia. Some of Lowden's photographs taken while on leave in London appear in this book. He died of wounds on 19 July 1917 after the battle of Messines. He is commemorated on the Menin Gate Memorial at Ypres, Belgium.

LOWE, Hughie. A 15-year-old labourer from Bowral, New South Wales, Lowe lied about his age and enlisted as a driver with the 4th Field Artillery Brigade in September 1915. He served in France until January 1918 when his mother notified authorities that he was under age. He was then sent home. He returned to Sydney, worked as a telephone technician, married and raised four children. His half-brother, Corporal William Lowe, was discharged because of the effects of shell shock in 1917.

LOWE, William. A 28-year-old surveyor from Redfern, Sydney, Lowe was among the original recruits of the 2nd Battalion in 1914. He fought at Gallipoli and in France where he was promoted to corporal. He began to suffer from the effects of shell shock in late 1916, and suffered a breakdown early the next year. His discharge papers state that he suffered from 'delusional insanity'. Lowe spent the rest of his life in a Sydney psychiatric hospital. His half-brother, Hughie Lowe, survived the war.

LYNCH, Patrick. A 21-year-old farmer from Warracknabeal, Victoria, Lynch enlisted in the 24th Battalion in March 1915. He was promoted to corporal at Gallipoli, and was at one point engaged in fighting with Turks in trenches less than ten metres away. He was killed in action on 20 September 1915 when a fuse bomb meant for a rival trench was accidentally dropped in his own trench. He is buried at Lone Pine Cemetery alongside Private Walter Turnbull and Corporal James Geddes who died as a result of the same incident.

McCALLUM, Aubrey Robert. A butcher from Winchelsea, Victoria, 22-year-old McCallum joined the 8th Field Artillery Brigade in August 1915. He served as a gunner, mostly at the Western Front, and returned to Australia in June 1919.

McCONNACHY, Albert ('Peter'). A 25-year-old miner from Broken Hill, McConnachy enlisted in the 10th Battalion in September 1914. He was made private and rejected a promotion to corporal while in Egypt early in 1915. Several hours after taking the heights of Gallipoli on 25 April, McConnachy was shot in the head and chest while smoking a cigarette. He is commemorated on the Lone Pine memorial. His younger brother Clifford, a member of the 11th Light Horse, survived the war.

McCONNACHY, Clifford Peter. A 19-year-old labourer from Torrensville, South Australia, McConnachy joined the 11th Light Horse in December 1914. He embarked from Brisbane in June 1915 as a private. He was initially attached to 11th Light Horse staff headquarters and later served as a machine-gunner. He returned to Australia in July 1919, but his older brother Albert ('Peter') was killed at Gallipoli on 25 April.

McCORMACK, Thomas Furlong, MM. McCormack, 25, a civil engineer from East St Kilda, Melbourne, enlisted with the 5th Field Company Engineers, in July 1915. He served at Gallipoli then France where he was promoted to second lieutenant in 1916 and decorated with the Military Medal in April 1917. He returned to Melbourne after the war.

McCRAE, Duncan. A farmer from Barrington, New South Wales, McCrae enlisted as a driver with the 5th Field Artillery Brigade in August 1915. McCrae, 20, saw action at the Western Front where he was wounded in early 1918. He returned to Australia in May 1918.

McCRAE, Geoffrey Gordon. A member of a Melbourne establishment and artistic family, McCrae, of Hawthorn, was serving an architectural apprenticeship before the war. He was wounded three times at Gallipoli; upon seeing McCrae in hospital, General Birdwood urged him to stay on. McCrae could not refuse and was promoted to major. He was shot through the neck in July 1916 as he led the 60th Battalion in a suicidal charge at Fromelles. McCrae is buried in the Rue-du-Bois Military Cemetery, France.

McELWEE, William Colin. A 25-year-old tailor from Middle Park, Melbourne, McElwee enlisted as a reinforcement in the 8th Light Horse in June 1915. By the time he arrived at Gallipoli, the 8th Light Horse had been decimated in the Nek charge. Private McElwee returned to Australia in April 1919.

McGARVIE, David. A dairy farmer from Pomborneit, Western Victoria, McGarvie enlisted in the 8th Light Horse, having been originally rejected because he had a hare-lip. Private McGarvie, 22, was a particularly good marksman. He emerged as an unlikely hero of the light horse charge at the Nek in August 1915, where he inflicted a number of enemy casualties using a rifle while lying beneath torrents of machine-gun fire, until shot himself. He returned to the Western District in November 1915 as a result of a badly wounded ankle, and resumed dairy farming.

McGOLDRICK, Albert Alexander, MM. An 18-year-old salesman and film projectionist from Ballarat, McGoldrick joined the 6th Field Ambulance as a private in March 1915. He initially served at base hospitals in Alexandria, Egypt, where hundreds of wounded Gallipoli servicemen were treated. En route to Gallipoli in September 1915, McGoldrick witnessed the sinking of the *Southland* troopship, which claimed the lives of thirty-two Australians in the Mediterranean. McGoldrick suffered from enteric fever at Gallipoli and was sent back to Australia to recover. He re-enlisted in 1916 with the 8th Field Ambulance and was wounded at Ypres in September 1917 when a shell struck his stretcher bearing team, killing four of his mates. In September 1918 he was awarded the Military Medal for carrying wounded Australians across the Hindenburg Line in the battle for St Quentin Canal. He returned to Ballarat after the war, raised a family and worked as a sports journalist and book keeper. McGoldrick later served as secretary of the Ballarat Turf Club and other racing clubs in the district from 1928 to 1968. He died in 1988 aged 91.

McINERNEY, John ('Jack') Morris. A chemist from Mt Gambier, near the South Australia/Victoria border, McInerney joined the 10th Battalion in August 1915. He was wounded late in 1916 and, despite his pessimistic outlook on his chances of survival, rose to the rank of lieutenant by the end of 1917. His fiancée, Olivia May Deane, was an Australian nurse serving in London. They were reunited briefly in 1917, and planned to marry after the war. McInerney was killed in action at Merris on 28 June 1918 at the age of 30.

McINTYRE, John Harold. One of a few soldiers who dared to take photographs during the 25 April Gallipoli landings (see photograph page 107). McIntyre, a 21-year-old ironmonger from Dulwich Hill, New South Wales, landed with the 1st Battalion. He was wounded twice at Gallipoli but recovered and attained the rank of 2nd lieutenant. He was killed in action on 5 November 1916 at Flers.

McMILLAN, Alexander Walton. A salesman from the Melbourne suburb of Hawthorn, McMillan, 20, joined the 3rd Division Artillery in February 1916. The photograph on page 51 was taken by Lieutenant McMillan as he sailed to the front on board the *Aeneas*. He survived the war.

McNIDDER, Hugh Montgomery. A 33-year-old miner from the Victorian town of Wonthaggi, McNidder joined the 24th Battalion in March 1915. Corporal McNidder, who was married, was badly wounded at Gallipoli on 20 September 1915 when a lighted bomb meant for the Turks was accidentally dropped in his trench, leaving three of his mates with fatal wounds. He returned to Australia in January 1916.

McPHEE, James Edmond, MM. A 22-year-old bank clerk from the Melbourne suburb of Essendon, McPhee joined the 4th Field Ambulance as a private in October 1914. He served at Gallipoli and the Western Front where General Birdwood decorated him with the Military Medal in 1918 for conspicuous bravery while assisting the wounded under fire. McPhee returned to Australia in October 1918, having attained the rank of sergeant.

MAKEHAM, John. Enlisted as a 27-year-old private in the 7th Battalion in August 1914. Makeham, a farmer by vocation, was wounded twice at Gallipoli. He recovered to serve at the Western Front where he was again wounded in mid-1917, badly enough this time to return to Australia. He attained the rank of quartermaster sergeant.

MARSDEN, Harold. Enlisted in the 9th Battalion in February 1916 as a private. He was originally from Sydney but joined up in Queensland. His personal details were: age 25, single, labourer, Roman Catholic; contact address: P. O. Chinchilla Queensland. He was killed instantly when a German shell landed on his position in Belgium, 20 July 1918. He was on telephone duty when the shell struck.

MARTIN, Norman Angus. A 22-year-old farmer from Cohuna, Victoria, Martin enlisted as a driver with the 8th Field Artillery Brigade in January 1916. He was promoted to sergeant and survived the war, returning to Australia in mid-1919.

MASTERS, Charles Alexander. Masters, like one in four other AIF recruits, was a native of Britain. Formerly of London, Masters settled in the Melbourne suburb of Elsternwick and worked as a blacksmith. He enlisted in the 2nd Field Artillery Brigade at the age of 28 in August 1914, and was killed in action near Flers, France, in November 1916.

MAXWELL, Duncan Struan, MC. A 22-year-old farmer from Tasmania, Maxwell enlisted as a private with the 52nd Battalion in August 1914, and quickly came under notice for his natural leadership ability and his coolness and efficiency in the trenches. Maxwell fought at Gallipoli, then on the Western Front where he was awarded the Military Cross in 1917 for repulsing three separate attacks by Germans on an Australian trench. He attained the rank of captain before returning to Australia in July 1918.

MAY, William. A Port Melbourne storeman, May enlisted with the 22nd Battalion in 1915 aged 29 as a quartermaster sergeant, and arrived at Gallipoli in time for the last few months of the campaign. He served at the Western Front where he became an honorary captain. May was repatriated in December 1919.

MERIVALE, John Laidley. An overseer from Darling Point, New South Wales, Merivale enlisted in the 4th Battalion as a 27-year-old private. His diary describes the dramatic fighting at Lone Pine. He was killed in action there on or around 8 August 1915, having attained the rank of lieutenant.

MILLAR, George Simpson. Millar's enlistment details were: 23, single, pastoral pursuits, Presbyterian. He joined the 5th Light Horse as a trooper, and like many servicemen in mounted units, he had come from a farm: 'Nowramie' in Clayfield, Queensland. After serving with the light horse at Gallipoli, he was commissioned with the British Imperial Army.

MILLER, Robert Percival. Miller enlisted in the 5th Australian Light Horse, aged 19, at the New South Wales township of Teven in 1914. He was wounded four times in action, twice severely. He went back to his unit after recovering from both injuries, and eventually returned to Australia a fortnight after the 1918 Armistice was signed, to his wife Marcella and to his occupation of farmer. He attained the rank of corporal.

MILLS, Charles, OBE. A professional soldier by occupation, 39-year-old Mills lived in Hampton, Victoria, with his wife. He enlisted as a captain in the 31st Battalion in August 1915 and arrived at Gallipoli for the tail end of the campaign. Mills was shot in the hand and taken prisoner in the battle of Fromelles in July 1916. The lieutenant colonel was released after the Armistice and was one of the last to be returned to Australia in December 1919. The following year he was awarded the Order of the British Empire in recognition of services rendered to fellow prisoners.

MILLS, David George. Enlisted in the 8th Battalion in August 1914 at the age of 23. Private Mills, a labourer, believed to be from Mirboo, Victoria, was wounded at Gallipoli on the day of the landings, and was shot a second time, fatally, while being stretchered to a dressing station at Anzac Cove.

MILNE, Edmund Osborne, DSO. A railway traffic inspector, Milne, 27, joined the 1st Railway Supply Detachment as a lieutenant in September 1914. He was from Orange, New South Wales, and like most AIF recruits his marital status was 'single'. He became a highly decorated officer—when he returned to Australia as a major in 1919, he had the Distinguished Service Order, the French Croix de Guerre and a Mention in Despatches beside his name.

MINIFIE, Percival Carl. A 26-year-old railwayman from Watchem, Victoria, Minifie enlisted in August 1914. He was attached to the machine-gun section of the 8th Battalion at Gallipoli, and was later transferred to the 1st Machine-Gun Battalion. He was promoted to lieutenant but was killed in action at Broodseinde in 1917.

MITCHELL, Fred. Mitchell enlisted in August 1915 on the day he turned 18. His twin brother Hawton joined up at the same time. A farmer from Wodonga, Victoria, Private Mitchell sailed to France as a reinforcement in the 24th Battalion. He died on 1 July 1916 in France after being hit by machine-gun fire.

MITCHELL, Hawton. Joined up as an 18-year-old private in the 8th Reinforcements to the 24th Battalion in August 1915 at the same time as his twin brother (see above). A farmer from Wodonga, Victoria, Mitchell died of wounds received near Chuignes, France, on 1 September 1918. He had been shot in the thigh.

MOLONY, Henry Patrick. Molony enlisted in the 5th Battalion in August 1914 at the age of 27 from Richmond, Victoria. Originally a private, he rose to the rank of lieutenant. He had been nominated for a Distinguished Conduct Medal at Gallipoli but military authorities stopped him receiving it after he refused to accept a reprimand over a trivial breach of duty in November 1915. He was wounded in action at Menin Road in September 1917 but remained on duty. He married in London in December 1917 and returned to Australia in January 1919.

MORRIS, Herbert Norman. Enlisted with the 2nd Field Artillery Brigade in February 1915 at the age of 26. Morris, a manufacturer from the Melbourne suburb of Hawthorn, fought at Gallipoli and the Western Front, and rose to the rank of major. He was discharged in November 1919.

MORRISON, Matthew Edward. Joined the 7th Reinforcements to the 13th Light Horse in August 1915 at the same time as his two cousins Fred and Hawton Mitchell (see above). Morrison, an 18-year-old farmer from Wodonga, Victoria, was used as a marksman and was Mentioned in Despatches for 'particularly good work on patrols' from September to November 1918. He survived the war and returned to life as a grazier. He married and raised three children. He became president of the Wodonga Shire Council shortly before his death in 1960 at the age of 64.

MULCAHY, Gilbert Payne. A 22-year-old clerk from Auburn, Victoria, he enlisted as a sergeant on the HQ staff of the 6th Brigade in February 1915. Mulcahy arrived in Cairo in time to witness the 2 April Wazzer riot, and served at Gallipoli then the Western Front. He returned to Australia in March 1919.

MULVEY, Frederic ('Eric') Christie. A hydrographic surveyor from Newcastle, New South Wales, Mulvey joined the 2nd Light Horse in Brisbane in August 1914. The 22-year-old private was killed in action at Quinn's Post on 14 May 1915. He is commemorated on the Lone Pine Memorial.

MUSGROVE, Reginald ('Dolph') Hainsworth. An engineer who listed his address as the Lidcombe Town Hall, New South Wales, Private Musgrove joined the

12th Light Horse in January 1915 at the age of 18. He served at Gallipoli where he was killed in action on 9 November. Musgrove is buried at Shell Green cemetery.

NEWSON, Basil William. A 31-year-old bank accountant from Cootamundra, New South Wales, Newson joined the 2nd Battalion in August 1914. He was shot through the jaw the day after the Gallipoli landings, and was invalided back to Australia. He re-embarked for England in January 1917 and served out the rest of the war in the Army Pay Corps. His rank was lance-sergeant.

OLDROYD, Roy Andrew David. A sugar refinery worker from Abbotsford, New South Wales, who was quick to join the rush to enlist in August 1914. Oldroyd became recruit number 283 in the 1st AIF Battalion, a Sydney unit. The 19-year-old private was hit by machine-gun fire at Gallipoli on 29 April 1915 and lost his right leg as a result of his wounds. He returned to Australia the following year and got his old job back. He married, raised a family, but struggled to adapt as an amputee. He died in 1949 at the age of 53.

O'MEARA, John Anthony. A 22-year-old labourer from Rochford, Victoria, O'Meara enlisted with the 7th Battalion as a sergeant. He was listed 'missing at sea' at Albany, Western Australia, on 25 October 1914 when his boat, the *Hororata*, was anchored and waiting for New Zealand ships to join the fleet. The exact circumstances of O'Meara's death are not recorded. He is commemorated on the Chatby Memorial at Alexandria, Egypt.

PEPPER, Henry Higham. Left a farm at Nar Nar Goon, Victoria, to enlist in the 7th Battalion. Described as 'reliable and cool' by his colonel, Pepper operated a Lewis machine-gun. He was killed in action on 9 August 1918 at Lihons Ridge after attempting to nullify German machine-gunners. Although shot in the hand, he kept firing, knocking out several enemy positions, until fatally wounded. Pepper, a 25-year-old lance corporal, was the only son of Mary Ann Pepper of Mordialloc.

PERRY, Bertram Harold, MM. A 21-year-old labourer from Horsham, Victoria, Perry enlisted as a private in the 14th Battalion in September 1914. He was wounded at Gallipoli but recuperated. His war record is marked by two outstanding achievements: the first, the awarding of the Military Medal for bravery at Bullecourt in 1917; then his secondment to the élite North Russian Relief Force in 1918. Perry, by then a sergeant, was involved in training White Russian forces against the Bolsheviks. He returned to Australia in late 1919.

ROBERTS, Henry John. An 18-year-old farmer from Leeton, New South Wales, Roberts enlisted as a corporal in the 18th Battalion in February 1915. He rose to the rank of sergeant but was wounded in early 1917 in France and discharged in March 1917.

ROBINSON, George Seaborne. A medical student at Melbourne Hospital prior to the outbreak of war, Robinson enlisted in the Australian Army Medical Corps at the age of 28 in 1915. His first overseas duty was to assist as a surgeon on board the *Karoola*. He was later attached as Regimental Medical Officer to the 11th Battalion, the unit he served with for the rest of the war. He was awarded the Military Cross (then later a bar to the MC) in 1917 for leading a party of men to assist wounded stranded amidst enemy gunfire at Louverval, France. In a letter that began 'Dear Robinson' he was congratulated on his award by General Birdwood. Robinson married Sister Mary Carey, an Australian nurse, in London before returning to Australia in 1919. He commenced a medical practice in Lockhart, New South Wales, then moved to Williamstown, Victoria, before re-enlisting as a medical officer in World War II. Robinson died in 1955 at the age of 68; his wife Mary died in 1966 aged 73. The Robinsons raised three children.

ROBSON, Frederick. A butcher from Rockhampton, Queensland, Private Robson joined the 15th Battalion in September 1914. Robson's diary candidly describes the brutality inflicted on some Turkish troops, particularly in the early part of the Gallipoli campaign. Robson was killed in action on 18 May. He is commemorated on the Lone Pine Memorial.

ROSS, John Lindsay. A 20-year-old school teacher from Ballarat, Victoria, Ross enlisted in 1914 with the 27th Battalion, an Adelaide unit, which had a vacancy for a signals lieutenant (the rank he attained in the citizen forces). He fought at Gallipoli and France where in 1916 he received a serious arm wound that necessitated him returning to Australia. He rejoined the 27th Battalion later that year, and returned to the front in January 1917. Ross was promoted to captain and got through the rest of the war. Despite his soldierly commitments, he was an avid photographer and correspondent to his parents. He married, started a family and resumed teaching, mostly in the area of manual arts. In 1934 he was principal of Brunswick Technical School (Melbourne) where, on the outbreak of World War II, he trained air force recruits in fitting. He died in 1976 at the age of 82.

RUSSELL, Frederick Robertson. A 23-year-old chauffeur from Bacchus Marsh, Victoria, Russell enlisted as a reinforcement in the 14th Battalion in July 1915. The product of an illegitimate birth (he grew up believing his true mother was his sister), Private Russell had a premonition that he would be killed in the fighting at Pozières. He was killed instantly hours later (10 August 1916) when struck in the head by shell fragments. He is commemorated by an elm tree on the Bacchus Marsh avenue of honour. Russell had a brother, Ivan, of the 9th Battalion, who survived the war.

SANGER, Arthur. A labourer from Fryerstown, Victoria, Sanger enlisted in the 23rd Battalion at the age of 25 in February 1915. He served at Gallipoli and the Western Front where he rose to the rank of sergeant before being killed in action on 4 October 1918 at Montbrehain in the AIF's last action of the war. He is buried at the Bellicourt British Cemetery, France.

SCHULER, Phillip Frederick. An *Age* journalist, Schuler lived in the Melbourne suburb of Hawthorn. At the age of 27, he accompanied the 1st Division to Egypt, on board the *Orvieto*. Some of his photographs from the voyage appear in this book. In 1915 he was given special permission from General Hamilton to visit Gallipoli and file reports back to the *Age*. Schuler was so full of admiration for the ways of Australian servicemen that he decided to join up himself. He enlisted in the 3rd Divisional Train, a service corps unit, in 1916 but died of wounds the following year. He is buried at the Trois-Arbres Cemetery, France.

SIBSON, Thomas Edward. A native of Leicestershire, England, Sibson was working as a farmhand in Victoria when war broke out. He seemed content to go on farming until June 1916 when he received a white feather (a symbol of cowardice). He then joined the 5th Battalion, trained at Seymour and sailed to the front as a reinforcement. He was wounded in France in 1916, but survived the war.

SIDDELEY, William McQueen Saxon. A 19-year-old private secretary from St Kilda, Melbourne, Corporal Siddeley sailed with the 5th Battalion, and later transferred to the Australian Medical Corps. He assisted the wounded at Gallipoli where he apparently became seriously ill. He returned to Australia in August 1915.

SIMPSON (Kirkpatrick), John. A 22-year-old fireman from South Shields, England, Simpson joined the 3rd Field Ambulance as a stretcher bearer from Brisbane in August 1914. Simpson, whose true surname was Kirkpatrick, came under notice at Gallipoli where he used a donkey to ferry wounded soldiers back to dressing stations. He was killed in action on 19 May 1915 when shot through the chest by a shrapnel bullet. Simpson and his humble donkey have been enshrined as symbol of courage and martyrdom. Simpson is buried at Beach Cemetery.

SINCLAIR-MacLAGAN, Edward George, DSO, CB, CMG, Croix de Guerre, DSM (American). A former British Regular Army officer and drill director at Royal Military College Duntroon, Sinclair-MacLagan commanded the 3rd AIF Brigade at the outbreak of war. The 45-year-old colonel possessed a down-to-earth sense of humour that struck a chord with the preponderance of miners and bush workers in his brigade. He remained in command of the brigade until 1917 when he was promoted to the command of the 4th AIF Division. He stayed with the 4th Division until 1919 whereupon he commanded the 51st (Highland) Division in Scotland.

SMITH, Arthur Henson. A 24-year-old clerk from East Malvern, Victoria, Smith joined the 2nd Artillery Brigade in August 1914. He participated in operations at Gallipoli, Belgium and France and survived the war, returning to Australia in late 1919.

SMITH, Edwin Richard, MM. A 23-year-old bank clerk from Mooroopna, Victoria, Smith enlisted as a private with the 22nd Battalion in December 1915. He was killed in action at Mouquet Farm on 26 August 1916. Smith was awarded the Military Medal posthumously. He is buried at the Pozières British Cemetery, France.

SMITH, George, MM. A plate layer from Melbourne, Smith enlisted in the 16th Battalion in March 1915 as a 19-year-old private. He was promoted to corporal in April 1917 but later court martialled for reportedly allowing a 'person committed to his charge' to escape. Smith was pardoned. He was awarded the Military Medal for bravery in May 1918 and shot in the abdomen three months later. He returned to Australia in 1919 and died in 1972 aged 75. Two of Smith's brothers also enlisted. Lance Corporal Charles Smith, 51st Battalion, was killed in action at Mouquet Farm on 3 September 1916; Sapper Norman Smith, 59th Company, Australian Railway Operations Division, was repatriated to Australia in 1919.

SMITH, Harry Joseph Sinclair. A star student and sportsman of Sydney Grammar School, Smith was working as a cadet draftsman at the outbreak of the war. He was also a Sunday school teacher at St Cuthbert's Church of England, Naremburn. He joined the 3rd Battalion in August 1914 at the age of 19, and held the rank of lance-corporal at Gallipoli. He died on 23 June 1915 as a result of a gunshot wound to the head.

SMITH, Percy Garfield. Smith, a labourer from Harrisville, Queensland, joined the 9th Battalion in September 1914 at the age of 26. He suffered facial wounds at Gallipoli in March 1915 but rejoined his unit for the last four months of the campaign. He was detached to the 3rd Brigade Signal Company in July 1917, and suffered shrapnel wounds when a shell struck his position three months later. Private Smith returned to Australia in October 1918.

STEVENS, William Johnston. Originally from England, Stevens was a 47-year-old widower when he enlisted with the AIF's Chaplains' Department in April 1915. The Presbyterian minister was attached to the 5th Brigade, and his job description included counselling, censoring letters and conducting services while under threat of enemy fire. Stevens died on 15 November 1917 of wounds sustained at Ypres. He is buried in Brookwood Military Cemetery, England.

SUMMERFIELD, Frederick Martin. A 19-year-old grocer from the Melbourne suburb of Malvern, Summerfield enlisted as a gunner in the 1st Division Ammunition Column in February 1915. He served at Gallipoli and the Western Front where he was promoted to lieutenant. He returned to Australia in March 1919.

SUTTON, Alfred, CB, CMG, VD. The highly decorated Alfred Sutton was a Brisbane doctor by profession. He came under attention for his leadership at Gallipoli where he commanded the 3rd Field Ambulance, which included Private John Simpson. Sutton also had a keen eye for an angle, and his photographs and diary extracts form a memorable record of the campaign. In July 1915 he was selected by General Legge to be the Assistant Director of Medical Services of the newly formed 2nd Division. The promotion did not take him any further away from the line of fire, and in 1917 the 53-year-old was Mentioned in Despatches on three separate occasions. He survived the war.

TATE, Sidney Ernest. Tate enlisted from Westmead, Sydney, in September 1916 in the 21st Battalion, having been earlier rejected because of poor eyesight. Private Tate, 25, worked as a builder's labourer and ship steward, and was married with two young sons. He died as a result of a gunshot wound to the head, near Amiens, three months before the war ended.

TONGS, Allan Lorenzo. At 49, Tongs was among the oldest volunteers of the AIF. He left a farm at North Motton, Tasmania, to join the 12th Battalion in August 1915. Tongs was promoted to sergeant and struggled under the strain of the fighting—a fact which his diary openly explores. He returned to Australia in September 1917.

TURNBULL, Walter (Willy). An Englishman by birth, Turnbull emigrated to Victoria and lived at The Basin, in the Dandenongs. He had been working as a clerk when he enlisted in the 24th Battalion in March 1915 aged 31. Private Turnbull died of wounds on 21 September 1915 after a fuse bomb meant for a rival Turkish trench was fumbled in his own trench. He is buried at Lone Pine Cemetery alongside Corporal Patrick Lynch and Corporal James Geddes who died in the same incident.

VIRGOE, Percy. A 30-year-old stock and station agent from Casterton, Victoria, Virgoe enlisted as a private with the 4th Light Horse. He was slightly wounded in the ankle at Gallipoli but bouts of dysentery, debility and rheumatism saw him invalided back to Australia in May 1916. After recovering, he re-enlisted in October 1916 as a sergeant in the Pay Corps, serving out the rest of the war in England and France.

WALKER, Horace Briggs. A civil servant from Semaphore, South Australia, Walker enlisted as a lieutenant in the 27th Battalion in December 1914. He was wounded in France in 1916 then again in 1917 before returning to Australia in July 1917 at the age of 27.

WEATHERITT, George Thomas, MM. An 8th Battalion private who rose through the ranks to lieutenant, Weatheritt, an 18-year-old grocer's deliverer from Boort, Victoria, enlisted in July 1915. He was shot in the back at Pozières in 1916 (his trouser button deflected what otherwise would have been a fatal impact), recovered, and went on to win the Military Medal for conspicuous bravery in 1917. Weatheritt returned to Australia in May 1919.

WESTWOOD, Arnold Douglas. A salesman from Bairnsdale, Victoria, Westwood enlisted with the 15th Field Ambulance in 1915. Private Westwood, whose diary describes his excitement at arriving in France, died of wounds received at Bullecourt on 5 May 1917. He was 22.

WHITE, Edward Charles Vincent. A 27-year-old driver who lived with his wife in the Melbourne suburb of Prahran, White enlisted with the 24th Battalion in February 1916. Known as 'Alphabet' among his mates, Private White was killed in action during the second Allied attack on Bullecourt on 3 May 1917, but his wife Annie was convinced he was still alive and placed 'Soldiers' Whereabouts' notices in Melbourne newspapers seeking news of her husband. As late as 1930 she was also corresponding with military mental hospitals in the belief that White might have been admitted under an assumed name.

WHITEOAK, Percy Robert, MM. A plasterer from the Melbourne working-class suburb of Preston, Whiteoak enlisted with the 6th Field Ambulance as a private in March 1916. Whiteoak was 24 when awarded the Military Medal for stretchering wounded men to safety while under fire in 1917. Whiteoak, who was promoted to lance-corporal, survived the war and returned to Australia in mid-1919.

WILDER, Herbert John. Enlisted as a reinforcement with the 58th Battalion in September 1916, Wilder, 32 and married, had been working as a labourer in Drummoyne, New South Wales. In France, he took on the dangerous job of Lewis machine-gunner and died from a gunshot wound to the neck at Passchendaele on 11 October 1917. Private Wilder has no known grave. His name appears on the Menin Gate memorial in Belgium.

WILLIAMS, Clarence John. A farmer from Burra, South Australia, Williams enlisted as a reinforcement in the 10th Battalion in August 1915. The 18-year-old private first served as an officer's batman then transferred to the infantry and fought in some of the major battles of the Western Front. He returned to Australia in February 1918.

WILSON, Septimus Frontine. Left a position as a bank accountant to enlist in the 2nd Light Horse at the age of 32. Like most early AIF volunteers, he had previous experience in the citizen forces (a stint in the 4th Light Horse unit). He sailed from Brisbane as a private in 1914, saw action at Gallipoli, but returned to Australia early in 1916 while AIF forces were being restructured in Egypt.

WOODINGS, George William. A farm labourer from Coromandel Valley, South Australia, Woodings, 23, enlisted in the 10th Battalion in August 1915. He was killed in action at Bullecourt in May 1917. Private Woodings' body was never recovered, but his name appears on the Villers-Bretonneux Memorial, France.

WOOLNOUGH, Ernest Ralph. The Port Adelaide warehouseman enlisted in the 27th Battalion in 1916 at the age of 38. He was promoted to sergeant in June 1916 but demoted himself to private in order to get on an earlier boat. Woolnough, who left behind a wife and two children, was promoted to sergeant in March 1917. He was reportedly killed instantly when struck in the head by a shell near Armentières on 28 March 1918.

YOUNG, Albert Victor. A labourer from the working-class Melbourne suburb of Brunswick, Young joined the 7th Battalion in August 1914. The 27-year-old private died on 22 May 1915 of wounds received at Gallipoli. He is buried at Chatby War Memorial Cemetery in Alexandria, Egypt.

Notes

Introduction

1 Lieutenant Lindsay Ross, 27th Battalion, letter, Abbassia, Egypt, 21 July 1915; Museum Victoria.

2 Lieutenant Austin Laughlin, 6th Battalion, letter, Ayrshire, England, 3 June 1917; private donor.

3 Driver Claude Ewart, 4th Field Artillery Brigade, diary, Pozières, France, — July 1916; Museum Victoria.

4 Corporal George Bailey, 8th Battalion, diary, Sutton Veny, England, 22 January 1918; private donor.

5 Unknown 24th Battalion soldier, letter, Gallipoli, 29 September 1918; private donor

6 Corporal Hugh McNidder, 24th Battalion soldier, letter, Egypt, 1 December 1916; private donor.

7 J. C. Waters, *Crosses of Sacrifice*, 1932, Angus & Robertson, Sydney, 1932, p. 99.

8 Greg Kerr, *Lost Anzacs: The Story of Two Brothers*, Oxford University Press, Melbourne, 1997, p. 48.

9 Quoted, Robin Gerster, *Big Noting: The Heroic Theme in Australian War Writing*, Melbourne University Press, Melbourne, 1987, p. 13.

10 Ibid.

11 Private Bert (Peter) McConnachy, 11th Australian Light Horse, letter, Cairo, 8 February 1915; private donors.

12 Trooper J. McGrath, unit unknown, diary, Alexandria, — 1916; private donor.

13 Private Percy Virgoe, 4th Australian Light Horse, diary, on board the *Grampian*, 28 September 1915; private donor.

14 C. E. W. Bean, *Gallipoli Mission*, ABC Enterprises and the Australian War Memorial, Crows Nest, 1991 (first published 1948), p. 110.

15 Lieutenant Cowey, Sergeant Palmer, *Nominal Roll of No. 9 Platoon, "C" Company, 3rd Battalion, Ist Inf. Bde*, 1915–18; private donor.

16 Newton Wanliss, *The History of the Fourteenth Battalion, A.I.F.*, The Arrow Printery, Melbourne, 1929, p. 281.

17 Private William Kerr, 49th Battalion, wallet inscription, 1915–19; private donor.

18 Bean, *Anzac to Amiens*, Australian War Memorial, Canberra, 1983 (first published 1946), p. 129.

19 Lieutenant John Merivale, 4th Battalion, letter, Gallipoli, 18 August 1915; Australian War Memorial.

20   Laughlin, letter, White Gully, — 1915; private donor.

21   Major General R. S. Buchan, *Junior Leadership on the Battlefield, Australian Army, 1990*, Australian Government Publishing Service, 1993, chap. 8, p. 4.

22   Ibid., chap. 6, p. 11.

23   Colonel E. G. Sinclair-McLagan, *Brigade Order Issued on the Eve of the Landing, April 25th, 1915*; private donor.

24   Private Thomas Sibson, 5th Battalion, letter, France, 9 May 1917; private donor.

25   Lance-Corporal Arthur Sanger, 23rd Battalion, diary, France, — 1916; private donor.

26   Virgoe, diary, Gallipoli, 4 June 1915; private donor.

27   Private George Levens, 7th Battalion, letter, Cairo, 27 February 1915; private donor.

28   Colonel Alfred Sutton, 3rd Field Ambulance, diary, Gallipoli, 15 May 1915; Australian War Memorial.

29   Lieutenant John Barton, 55th Battalion, diary, France, — March 1918; Australian War Memorial.

30   Sergeant Allan Tongs, 12th Battalion, diary, France, — 1916; State Library of Victoria.

31   Corporal Hedley Kitchin, 6th Battalion, diary, Gallipoli, 24 April 1915, as quoted on page 72 of Kerr, *Lost Anzacs: The Story of Two Brothers*.

32   Sergeant Albert Goodsir, 33rd Battalion, diary, France, 27 August 1918; Australian War Memorial.

33   Major Geoff McCrae, 60th Battalion, letter, France, 19 July 1916; Australian War Memorial.

34   Captain Albert Jacka, 14th Battalion, letter, France, 14 December 1917; private donor.

35   McConnachy, letter, Cairo, 4 January 1915; private donor.

36   Private James Murray Aitken, letters, Gallipoli, 29 April, 15 May, — July 1915; France, — July 1916; Australian War Memorial.

37   Private Roy Oldroyd, 1st Battalion, letter, Manchester, 17 June 1915; private donor.

38   From transcript of taped interview with David McGarvie by history student Alison McKenzie, 1976; private donors.

39   Ian Affleck, Curator Photographs, Australian War Memorial, interview with author, 1998.

40   C. M. H. Clark, *A History of Australia V*, Melbourne University Press, Melbourne, 1981, p. 390.

41   Laughlin, letter, Lemnos, 25 November 1915.

42   Lance Corporal Henry Pepper, 7th Battalion, letter, France, — 1916; State Library of Victoria.

43   Private Arthur Findlay, 22nd Battalion, diary, France, — June 1916; Australian War Memorial.

44   Major Ernest Gregory, 8th Light Horse, diary, Gallipoli,—1915; private donor.

45   In *Gallipoli*, the 1981 film that evoked Australia's defeat in Turkey, director Peter Weir's camera breathes life into the *mise-en-scène* of some notable old photographs. It is no coincidence that he drew from them, as well as some stand-out passages from Captain Bean's written history of Gallipoli, under the guidance of war historian and writer Bill Gammage. Several easily recognised shots from Gallipoli's annals: the iconographic Simpson and his donkey and Australians making jam-tin bombs, to name two, come to life during a pan of Anzac Cove, and the Capa shot of the mortally wounded Spanish soldier is re-enacted in the final frame of the movie when its hero Archy sprints, as if in a foot race, to certain death at the Nek.

1 OUTBREAK

1 C. M. H. Clark, *A History of Australia V*, p. 372.

2 Private Reginald Cooke, 5th Battalion, diary, Melbourne, 4 August 1914; Museum Victoria.

3 Enlistment standards were lowered in February 1915 in an attempt to bolster dwindling recruitment levels. The age requirements were then 18 to 45, the minimum height lowered to 5 feet 4 inches (160 cm), while the minimum chest measurement fell to 33 inches (84 cm).

4 Private Frederick Mulvey, 2nd Light Horse, letter, Lismore, New South Wales, 28 August 1914; Australian War Memorial.

5 Private Thomas Sibson, 5th Battalion, letter, Seymour, Victoria, 7 July 1915; private donor.

6 Sibson, letter, Lemnos, 26 December 1915.

7 Private Allan Horner, 6th Battalion, diary, Broadmeadows, Victoria, 3 October 1914; private donor.

8 Lance Corporal Harry Smith, 3rd Battalion, diary, on board the *Euripides*, 19 October 1914; private donor.

9 Aitken, diary, on board the *Ascanius*, 1 November 1914; Australian War Memorial.

10 Private Harold Marsden, 9th Battalion, letter, before embarking on the *Itonus*, Queensland, 6 August 1916; private donor.

11 Private Albert Young, 7th Battalion, diary, on board the *Hororata*, 26 October 1914; State Library of Victoria.

12 Private Frank Lesnie, 17th Battalion, letter, on board the *Kanowna*, 17 July 1915; Australian War Memorial.

13 Private Jack McInerney, 10th Battalion, letter, on board the *Malwa*, 12 December 1915; Australian War Memorial.

14 Sergeant Jack Chugg, Ist Light Horse Field Ambulance, diary, on board the *Suthern*, 31 October 1914; Museum Victoria.

15 Aitken, diary, on board the *Ascanius*, 7 November 1914.

16 McInerney, letter, on board the *Malwa*, 12 December 1915.

17 Chugg, diary, on board the *Suthern*, 9 November 1914.

18 Sergeant Thomas Allsop, 11th Battalion, letter, Cairo, 14/15 December 1914; private donor.

19 Private Reg Musgrove, 6th Light Horse (later 12th A.L.H), letter, on board the *Ceramic*, 7 July 1915; private donor.

20 McInerney, letter, on board the *Malwa*, 12 December 1915.

21 Private Henry Geyer, 14th Battalion, letter, Heliopolis, Egypt, 27 February 1915; private donor.

22 Gregory, diary, on board the *Star of Victoria*, 29 March 1915.

2 EGYPT

1 Private Harold Jude, 8th Battalion, album, Egypt, 1914; State Library of Victoria (original album held by private donor).

2 Ross, letter, Abbassia, 26 July 1915.

3 Driver Duncan McCrae, 5th Artillery Brigade, letter, Egypt, 11 February 1916, private donor.

4 Ross, letter, Abbassia, — August 1915.

5 McConnachy, letter, Egypt, 24 January 1915.

6 Young, diary, Egypt, 11 December 1914.

7 McInerney, diary, Egypt, 7 March 1916.

8 Geyer, letter, Egypt, 27 February 1915.

9 Lesnie, letter, Egypt, 1 November 1915; Australian War Memorial.

10 AIF medical records show that venereal disease was rife among the AIF before the arrival at Cairo, and well after its departure. Treatment reports furnished in 1914 at Colombo found that VD formed the highest incidence of hospital admissions, followed by measles (A. G. Butler, *Official History of the Australian Army Medical Services 1914–18* Vol. 1, Australian War Memorial, 1930, p. 39). In the last six months of the war, the average weekly attendance at Australian VD and gonorrhoea treatment centres in London was a staggering 4623 (W. G. Macpherson et al., *Medical Service Diseases of the War,* Vol. 2, His Majesty's Stationery Office, London, 1923, p. 127).

11 Levens, letter, Egypt, 27 February 1915; private donor.

12 Mulvey, letter, Heliopolis, Egypt; 14 March 1915.

13 Mulvey, letter, Heliopolis; 27 February 1915.

14 McConnachy, letter, Cairo; 4 January 1915.

15 Private Harold Aisbett, 39th Battalion, diary, Cairo, — June 1916; private donor.

16 Makeham, diary, Mena, — April 1915.

17 Mulvey, letter, Heliopolis, 2 April 1915.

18 Major G. McCrae, letter, Mena, 3 April 1915.

19 Chugg, diary, Cairo, April 1915.

3 GALLIPOLI

1 Ross, letter, Gallipoli, 12 September 1915.

2 Private David Mills, 8th Battalion, diary, Lemnos, — April 1915; State Library of Victoria.

3 Lance-Corporal H. Smith, diary, Lemnos, 18 April 1915; private donor.

4 Kitchin, diary, Gallipoli, 24 April 1915, as quoted in Kerr, *Lost Anzacs: The Story of Two Brothers*, p.72.

5 Lieutenant Albert Heighway, 7th Battalion, letter, Alexandria, Egypt, 6 May 1915; private donor.

6 Mills, diary, Gallipoli, 25 April 1915.

7 Lieutenant Consett Riddell, 6th Battalion, letter, No. 15 General Hospital, Alexandria, 5 May 1915; private donor.

8 Sergeant Basil Newson, 2nd Battalion, letter, Kasr-El Nil Army Hospital, Cairo, 6 May 1915; private donor.

9 Private Fred Robson, 15th Battalion, diary, Gallipoli, 27 April 1915; Australian War Memorial.

10 Bill Gammage, *The Broken Years*, Penguin Books, Ringwood, 1975, p. 97.

11 Aitken, letters, Gallipoli, 17 May, 29 August 1915.

12 Newson, letter, Gallipoli, 6 May 1915.

13 Corporal William Siddeley, 14th Australian Army Medical Corps, diary, Gallipoli, 27 April 1915; Museum Victoria.

14 Sutton, diary, Gallipoli, — April 1915.

15 Private Septimus Wilson, 2nd Light Horse, letter, Gallipoli, 31 August 1915.

16 Corporal Charles Lewis, 13th Battalion, letter, Gallipoli, 15 July 1915; Australian War Memorial.

17 Sutton, diary, Gallipoli, 4, 19 May 1915.

18 Sutton, diary, Gallipoli, 15 May 1915.

19 Young, diary, Alexandria, — May 1915.

20 Siddeley, diary, Gallipoli, 8, 9 May 1915.

21 Colonel Ernest Herrod, 7th Battalion, letter, Gallipoli, 10 May 1915; private donor.

22 Newson, letter, Gallipoli, 6 May 1915.

23 Laughlin, letter, Lemnos, 25 November 1915.

24 Lieutenant Henry Molony, 5th Battalion, diary, Gallipoli, 2 July 1915; State Library of Victoria.

25 Lewis, letter, Gallipoli, undated.

26 Cooke, diary, Gallipoli, 9 August 1915.

27 Aitken, letter, on board the *Corsican*, 30 March 1916.

28 Pepper, letter, Gallipoli, — 1915.

29 Private William Callinan, 6th Field Ambulance, diary, Gallipoli, — December 1915; State Library of Victoria.

30 Private Gerard Cochrane, 5th Battalion, diary, Gallipoli, — 1915; private donor.

31 Unknown 24th Battalion soldier, letter, Gallipoli, 29 September 1915; private donor.

32 Lieutenant John Merivale, 4th Battalion, letter, Gallipoli, 18 [?] August 1915; Australian War Memorial.

33–5 Ibid.

36 McGarvie, from transcript of interview with Alison McKenzie.

37 Richard E. McGarvie, former Governor of Victoria, descendant of Private David McGarvie, interview with author, 1999.

38 Gammage, *Broken Years*, p. 76.

39 Sergeant George Hill, 7th Battalion, letter, Gallipoli, 22 August 1915; private donor.

40 Surveys among World War II soldiers found that combat efficiency peaked after twenty to thirty days of action, and deteriorated towards a state of exhaustion after fifty to sixty days (as quoted in Richard Holmes, *Firing Line*, Pimlico, London, 1994, p. 214).

41 Unknown 24th Battalion soldier, letter, Gallipoli, 29 September 1915; private donor.

42 McNidder, letter, location unknown, 1 December 1916.

43 Ross, letter, Gallipoli, 6 December 1915.

44 Makeham, diary, Gallipoli, — December 1915

4 WESTERN FRONT

1 Molony, diary, Egypt, 4 March 1916.

2 McInerney, letter, Egypt, — 1916.

3 General Birdwood conceived a plan to split each battalion in half so that inexperienced troops could benefit from being around Gallipoli originals. Many old soldiers were resentful; first they had been prised away from the peninsula, and now their regimental brotherhood was being torn apart. But three divisions were turned into six under the Birdwood plan, and the aggrieved begrudgingly made way for the new chums.

4 McInerney, letter, France, 15 April 1916.

5 Sergeant Gilbert Mulcahy, 6th Brigade, diary, France, 25 March 1916; Museum Victoria.

6 Molony, diary, France, 30 March 1916.

7 Lieutenant George Weatheritt, 8th Battalion, diary, France, — March 1916; private donor.

8 William Callinan, 6th Field Ambulance, diary, France, 27 March 1916; State Library of Victoria.

9 Private Arnold Douglas Westwood, 15th Field Ambulance, diary, France, 30 June 1916; private donor.

10 Aitken, letter, France; 11 April 1916.

11 Ross, letter, France, — April 1916.

12 Holmes, *Firing Line*, p. 380.

13 QM Sergeant Ernest Jones, 10th Battalion, letter, France, 22 May 1916; private donor.

14 Ewart, diary, France, 9 July 1916.

15 Ross, letter, France, — 1916.

16 Aitken, letter, France, 31 May 1916.

17 Trench raid reconstructed from letter from Lieutenant A. Laughlin, to father, from hospital in Boulogne, France, 16 June 1916; private donor.

18 Bean, *Official History of Australia in the War of 1914–18*, Vol. III, Angus & Robertson, Sydney, 1939 (first edition 1929), pp. 252–5.

19 Ewart, diary, France, 17 July 1916.

20 Major G. McCrae, letter, France, 19 July 1916.

21 Private George Blair, 60th Battalion, diary, France, 19 July 1916; private donor.

22 Brigadier General H. E. ('Pompey') Elliott, 15th Brigade, letter, France, 21 July 1916; Australian War Memorial.

23 Weatheritt, diary, France, — July 1916.

24 Ibid.

25 Gammage, *Broken Years*, p. 166.

26 Aitken, letter, France, — July 1916.

27 Ibid.

28 Private Edwin Smith, MM, 22nd Battalion, letter, France, 10 July 1916; private donor.

29 Tongs, diary, France, — August 1916.

30 Makeham, diary, France, — 1916.

31 Aitken, letter, France, 3 September 1916.

32 Aitken, letter, Gallipoli, 29 April 1915.

33 Tongs, diary, France, — August 1916.

34 Private Alex McGoldrick, 8th Field Ambulance, diary, Belgium, — 1917, private donor.

35 Interview with Private A. McGoldrick by son, Alex junior (transcript supplied to author).

36 Ewart, diary, France, — 1916.

37 R. J. Currie et al., 6th Field Ambulance, obituary letter to Private William Callinan's parents, France, 13 August 1916; State Library of Victoria.

38 Kerr, *Lost Anzacs: The Story of Two Brothers*, p. 6.

39 Private Clarence Williams, 10th Battalion, diary, France, reference to 1916–17 period, reconstructed after the war; private donor.

40 Weatheritt, diary, France, December 1916/January 1917.

41 Ewart, diary, France, dates illegible.

42 Sergeant Phillip Murray Knight, 1st Battalion, letter, France, 28 November 1917; State Library of Victoria.

43 The push for conscription was defeated by 72 500 votes in a referendum in October 1916. Prime Minister Hughes continued to campaign but a second plebiscite in December 1917 produced a resounding 'No' majority of 166 600 votes. The two battle-front referendums registered modest 'Yes' majorities in favour of conscription.

44 McInerney, letter, Salisbury Plain, England, 13 May 1917.

45 Williams, diary reference to battle of Bullecourt, reconstructed after the war.

46 Makeham, diary, France, — 1916.

47 Major Donald Coutts, 6th Field Ambulance, diary, Belgium, 22 March 1917; private donor.

48 Sergeant Albert Goodsir, 33rd Battalion, letter, Paris, 3 August 1917; Australian War Memorial.

49 Makeham, diary, France, — April 1917.

50 Private Allan Hislop, 25th Battalion, diary, Belgium, 29 May 1916; State Library of Victoria.

51 Ross, letter, France, — July 1918.

52 Ewart, diary, France, — 1916.

53 Ewart, diary, France, undated.

54 N. E. Smith, report to Australian Red Cross Society, in relation to death of Private Herbert (John) Wilder, 58th Battalion, in France, 7 May 1918; private donor.

55 Clark, *A History of Australia V*, p. 392.

56 Tongs, diary, France, — August 1916.

57 Sergeant James Edmond McPhee, 4th Field Ambulance, diary, France, —1918; State Library of Victoria.

58 Ewart, diary, France, undated.

59 Wanliss, *The History of the Fourteenth Battalion, AIF*, pp. 112–13.

60 Dale James Blair, 'Beyond the metaphor: football and war, 1914–1918', *Journal of the Australian War Memorial*, Issue No. 28, April 1996, p.4.

61 Gunner Sydney Cockburn, MM, 3rd Field Artillery Brigade, diary, Glasgow, 29 September 1917; private donor.

62 Cockburn, diary, Belgium, 2 January 1918.

63 Cockburn, diary, Belgium, 29 December 1917.

64 Lieutenant John Barton, 55th Battalion, diary, France, 31 December 1917; Australian War Memorial.

65 Bailey, diary, England, 22 January 1918.

66 Butler, *Official History of the Australian Army Medical Services 1914–18*, Vol. 1, p.72.

67 Ibid., table no. 27.

68 McInerney, letter, France, —1918.

69 Private Percy Smith, 9th Battalion, letter, Sutton Veny, England, 24 February 1918; private donor.

70 Peter Dennis et al., *The Oxford Companion to Australian Military History*, Oxford University Press, Melbourne, 1995, p. 225.

71 Cockburn, diary, France, 29–30 March 1918.

72 Barton, diary, France, — April 1918.

73 Bailey, diary, France, 28 April 1918.

74 Kerr, *Lost Anzacs: The Story of Two Brothers*, p. 6.

75 Bean, *Anzac to Amiens*, pp. 456, 469, 470.

76 Gunner Aubrey McCallum, 8th Field Artillery Brigade, letter, France, — April 1918; private donor.

77 Ross, letter, France, 14 July 1918.

78 Bailey, diary, France, 30 April 1918.

79 Williams, diary, France, — June 1917.

80 Major George Robinson, Regimental Medical Officer, 11th Battalion, letter, France, 29 July 1918; private donors.

81 Bean, *Anzac to Amiens*, p. 473.

82 Sydney letter from 'Dolly', sister of Corporal George Smith, 16th Battalion, dated 27 September 1918; private donor.

83 Technically, the 1st Battalion agitators should have faced a firing squad for mutiny, but they were charged with the lesser crime of 'desertion'. A few of the ringleaders were impris-

oned until being pardoned by King George V on Anzac Day 1919. An earlier but lesser-known mutiny had been staged by officers and men from three platoons of the 59th Battalion in July 1918.

5 THE MARK OF WAR

1 Ross, letter, Glasgow, 19 November 1918.

2 Coutts, diary, France, 31 January 1919.

3 Quarantine regulations prevented the return of animals to Australia after the war, hence many light horsemen shot their mounts rather than leave them to neglect.

4 Sergeant Bert Perry, Elope Force, diary, Russia, — December 1918; Australian War Memorial. Perry was part of a mission to bind Russian forces to form a new Eastern Front, but by mid-1919, the White Russians had begun to murder their Allied advisers.

5 Quoted in Kerr, *Lost Anzacs: The Story of Two Brothers*, p. 173.

6 Lance-Corporal Percy Whiteoak, 6th Field Ambulance, diary, on board the *Königin Luise*, 28 June, 5 July 1919; private donor.

7 Gerster, *Big Noting: The Heroic Theme in Australian War Writing*, p. 167.

8 Makeham, diary, on board the *Persic*, — February 1918.

9 Ashley Ekins, 'The end of the Great War: Australian soldiers and the armistice of November 1918', *Wartime* magazine, No. 4, Summer 1998, Australian War Memorial, Canberra, p. 13.

10 Kerr, *Lost Anzacs: The Story of Two Brothers*, p. 226.

11 Butler, *Official History of the Australian Army Medical Services 1914–18*, Vol. 1, p. 834.

12 The 14th Battalion suffered 1049 fatal casualties in World War I (41 officers and 1008 other ranks), out-totalling its original enlistment quota of 1000.

13 C.E.W. Bean as quoted in Ken Inglis, *Anzac Remembered*, History Department, Melbourne University, Melbourne, 1988, p. 26.

14 Bob Bryant, interview with author, 1998. Collins Street anecdote relayed to Bryant's father Quartermaster Sergeant Jim Bryant, who served under Elliott.

15 Elliott's own health had been deteriorating. He suffered from depression and high blood pressure, which doctors believed contributed to his suicide while in hospital in March 1931.

16 Medical officer, Mont Park Military Mental Hospital, Melbourne, letter, 15 January 1930, to Mrs A. M. White, Preston; private donor.

17 Marcia Wordsworth, interview with author, 1999.

18 Pam Rudgley, interview with author, 1999.

19 Grace Connor, interview with author, 1999.

20 Alex McGoldrick junior, interview with author, 1999.

21 Mrs L. J. Simpson, of New York, letter to Gunner Sydney Cockburn, Camberwell, Victoria, 3 April 1919; private donor. The letter alludes to Cockburn gathering personal items, including photographs, of a dead American soldier and sending them to the soldier's widow in New York. 'I can never thank you enough but our dear father who watches over you all will repay you for your kindness', wrote Mrs Simpson. Cockburn fought alongside American soldiers in 1918.

22 Tongs, diary, France, undated.

Notes to Captions

1   John Entwistle, Melbourne tattooist, interview with author, 1999.

2   Private Sydney Tate, diary, France, October 1917; private donor.

3   Marie Rumsey, interview with author, 1998.

4   Ibid.

5   From transcript of taped interview of David McGarvie by history student Alison McKenzie, 1976, private donors.

6   Edward Edwards, letter, St Kilda, Victoria, 15 July 1915; private donor.

7   Sergeant James McPhee, 4th Field Ambulance Brigade, diary, Belgium, 7 June 1917, 28 September 1917; State Library of Victoria.

8   Driver Edward Chave, 1st Light Horse, photo postcard, Cootamundra Military Camp, New South Wales, September 1915; private donor.

9   Driver Edward Chave, photo postcard, Cootamundra, New South Wales, 17 October 1915; private donor.

10 Lieutenant Lindsay Ross, 27th Battalion, diary, on board the *Ulysses*, 26 December 1917; State Library of Victoria.

11 Captain Geoff McCrae, 7th Battalion, letter, Cairo, 16 March 1915; State Library of Victoria.

12 Private Percy Virgoe, 4th Light Horse, diary, undated; private donor.

13 Private Austin Laughlin, 1st Division Signal Company, photo postcard, Cairo, 1915; private donor.

14 Lance Corporal Harry Smith, 3rd Battalion, diary, Cairo, 6/7 December 1914; private donor.

15 Private Harold Jude, 8th Battalion, collection of photographs, Cairo, 1915; State Library of Victoria.

16 Ross, letter, Cairo, 25 July 1915.

17 Unknown soldier, photo postcard, Cairo, 11 March 1915; Museum Victoria.

18 C.E.W. Bean, *The Story of Anzac: The Official History of Australia in the War of 1914–1918*, Volume 1, Queensland University Press, Australian War Memorial, 1981 (first published 1921), pp. 536–7.

19 As quoted in Kerr, *Lost Anzacs: The Story of Two Brothers*, p. 64.

20 Lieutenant John Merivale, 4th Battalion, letter, Gallipoli, 31 May 1915; Australian War Memorial.

21 Colonel Alfred Sutton, 3rd Field Ambulance, diary, Gallipoli, 4 May 1915; Australian War Memorial.

22 Private Tom Leahy, 10th Battalion, letter, Gallipoli, undated; private donors.

23 Private Roy Oldroyd, 1st Battalion, letter, England, 1915; private donor.

24   Oldroyd, letter, England, 11 June 1915.

25   Oldroyd, letter, England, June 1915.

26   Bertha Moran, interview with author, 1998.

27   Laughlin, letter, Lemnos, 25 November 1915.

28   Sutton, diary, Gallipoli, 15 May 1915.

29   Smith, diary, Gallipoli, 12 June 1915.

30   Private Edwin Harmer, 5th Battalion, letter, Malta, 30 June 1915; private donor.

31   Lieutenant Henry Molony, 5th Battalion, diary, Gallipoli, 21 October 1915; State Library of Victoria.

32   Ross, letter, Melbourne, 5 September 1932.

33   Ross, letter, on board the *Geelong*, 31 May 1915.

34   Driver Claude Ewart, 4th Field Artillery Brigade, diary, France, 1916, Museum Victoria.

35   Ewart, diary, France, 1916.

36   Laughlin, letter, hospital, Boulogne, France, 16 June 1916.

37   Quartermaster Sergeant Ernest Jones, 10th Battalion, letter, Cairo, November 1915; private donor.

38   Private George Blair, 60th Battalion, photo postcard, France, 1916; private donor.

39   Blair, diary, Western Front, 15 March 1917.

40   Blair, 'Field Medical Card', No. 3 Stationary Hospital, C.E.F., France, 5 March 1917.

41   Lyn Gibbs, interview with author, 1999.

42   Private Hawton Mitchell, 24th Battalion, letter, France, July 1916; private donor.

43   Mitchell, letter, England, — 1916.

44   Trooper Matthew Morrison, 13th Light Horse, diary, France, 17 January 1917; private donor.

45   Morrison, diary, France, 21 March 1917.

46   Morrison, diary, France, 22/23 March 1918.

47   Mitchell, letter, France, August 1918.

48   Captain Geoff McCrae, 60th Battalion, letter, Gallipoli, 2 July 1915; Australian War Memorial.

49   McCrae, letter, France, 13 July 1916.

50   McCrae, letter, France, 19 July 1916.

51   Hugh McCrae, 'Hugh McCrae Hangs a Garland Round a Brother's Memory', letter, Melbourne, 1916; Australian War Memorial.

52   Lance Corporal Henry Pepper, 7th Battalion, letter, France, 1 June 1916; private donor.

53   Lily Agnes Russell, Bacchus Marsh, Victoria, letter to Private Fred Russell in France, 7 July 1916.

54   Captain Albert Jacka, 14th Battalion, letter, France, 14 December 1917; private donor.

55   Will C. Groves, 14th Battalion, letter, State School 3752, Glen Brae via Waubra, 22 October 1919; private donor.

56   A.G. Butler, *Official History of the Australian Army Medical Services 1914–18*, Vol. 1, Australian War Memorial, Canberra, 1930, p. 73.

57   Gunner Sydney Cockburn, 4th Field Artillery Brigade, diary, Larkhill Camp, England, 9 March 1917; private donor.

58   Mrs Elizabeth Herrod, Brittania Creek, Victoria, letter to J.M.Lean, AIF administration, 27 March 1917; private donor.

59   Eric Hansford, 14th Battalion, letter, France, 18 July 1917; private donor.

60   Affleck, interview with author 1999.

61 Private Harry Devine, 22nd Battalion, photograph, Western Front, undated; private donor.

62 Sergeant J. W. Harvey, MM, *The Red and White Diamond: The Official History of the 24th Battalion...Australian Imperial Force*, Alexander McCubbin, Melbourne, 1920, p. 226.

63 Ross, 27th Battalion, letter, 3rd London General Hopsital, Wordsworth, England, 28 May 1916.

64 Ross, letter, France, 17 June 1918.

65 Private Ralph Woolnough (later Sergeant), 27th Battalion, letter, Melbourne, 4 August 1916; private donor.

66 Private Murray Aitken (later Lieutenant), 11th Battalion, letter, Cairo, 27 January 1915; Australian War Memorial.

67 Aitken, letter, on board the *Corsican*, 30 March 1916.

68 Aitken, letter, France, April 1916.

69 Aitken, letter, Glasgow, 17 May 1916.

70 Ross, letter, Belgium, January 1919.

71 Private Charles Jackson, Australian Mechanical Transport Company, diary, France, 31 January 1919; private donor.

72 Morrison, diary, Belgium, 20/21 January 1919.

73 Morrison, diary, Wodonga, Victoria, 3 July 1919.

74 Corporal William Lowe, 2nd Battalion, letter, France, 19 September 1916.

INDEX